EMOTIONAL WORLDS

Are emotions human universals? Is the concept of emotion an invention of Western tradition? If people in other cultures live radically different emotional lives, how can we ever understand them? Using vivid, often dramatic, examples from around the world, and in dialogue with current work in psychology and philosophy, Andrew Beatty develops an anthropological perspective on the affective life, showing how emotions colour experience and transform situations; how, in turn, they are shaped by culture and history. In stark contrast with accounts that depend on lab simulations, interviews, and documentary reconstruction, he takes the reader into unfamiliar cultural worlds through a narrative approach to emotions in naturalistic settings, showing how emotions tell a story and belong to larger stories. Combining richly detailed reporting with a careful critique of alternative approaches, he argues for an intimate grasp of local realities that restores the heartbeat to ethnography.

ANDREW BEATTY has done five years' fieldwork in Indonesia. He teaches anthropology at Brunel University London and is the author of four other books, most recently *A Shadow Falls: In the Heart of Java* (2009) and *After the Ancestors: An Anthropologist's Story* (Cambridge, 2015).

NEW DEPARTURES IN ANTHROPOLOGY

New Departures in Anthropology is a book series that focuses on emerging themes in social and cultural anthropology. With original perspectives and syntheses, authors introduce new areas of inquiry in anthropology, explore developments that cross disciplinary boundaries, and weigh in on current debates. Every book illustrates theoretical issues with ethnographic material drawn from current research or classic studies, as well as from literature, memoirs, and other genres of reportage. The aim of the series is to produce books that are accessible enough to be used by college students and instructors, but will also stimulate, provoke and inform anthropologists at all stages of their careers. Written clearly and concisely, books in the series are designed equally for advanced students and a broader range of readers, inside and outside academic anthropology, who want to be brought up to date on the most exciting developments in the discipline.

Series Editorial Board

Jonathan Spencer, University of Edinburgh
Michael Lambek, University of Toronto

Emotional Worlds

Beyond an Anthropology of Emotion

ANDREW BEATTY

CAMBRIDGE
UNIVERSITY PRESS

University Printing House, Cambridge CB2 8BS, United Kingdom

One Liberty Plaza, 20th Floor, New York, NY 10006, USA

477 Williamstown Road, Port Melbourne, VIC 3207, Australia

314–321, 3rd Floor, Plot 3, Splendor Forum, Jasola District Centre, New Delhi – 110025, India

79 Anson Road, #06–04/06, Singapore 079906

Cambridge University Press is part of the University of Cambridge.

It furthers the University's mission by disseminating knowledge in the pursuit of education, learning, and research at the highest international levels of excellence.

www.cambridge.org
Information on this title: www.cambridge.org/9781107020993
DOI: 10.1017/9781139108096

© Andrew Beatty 2019

This publication is in copyright. Subject to statutory exception and to the provisions of relevant collective licensing agreements, no reproduction of any part may take place without the written permission of Cambridge University Press.

First published 2019

Printed in the United Kingdom by TJ International Ltd. Padstow Cornwall

A catalogue record for this publication is available from the British Library.

ISBN 978-1-107-02099-3 Hardback
ISBN 978-1-107-60537-4 Paperback

Cambridge University Press has no responsibility for the persistence or accuracy of URLs for external or third-party internet websites referred to in this publication and does not guarantee that any content on such websites is, or will remain, accurate or appropriate.

For Mercedes

Contents

Preface and Acknowledgements		*page* ix
Introduction		1
Part I Groundings		23
1	Emotions in the Field: Recognition and Location	25
2	Nias: Emotions Dramatized	46
3	Java: Emotions Analyzed	76
Part II Narrative		105
4	The Case for Narrative	107
5	Persons and Particulars	125
6	The Narrative Understanding of Emotion	150
7	Writing Emotion	168
Part III Perspectives		195
8	Affect: A Wrong Turn?	197

Contents

9	Concepts, Words, Feelings	228
10	The Uses of Empathy	260
	Conclusion	278
	References	283
	Index	299

Preface and Acknowledgements

This book is a study of how emotions operate in the world, how they differ from one place to another, how they are a part of what makes those places different. Anthropological in its comparative coverage and reflexive stance, the book joins a broader conversation with writers and researchers in other scholarly fields who are interested in emotion. Readers with backgrounds in psychology, philosophy, sociology, and history will, I hope, get something out of it. Anthropologists may be surprised (amused, ruffled, piqued: let's hope for a spread of emotions, excepting that dubious candidate, boredom). It is not, in any sense, an orthodox textbook or introduction. Rather, it develops a distinctive approach, plunges readers into the thick of debates, and brings them close to the ethnographic field at its most intimate. The 'beyond emotion' of the subtitle expresses both a wish to escape the limitations of the central concept and a call for a more emotionally engaged ethnography, an enhanced realism that captures the richness of the fieldwork encounter and the complexity of human relations.

For most people, emotions and how we think about them begin with the family. So it is with this project. My wife Mercedes accompanied me on fieldwork in Nias and shared its most intense moments, high and low (in Nias there is no middle). Our children, Sofia and Daniel, came with us to Java, a golden period that contributed much to an understanding of Javanese emotional ways. For this book, Mercedes and Daniel helped

Preface and Acknowledgements

clarify arguments and made decisive suggestions and cuts. I owe much to their acuity and tact. Thanks to those we lived among for several years, mainly in the 1980s and 1990s, and have known for over a generation, cannot easily be specified: affection, regret, yearning, hope, and a kind of love would all be part of it. I am grateful to the people of Bayu (Java) and Orahua (Nias) for their patience and shared curiosity; more than anything, for their friendship. The correct acknowledgement in Nias would be the downbeat formula (to be explained later), 'there is no resentment'; in Java, an even lower-key 'begging your sincere pardon, inside and out, for my shortcomings' must do. These local sentiments, as well as the others enumerated, are a reminder that the experience of fieldwork vastly exceeds its narrow purposes. May anthropology rise to the challenge.

I have drawn haphazardly on the following publications, reworking, borrowing, and sometimes contradicting their original arguments. 'Emotions in the field', *Journal of the Royal Anthropological Institute* 11: 17–37 (2005); 'Feeling your way in Java: An essay on society and emotion', *Ethnos* 70: 53–78 (2005); 'How did it feel for you: emotions, narrative, and the limits of ethnography', *American Anthropologist* 112: 430–443 (2010); 'The tell-tale heart: Conversion and emotion in Nias', *Ethnos* 77: 1–26 (2012); 'Current work in anthropology: reporting the field', *Emotion Review* 5 (4): 414–422 (2013); 'Anthropology and emotion', *Journal of the Royal Anthropological Institute* 20: 545–563 (2014); *After the Ancestors: An Anthropologist's Story* (Cambridge University Press, 2015). I am grateful to the publishers Sage (*Emotion Review*: http://journals.sagepub.com/home/emr), Wiley Blackwell (*American Anthropologist, JRAI*), Taylor & Francis (*Ethnos*: www.tandfonline.com/toc/retn20/current), and Cambridge University Press for permission to use this material. My thanks to an anonymous CUP reviewer for very useful advice, which I have tried to follow. Finally, heartfelt thanks to series editors Michael Lambek and Jonathan Spencer, and to Andrew Winnard, my editor at CUP, for their encouragement, guidance, and patience.

Introduction

We begin, where anthropology properly begins: in the field. In a cavernous wooden hall, six feet above the ground, two men are contending in loud but measured voices. Their audience, roughly disposed about them in two camps, is attentive and respectful. The orators speak in turn, and each seems to address his own side rather than the opponents. Listeners murmur approval and wag their heads, bending to eject mouthfuls of blood-red beteljuice through holes in the floor. Each speaker nominates a confederate who echoes the more resonant phrases in overlapping cries, an antiphony that winds up the tension or clinches a point. But nobody interrupts. There is an etiquette, a procedure. The tone is reasonable if emphatic like that of a prosecutor, but the content is otherwise. An orator appeals, via the sympathies of his own side, to the 'hearts' of the other camp, anatomizing his cares, naming feelings unvoiced in English: hearts that are 'bright', 'cracked' or 'shrivelled'. The verbal formulas suggest something emotional; but neither context nor empathy can supply us with a meaning. The talk is all about debts and gifts, calculations of brideprice. As the antagonists give way to the next pair the tone shifts, but the heart, in all its phases, still figures. Speeches now alternate between ruminative soliloquy and abrupt violence, as when one man darts forward, eyes blazing, and stamps the floor (provoking a furious grunting from below where the pigs are corralled). A lull follows, listeners fish in their betel pouches or spit a longheld

Introduction

gobful. Unperturbed by the outburst the calmer opponent now replies in milder tones: 'As our friend was saying, *their* hearts are scorched. But we too have our stories. Are *our* hearts not squeezed?' '*Squeeeeezed!*' returns his echo.

That was Nias. Another fieldwork snapshot, this time Java. In a formal parlour – all patterned tiles and curlicued teak chairs – a mother corrects her little son in front of visitors for failing to greet them. The visitors are impassive, blandly smiling behind the steaming glasses of tea they are too polite to sip. But the mother wants to make a point. 'Ashamed!' (*isin*) she declares to no one in particular; then, straightening the boy's shoulders, gently pushes him out to the sound of laughter. A simple scene, but hard to read. Who exactly is ashamed, or meant to be? Is the declaration of *isin* a reference to the boy's feelings or his mother's, a projection of her feelings onto him, a cover for those feelings, a judgment of the situation, an admonition, or an exhortation – amplified by laughter – to feel or act a certain way? In a similar incident a little girl, eyes downcast, is urged to stand up in a show of 'respect' to a stranger (again the word is announced). In a third, a child is prompted to show 'gratitude'. What is going on? Having learned the language we know roughly what the words mean – we know how to use them – but what is their function here: Descriptive, performative, educative? What is the psychological reality of the named process? How are word, context, and feeling connected?

Nitpicking questions like this do not normally trouble us as we go about our lives. By adulthood most people have enough savoir-faire to grasp quickly, if not always accurately, what is going on; but put them in a slightly unfamiliar setting – up an age-group, down a class, sideways across occupations – and the chances of being tone-deaf to some of the cues increase. In an alien field location all cues are potentially misleading. You might think you understand, but what do you understand?

The difficulties of recognizing and interpreting emotional episodes in the field – if we are alert to them – open onto general problems of

Introduction

method; and they mask deeper questions about the nature of emotion and the coherence of the emotion concept. So much hangs on a word or gesture, but how quickly we pass to generalities, skipping over the awkward detail! Doubts about the cultural appropriateness of our categories and the barriers to shared experience complicate all fieldwork, but in the case of emotion they seem especially acute. Their challenge should not be underestimated. For if we cannot reliably parse emotions away from home, or naively assume that we know what counts as such, our generalizations are unfounded and will in turn lead us to misconstrue other cases. Mistake the emotion and you mistake the scene; misread the scene and you confound the disposition of the actors; get that wrong and you bungle the whole story. But the challenge is not just practical, nor even theoretical (Who is to say what element has priority in the sequence of errors?). The ability to recognize and comprehend emotion affects the quality of our engagement with others, the sense we make of experience, and the life that goes into our ethnography. For the anthropologist the problem of what constitutes emotion begins and ends in the field.

My examples – one exotic, dramaturgically complex, the other simple, even banal – come from two very different societies, both, as it happens, in Indonesia. The opacity of one and the seeming transparency of the other present different kinds of difficulty. Before the calculated passion of the orators we are clueless, yet long-term familiarity does not help much. The German missionary Heinrich Sundermann lived long enough in Nias to translate the Bible into *li niha* ('the speech of humans') but he remained baffled by its heart-speech. German hearts and human hearts were not the same. (Nor, as I would discover a century later, were English hearts.) By contrast, in the temperamentally cooler – but still equatorial – setting of the Javanese parlour, we have an immediate sense of familiarity: there seems to be nothing to explain. And if we misrecognize what is going on there will be no consequences, so no likelihood of being put right. Where Niasans take great pains to analyze and embroider your mistakes – a kind of mettle-testing not

3

Introduction

unrelated to the agonistic style of debate – a polite Javanese host, to save further trouble, only points out your worst *faux pas*. Either way, the fieldworker is wrongfooted. One society presents an intractable problem, the other an invisible one.

We shall have more to do with Nias and Java, with hearts and manners (and whether those hearts are really manners, those manners hearts). For the moment, grant an experiential fact. Against the caution of cultural relativism that, emotionally speaking, nothing is what it seems, field researchers do somehow, sometimes, manage to connect, even against the grain of their theoretical prejudices. The practical wisdom of fieldwork outlasts the tides of theory, a battered rock against its waves. Accordingly, the approach I develop in this book builds on ethnography's unique strengths: personal involvement, long-term familiarity, local knowledge, time-depth. The approach taken is a *narrative* one. Rather than focusing on artificially demarcated emotions, I consider *emotional episodes* within broader, often competing narratives. I develop my argument through a consideration of key texts and through analysis of my own fieldwork in these two contrasting settings: the tribal society of Nias, an island to the west of Sumatra, and the culturally plural, peasant society of rural Java. Both places make emotions, broadly understood, a cultural focus. In Nias (Chapter 2), emotions serve as a vehicle of political rhetoric in what was, until yesterday, largely an oral culture. In Java (Chapter 3), certain focal emotions ('shame', 'reluctance') serve as social antennae enabling mutual adjustments among villagers in a fractious, ideologically competitive setting. Like other Asian civilizations, Java also possesses a sophisticated psychology that offers an alternative perspective on human nature. In both societies, the psychological reality of certain key emotions appears to be indeterminate and ethnographically dubious, which prompts questions about the constitution of emotions and their cross-cultural comparability.

Although other examples will be drawn from around the world (notably the Utku and Bedouin in Chapter 5), the book has a Southeast

Asian and Pacific bias. For this I make no apology. My own emotional explorations over many years have been among island peoples, and most of the pioneering work on emotion has been carried out in places like Tahiti, Bali, and Luzon. Happily, in a comparative venture of this kind, relevance is not established by quantity. Tiny Ifaluk, a pixel in the Pacific with a few hundred souls, has as much to tell us about emotion as certain other societies numbering millions. In the ethnographer's scales an island can outweigh a continent.

What is an emotion?

It is customary to begin any contribution to this subject with a definition, as William James did in his famous essay of 1884, *What is an Emotion?* (In fact, it's customary to begin by quoting James.) His counter-intuitive answer – emotions don't bring about bodily changes, as common sense assumes (tiger $\rightarrow$ fear $\rightarrow$ thumping heart), rather, 'our feeling of the same changes as they occur IS the emotion' – sparked a century of controversy. Yet despite the wealth of accumulated theory and experimental data we are not much nearer an agreed answer to James's question. Indeed, the problem has become a lot more complicated as the heterogeneity of emotions has become clearer.

Emotions colour our thoughts, shape our reactions, load our dreams with obscure significance, urge decisions, trigger action, frame the moment, revise the past, and alter the state of affairs. Inside us like thoughts and sensations yet somehow out there like speech and action, emotions are and do many things. But what are they? Among the leading answers: feelings, judgments, biological reactions, brain states, social roles, functional orientations, action tendencies, evolved responses to opportunity and danger, performances, transactions, cognitions, strategies, and words. Each has been offered as a definition ('emotions are a kind of X'), and all have a claim, though the truth of the matter is not to be discovered by adding them up, which would make

Introduction

emotions equivalent to practically everything human. To parse emotions, sort the sheep from the goats, we must be able to distinguish between feelings (or cognitions or judgments or roles) that are emotional and those that are not, or between dispositions to action that stem from emotion and those more coolly motivated. Pointing to thought, feeling, or action as your definition gets you no further. What *kind* of feeling or thought do you mean? Well, an emotional one, of course.

If definitions of emotion tend to be circular, perhaps emotions are simply givens in the world, fundamental ingredients of experience that we know without being able to define, as Augustine famously said of time. Yet the overarching category of emotion – self-evident to modern English speakers – is unnamed in many other traditions, as are numerous instances of what *we* would call emotions, such as love, guilt, even sadness. The Chewong of Malaysia are said to possess seven emotion words; English has over 2,000 (Russell 1991: 428). What to make of the discrepancy? The lack of translation equivalents in other languages might be an historical curiosity, a cause for smug celebration, or an obstacle in the way of a general theory. It could be that each emotion – anger, jealousy, joy – forms a natural kind, whether or not we name it. It could also be that anger and joy belong to a broader natural class of phenomena, Emotion, named in some traditions, undiscriminated in others. Only the dizziest postmodernist would deny that genes and kangaroos existed before they were known and named; so why should nostalgia, embarrassment, *Schadenfreude* and *amae* (Japanese for dependent love) require cultural formulation for their existence? As I explore in Chapter 9, much depends on *how much* depends on words.

Changing cultural perspectives

The slippery problem of definition, even of recognition, is mirrored in doubts over how we should *feel* about emotion, an ambivalence that has a history so deep and ramifying that it almost defines a civilization.

Greeks v. Persians, rationalists v. Romantics, reason and passion, culture and nature. Similar binaries figure in other traditions – Islam for one – but they are peculiarly central to Western self-definition, echoing down the millennia as if responding to some deeper prompting unbounded by history. Emotion (variously conceived and emphasized) is a touchstone of cultural value, a sluggish barometer of social change; in our own time, a spinning weathervane. For however indelible the categories and motifs, recent decades have seen an unmistakable resurgence of interest in the emotional. Once confined to psychology and philosophy, emotion has seized centre-stage in scholarly areas as different as geography and cultural studies, literary theory and artificial intelligence. In the applied fields of nursing, management, and market research, workshops on 'emotional labour' are now routine. Emotion is an obsession of our media-saturated world. Footballers undergo rage-counselling; men in suits train in 'emotional intelligence'; text messages are studded with emojis.

But the shift in sensibility, the growing cultural importance given to reflective emotion that historians have traced over the *longue durée*, and which sociologists have linked to the rise of bourgeois society and, latterly, consumerism, has ushered in a period of enormous confusion. On the crest of the Enlightenment, Kant knew where he stood: emotions were an 'illness of the mind'. But the contemporary scene is one of bewilderment. A listing of emotion titles on amazon.com – a market in present anxieties – brings up a puzzling mixture, ranging from the doubtful (*Emotions: Can You Trust Them?*) and alarmist (*Your Killer Emotions*), to the desperate (*SOS Help for Emotions*), and plain paranoid (*Enemies of the Heart: Breaking Free from Emotions that Control You*). Subtitles register alienation (*What Your Feelings Are Trying to Tell You*), emotional constipation (*How to Release Your Trapped Feelings*), and a dark night of the soul (*Why You Feel the Way You Do and What God Wants You to Do about It*). Remedies – at least the worldly kind – tend to the managerial (*The 4-Step Program to Take*

Charge of Your Emotions). 'Control' figures prominently (*Controlling Emotions so They Don't Control You; How to Control and React to the Size of Your Emotions).* Where the self-help manuals stir panic only to dispel it, for a modest outlay, popular science promises a solid, governable reality, preferring no-nonsense titles like *The Emotion Machine* and *Molecules of Emotion.* All seem to be telling us that emotions are inscrutable, predatory, and alien; above all they are *things*: things we mostly do not want to have.

One of the difficulties with getting a grip on emotion is that – for those deep civilizational reasons – our feelings about feelings tend to slant our understanding of their nature and significance, confusing the role they play with the role we think they ought to play. From the time of the Stoics, emotion and ethics have been deeply entangled. One reason why it is hard to grasp what emotions *are* is because, as food for thought, they are inescapably emotive.

Developing a scholarly approach: The example of history

To say that anthropology is not immune to this problem is no more than to say that it has a history. Like the other social sciences it operates with the tools of ordinary language, sometimes struggling to shed their historical baggage, sometimes as heedless of the linguistic medium as the proverbial fish in water. 'Culture', 'society', and 'religion', heading the list of key terms, seem made for debate; they are, in a famous phrase, essentially contested concepts. But 'emotion' is transparent. Or so we assume. And with transparency comes theoretical invisibility. You won't find a relevant entry in the index of most ethnographies.

One way of making the shape of a concept visible is to look at its history. How did people in the past think about emotions? How did emotions play out in social life? Is there compelling evidence of emotional climate change? These historical questions are not very different from the kind posed by anthropologists; and if the past is another

Introduction

country social historians can be reckoned ethnography's time-travellers. Historians of emotion attend to public and private sentiment, changing norms of expression, and what used to be called folk psychology (a concept nowadays considered a little too tidy). Rather than the conventional documents of social history – the wills, deeds, and pamphlets that graph the rhythms of civil society – their evidence is gleaned from the marginalia of everyday life – letters, jottings, diaries, and popular song – besides the worked-up presentations of literature and art (Matt 2011; Matt & Stearns 2014; Plamper 2015; Reddy 2001; Rosenwein 2006; Stearns 2008). Historical research also works backwards, genealogically, retracing the roots of contemporary notions to show how, for example, from the eighteenth century, 'emotions' gradually replaced the 'passions': concepts with quite different resonances and ideological functions (Dixon 2003, 2012).

Modern historians have become adept at finding emotional clues in the minutiae their forbears passed over in silence. Masters of the craft, like the French writers of the *Annales* school, offer a picture of vanished worlds as vivid as any ethnography and a reminder that making the past speak is a matter not only of knowing how to listen but of narrative and imaginative engagement.

An anthropological approach to emotion complements this vital historical work. It differs in its focus on the here and now, above all in its contact with everyday life. However personally invested in the past, the historian stands at a distance from the objects of enquiry. For the most part life is not written down but lived between the lines; the written record, such as it is, provides an ambiguous witness to how people felt and thought. As Eamon Duffy laments, 'routine . . . leaves few records, even though most of what is fundamental to ordinary existence is a matter of routine – undocumented, invisible and, as a consequence, far too easily discounted by the historian seeking to touch the texture of the life of the past' (2002: 67). Does a sparse diary entry on the death of a child imply lack of grief; or does grief go without saying

9

Introduction

(Pollock 1983)? Were emotional lives substantially different in the past? Duffy does a magnificent job in evoking the religious ethos of life in a sixteenth-century English village, piecing together the 'busy piety' of villagers from parish records and clerical accounts. Plenty of texture there, to be sure. But like any historian he faces 'the difficulty in all attempts at close encounter with the people of the past, of grasping what it was that mattered most to them' (Duffy 2002: 68), a problem compounded by history's silence on what the unlettered thought and felt.

The elusive object, the problem of reporting

In writing about emotions, anthropologists have the singular advantage of *being there*: they live the life, share the joys and sorrows. Freed of the written record (or unfazed by its absence) they ought to be better attuned to what goes without saying – or at least what goes without writing. Yet as ethnographers privately admit, in the retelling much of the life drains away. Emotion, like poetry, gets lost in translation. The living evidence can be as inscrutable as the laconic diary entry; either that or the analytical gaze withers its object. And there are further hazards. If historians fret about anachronism, the anthropologist's cardinal sin is ethnocentrism, the projection onto cultural others of one's own ways of thinking and – we must add – *feeling*. Against parochialism in *thought* there are ample safeguards: the comparative perspective, a century of field research, the massed chorus of world ethnographers. But feeling is trickier. For one thing, the doctrine of the Psychic Unity of Mankind espoused by Franz Boas, founding father of American anthropology, and generations of his followers, inhibits inquiry. The doctrine recognized diversity of cultural content but not of psychological faculties, which Papa Franz saw as biologically given, therefore invariable. Psychic unity implied emotional uniformity. But who is to say what counts as psychic or what constitutes unity? And where do emotions begin and end: in the mind, the situation, the cultural values? The

Introduction

discovery of the plasticity of the human brain under the pressure of culturally specified environments makes a simple universalism hard to sustain, however politically attractive. People grow up in different social and cultural contexts; most brain development takes place after birth. Our emotional lives may be far more variable than the Boasians allowed.

So the methods of the anthropologist, no less than those of the historian, bring their own difficulties. Anthropologists, too, are often engaged in reconstruction, working in the afterglow of an emotion. They also deal with conflicting interpretations, the distortions of memory, self-interested testimonies, the invisibility of feeling, and the imprecision of words. In fact, they deal *in* these problems, which are the very stuff of debate. For all the hazards of peering into the past, 'being there' is no simple remedy.

As these preliminaries suggest, a book about emotion written by an anthropologist requires a certain humility about what has been achieved and what can be done. The sheer difficulty of thinking and writing about emotion anthropologically is one of my central themes. Indeed, a method that combined conceptual analysis with ethnographic illustration – standard operating procedure – would produce something rather impoverished: either a lowest common denominator model of *l'homme moyen sentimental* or a gallery of exotic freaks. Why emotions require a different approach from, say, religious ritual or village politics will, I hope, become clearer. I shall argue that we need something less topically focused, more open to other possibilities. How could it be otherwise when emotions are all about us, part of us, the very air we breathe. Moreover, the growing interest in emotion across the humanities and sciences reminds us of the necessity of wide reading in other disciplines that fasten on diverse aspects of emotion. Accordingly, an anthropological look at emotion cannot be a mere anthropology *of* emotion, a fenced-in corner of psychological anthropology. Once we grant that emotions are central to human experience we cannot confine them in this way. The propositions, critiques, and reports from the

Introduction

frontline I shall offer belong to a bigger project, which is to contribute to a humane and emotionally engaged anthropology. What is needed, I shall argue, is a form of writing that captures dimensions of life too often left to fiction, parcelled out among experts in other fields, or left out of account altogether: something like that narrative and imaginative engagement that enables the historian to make the past present. Our challenge, as anthropologists, is to make the *present* present: to render experience faithfully, to fill in what the diarists and parish clerks left out. This implies more than a dogged positivism, the reporter's creed of 'tell it like it is'. The interesting truths are complex, murky, often unrecognizable to those involved. I have never understood those earnest souls who take their manuscripts to the field before publication for prior approval. No truth-respecting novelist would do such a thing. (My father-in-law's *roman à clef*, set among his familiars in Mexico City, was systematically misunderstood by its 'characters', each seeing themselves in another – a story in itself.) Art imitates life, but imitation is not duplication.

The job of this book is therefore preparatory and loosely programmatic as well as critical and comparative. I do not offer a full-blown ethnographic account or a set of prescriptions. My task is like that of the tropical hill farmers I once lived among: slash-and-burn clearing, trial-and-error planting, a spot of salutary headhunting. Anthropology is a multifarious enterprise, an unruly swidden not a velvet paddyfield. There is no best way. Who knows what might sprout should others wander into the field?

Prospects and impediments

But before we begin, a cautionary word and a glimpse of quandaries to come. Just as you cannot simply aggregate *definitions* in the hope that something sticks, nor can you combine *approaches* so as to cover all the bases. There may be no best way, but there are many bad ways. And the difficulty of arriving at a compendious and truthful account of emotion, or one that admits a diversity of perspectives, is compounded by the problem of cross-purposes that any synthesis faces. This goes beyond the usual contention that Theory A provides a better mapping than Theory B of the same terrain. Approaches to emotion in the social sciences are peculiarly incompatible. Scholars of 'discourse' and partisans of 'embodiment' are fighting with different weapons, an army against a navy, at odds over what constitutes the territory. So too with evolutionary psychologists and 'affect theorists'. The fable of the blind men and the elephant, routinely trotted out in reviews of emotion research, actually underrates the problem. It does, after all, assume that there *is* an elephant, and that each blind man is right about his portion – the ear, the tail, or the trunk. But suppose there is no elephant, or that the parts do not add up to a whole or belong to different beasts? What if thoughts, feelings, expressions, cultural models, and contexts are only contingently related? The thought-people will not be talking about the same thing as the feelings-people; cultural constructionists fly through the revolving door as the evolutionists exit.

In this book, I shall consider emotion in its different guises and from different perspectives (of language, empathy, pragmatics), not in a scattershot hope that something will score a hit, but in recognition of the diversity of emotion in form, context, and use. I do not come down decisively for or against a natural kind view of emotion (Barrett 2006), or even for or against the coherence of the emotion concept – a rather different question (Griffiths 2004: 234). A strategic scepticism justifies my eclectic coverage and an inclusive narrative approach. In any case, a preliminary anthropological demarcation would be futile when the point of this book is to open things up, recovering some of the essential detail of person, history, and circumstance that has been lost in reductive approaches. In his *Economy and Society* (1968: 399), Weber wrote of religion: 'Definition can be attempted, if at all, only at the conclusion of the study.' Swearing off definition, I hope nonetheless to provide more

Introduction

than a descriptive account. My argument will be that the grainy particulars are not simply *illustrative* or reflective of broader processes (biological, social, cultural), but *constitutive* of emotional experience. If we are to make headway in understanding, generalizations have to incorporate rather than transcend the level at which emotions are evoked and take effect, or risk caricaturing them. For an anthropologist, it therefore makes sense to cast the net wide, to consider the diverse ways in which feelings, motivations, evaluations, and situations come together, and how such combinations are locally understood and produced within cultural worlds by particular people, however they may be scientifically classified at more inclusive levels.

Without setting out a theory of what emotions are, I hope nonetheless to redraw some boundaries and knock over a few fences. My constant resource, point of departure and return, is the ethnographic field: not just the living laboratory of jungle, factory or desert oasis, but the knowledge acquired and deployed, often thoughtlessly, in the human encounter that always exceeds the bounds of theory and gives the lie to airy abstractions.

What can anthropology add to existing theories of emotion?

But why an *anthropological* approach? Surely anthropology can add little to the mountains of psychological, neuroscientific, and historical research. And who cares anyway about the anger or shame of an obscure people on the far side of the globe? What have the margins (but *whose* margins?) to say to the centre? Anthropology's contribution, on such a view, must be small. Yet at least in the human sciences it has proved critical, not merely as an inventory of exceptions ('The Ifaluk don't think like that!'), but as a distorting mirror. As psychologists and philosophers have increasingly recognized, examples from around the world have shown that standard emotion categories have a limited value

Introduction

beyond our shores. The challenge offered by ethnography is not merely the puzzle of the exotic. In grappling with other worlds, anthropology has unmasked our own taken-for-granted ways of thinking about thinking, feeling about feeling. In the villages, barrios, clinics, and schools where anthropologists toil, concepts of mind, body, individuality, and personhood have all been thrown into illuminating question. The study of emotion is at the heart of this critical endeavour.

Anthropology has also shared in broader critiques of gender, race, and the human subject that have complicated and enriched the study of other cultures. Changes in the way we understand subjectivity and emotional communication have altered the way we conduct fieldwork and understand the process of coming to learn other lifeworlds (Biehl, Good and Kleinman 2007; Davies & Spencer 2010; Okely 2012; Wilce 2009). This is all well and good. But to think differently about emotion – to press home the anthropological advantage – is, necessarily, to adopt new writing strategies. Or so I shall argue in pursuing the narrative thread. What is needed is 'deep' rather than 'thick description', a firmer sense of presence, a counter to the smiley.

The approach of this book

This book therefore offers something more than a reconsideration of emotion in the light of anthropology's provocative findings. It builds on a growing literature, but it also offers a critique of that literature and proposes a distinctive way forward. Anthropologists have disputed the nature of emotion for many years, but their disagreements have been muddied by their focus on different aspects of emotion sequences (here an ear, there a tail). Theorizing is out of step with ethnographic knowledge, and it jars with our practical understanding of human relations. To make progress we need to reintegrate conceptual critique with ethnographic analysis, bringing theoretical concepts closer to practical realities. I argue for an expanded vision of emotions as frames of

Introduction

understanding, social antennae, monitors of comportment, vehicles of political rhetoric, discursive justifications, and indicators of social boundaries.

New developments notwithstanding, the contention of this book will be that, despite some limitations, anthropology already possesses an array of powerful tools to capture and theorize emotion in context. The difficulty has been in the execution. A shrinking from the ethnographic actuality and a retreat into definitional debates have vitiated both theory and the reporting on which it is based. We have taken our eye off the ball. A necessary first step in rethinking emotion, therefore, is the critical one of testing claims against ethnography. Do discourse-centered approaches adequately sample naturalistic language (Chapter 5)? Do proponents of empathy tap into the right experiences (Chapter 10)? Does the 'turn to affect' turn up something new (Chapter 8)? Do person-centered interviews preserve the contexts that alone give emotions their meaning (Chapter 7)? What happens when the ethnographer stands aside from the living reality to formulate and compare? What gets lost in translation?

To put one's finger on the point where reality has been let slip is to point a way back towards ethnographic credibility. Without this credibility our theoretical efforts are castles in the air. A surprising finding of this book will be that, with scarce exceptions (fortunately good ones), the landmark studies of emotion in anthropology depend on very few worked-out ethnographic cases. Theories are too often based upon hypothetical or out-of-context examples. The concepts so generated have, in turn, yielded meagre ethnographic results, serving as blinkers not lenses. This paradox forces us to step back and ponder the diverse, uncertain sources of our knowledge about emotion. And it prompts us to look for reasons why emotion has proven particularly difficult to capture in ethnography.

My approach will therefore be critical in two senses: it offers a close reading of empirical studies, and it tests the value and robustness of anthropological concepts and rival approaches. A parallel positive endeavour will be to suggest new ways – or sometimes old ways rebooted – of reporting and analysing emotion. The point is not merely to fill in another gap, notionally equivalent to 'markets' or 'migration'. The aim is, rather, to explore how we can recover for anthropology some of the human significance and density that a fuller account of emotions, such as we find in literature, can give – in effect, to restore the heartbeat to ethnography. This is a problem of writing as well as method, 'art' as well as science. The richness and subtlety of motivation and feeling that we take for granted in our dealings with others has so far eluded all but a few ethnographers. Human complexity has been sacrificed to models, cases, and types. But a gain in verisimilitude demands not just better ethnographic tools but a fresh approach to writing and composition.

An interdisciplinary venture

Since this book is intended for an audience outside as well as inside anthropology, joining an ecumenical conversation on emotion, I must explain my terms of engagement. The narrative approach I develop does not depend on a view of emotions as discrete biological events governed by mechanisms that evolved to deal with threats and opportunities: 'basic emotions' for basic situations (Ekman 1999). (Basic emotions theorists typically postulate anger, fear, surprise, disgust, sadness, and joy as universals.) But nor does it embrace an out-and-out cultural relativism that would relegate the concept of emotion, as well as those listed instances, to an Anglophone folk psychology (Lutz 1988; Shweder 2004; Wierzbicka 1999). What I shall have to say about emotion from an anthropological point of view does not stand or fall on a consistent, or even 'correct', view of what emotions are – the reason being that I do not deal with emotions or their components as discrete entities: I am concerned with broader sequences of behaviour in which emotions play

Introduction

a role. The putative boundaries of emotions are not my concern. What emotions are taken to be, in any case, depends on what level of analysis you are using, what order of reality you are describing. For a linguist, emotions might be defined (or at least characterized) semantically; for a psychologist, by a mental state; for a neurologist, by changes in the nervous system; for a dramatist, by a plotted encounter. I shall try to show, nonetheless, that good ethnographic reporting of emotion episodes has a validity and integrity of its own that new scientific discoveries do not automatically threaten. Only when the ethnographer applies a misconceived theory is the report vitiated, usually by oversight or exclusion – as when we are told that emotions are simply and solely judgments, feelings, or social roles.

Thus far non-committal – my concern being to preserve a measure of independence and maximize anthropological advantage – readers will no doubt expect me to admit where I think the weight of evidence in emotion studies currently lies, even if that means testing their patience a little. Against the stronger forms of relativism and scepticism, the contention is that emotions do indeed hang together, whether at the level of experience or below decks where the interaction of diverse processes mostly happens out of consciousness (Frijda 1986, 2008; Scherer 2005, 2009). Except in a few curious ethnographic cases, duly to be considered, emotions hang together both subjectively and objectively. My perception of offence, my tensing up and getting hot under the collar, the feeling of being angry, and the urge to retaliate are of a piece: a coherent, shapely, temporal sequence, like a wave. Likewise the biological processes that underlie the sequence (Grandjean & Scherer 2009: 387). The coherence of emotions is *emergent*, like a picture that comes into focus, holds a while, then morphs into a different picture – a different emotion – as the focus shortens or the object of emotion changes (Barrett 2017; Clore & Ortony 2008). This transient coherence is not the determinate unity of an entity with physical or categorical boundaries like a tree, a mosque, or a game of chess; but nor is it

Introduction

the invention of fancy, like the Big Dipper in James Russell's sceptical analogy (2003), picked out among the stars but lacking scientific validity.[1] Our sense of what is happening to us, and perhaps our categorizing the event as 'anger' or 'shame' – whether verbalized or not – give direction and meaning to the emotion, communicate intent, and urge action. The form of subjective experience and the terms of its enactment – the phenomenology of emotion – are embedded in social life and learned through engagement with others. Unlike the stars, which are indifferent to our thoughts and plans, emotions are made up of them. In this heavily qualified sense, 'emotions are real' (Barrett 2012).

This affirmation of a multiplex reality salvages the bridge to cross-cultural understanding that relativism would sweep away. It also avoids the empiricist limitations of basic emotions theories that tend to ignore all that concerns the anthropologist – motives, plans, meaning, the social drama (Oatley 1992 a prominent exception). Still, however we want to delimit emotion, beyond a functional interdependence among ingredients it is difficult to specify what that grand coming together amounts to, especially since the contributing processes – perception, autonomic response, motivation – are not unique to emotion. Unsurprisingly, an agreed formal definition remains elusive (Dixon 2012; Manstead, Frijda & Fischer 2004; Solomon 2004).

Most scientific approaches to emotion allow some role for cultural diversity, the anthropologist's traditional entrée. What varies is the degree to which culture is admitted to be more than window-dressing. Ekman's basic emotions theory limits the role to 'display rules', conventions governing emotional expression. Likewise, Jamesian 'feeling theories' make the socio-cultural context superficial or secondary to what is going on inside the organism (Damasio 1999).

---

[1] Russell's objection is meant to apply to a scientific borrowing of the *everyday concept* of emotion; see also Widen & Russell (2010).

Introduction

In cognitive theories, by contrast, it is the subject's appraisal of a situation that characterizes the emotion. For the cognitivist, the emphasis falls on how the eliciting event – the offence, the kiss, the goal – looks to the subject and how she will respond, rather than how she feels, how quickly her heart is beating, or what face she is pulling. Cognitivists allow a greater role to cultural shaping, language, and individual variation in the constitution of emotion.

Magda Arnold, the inspiration for later appraisal theories, wrote in 1960: 'To arouse an emotion, the object must be appraised as affecting me in some way, affecting me personally as an individual with my particular experience and my particular aims' (quoted in Cornelius 1996: 112). The first anthropologist to take up this idea of contextualized self-involvement was Michelle Rosaldo, who defined emotions as 'embodied thoughts, thoughts seeped with the apprehension that "I am involved"' (1984: 143). Two philosophical formulations in the cognitivist tradition are also worth quoting, as they bear directly on a narrative approach. For Aaron Ben Ze'ev, 'an emotion is always related to a certain personal frame of reference against which its significance is evaluated' (2010. 44). For Robert Roberts, emotions are 'concern-based construals of ourselves, others and our situations' (1988: 208). The practice of standard ethnographic reporting, be it noted, typically underrates the 'personal frame of reference', quickly diverting to the *general* frame (e.g. the value system, gender politics, kinship categories) or assuming that personal significance is consistent from one instance to another. By eliminating personal entanglements, life history, and point of view, standard ethnography empties emotions of meaningful content.

To avoid this error, and also to get around definitional and boundary problems, I make the minimal unit of description the *emotional episode*. This capacious framework has the double advantage of making no assumptions about what an emotion is while including within a relatively small scale all that interests us in human behaviour – feeling, meaning, relationship, circumstance, action, implication, history. It

Introduction

allows a focus on the constituents of social life without presuming what they individually are, or even *that* they individually are (what is a relationship without circumstance? what is action without meaning?). If it turns out that emotions are not brute reflexes, evolved action programmes, or pragmatic ploys, but are assembled on the wing in ways scientists of ten or fifteen years ago cannot possibly have known (Barrett 2017), and that componential, appraisal, and semantic theories, not to mention discrete emotion theories, are up for revision, that need not disturb us. If the anthropologist is working on a broader canvas, the pointillist details disappear into the whole.

Part I

Groundings

ONE

Emotions in the Field
Recognition and Location

The unsettling power of ethnography in social research, its capacity to unseat assumptions and surprise with facts, derives from its odd mix of methodological holism and microscopic documentation, breadth of interest and intensity of focus. We ended the Introduction by imagining the 'whole' (emotional episodes interwoven within a narrative; the dots blended in a pointillist painting); now we zoom back in on the detail. The aim is to reveal the microscopic complexity of emotions, the brushmarks a synoptic view blurs. By doing so we can begin to explore what it is that makes emotions heterogeneous within a cultural setting and more systematically divergent across cultures. A close focus will give us a better fix on some of the challenging anomalies that ethnography casts up before we head into the field in Chapters 2 and 3 with the extended examples of Nias and Java.

As well as using ethnography, in seeking out the fine-grained details I shall draw upon literature – as I do throughout this book – taking advantage of the 'privileged access' (first-person point of view, knowledge of others' thoughts) denied to ethnography. Artistic insight is its own justification. But we can take encouragement from a comment of the poet-critic William Empson, who lived much of his life in the Far East. 'The main purpose of reading imaginative literature', he wrote, 'is to grasp a wide variety of experience, imagining people with codes

Groundings

and customs very unlike our own' (quoted in Bromwich 2017). Sounds very like ethnography.

The complexity of emotions

How can we begin to grasp the complexity of something as nebulous and fleeting as an emotion? How can we locate it in action, in circumstances and personality? Before analyzing an example it might be helpful, initially, to make some distinctions between emotions and other affective phenomena.

Emotions are of the moment. Unlike thoughts, attitudes, and preferences, which need not be present to be attributed ('he thinks he is good at tennis'), an emotion is only attributable while it is happening – much like a perception. But ordinary language is misleading. A 'jealous husband' has a *disposition* to jealousy: he does not experience jealousy the whole time. His being a jealous husband is an attribution of character and inclination, not of occurrent emotion. If I am said to love someone, that does not imply I am always and only feeling love (unless I am 'in love', a more acute and comprehensive case); rather I am disposed to feel love and act accordingly on occasion. Being angry, being an angry person, feeling angry and acting angry are not the same things. Emotion, feeling, character, disposition, and performance are linked but not equivalent.

Affective feelings that persist beyond a given situation, or appear unconnected with circumstances, are designated *moods*. An episode of anxiety and an anxious mood are qualitatively similar, but their constitution is different. Whereas emotions usually have an object (the beloved, the dentist, a parking ticket), moods have a vaguer application or none. Their elicitation, content, and biology are different from the briefer events we call emotions.

In philosophical jargon, emotions are 'intentional': they are *about* something, they 'have the feature of *directedness*' (Pugmire 1998: 12, 60;

Solomon 1993). This intentionality may even apply to emotions we are not aware of. My disappointment in a missed opportunity is manifest only in my irritability. Late for a reunion, I am angry with myself (the object) but take it out on the driver (the target). Dreams, non-conscious, are drenched in emotion though the objects of feeling often seem unaccountable. And in the complex case of mixed emotions, one feeling may predominate while not quite displacing another; they may alternate in consciousness like an oscillating figure and ground as this or that aspect of a situation comes to mind.

The interplay between levels of consciousness of emotion and the shifting of attention between emotional objects combines to make human behaviour endlessly fascinating, unpredictable, and easily misunderstood. Tolstoy is particularly acute on unrecognized emotions, showing how their undercurrents disturb the surface of behaviour and elude conscious formulation. Here, for example, in *War and Peace,* he describes the thought processes, bodily habitus, and mixed feelings of Pierre in the presence of his wife's admirer, the social climber Boris Drubetskoy (whom he resists regarding with suspicion):

The smile she gave him [Boris] was the same as she bestowed on everybody, but sometimes it gave Pierre an unpleasant feeling . . .
. . . strange to say, the presence of Boris in his wife's drawing room (and he was almost always there) had a physical effect upon Pierre: it seemed to paralyse his limbs, to awaken all his self-consciousness and take away his freedom of movement.
'Such a strange antipathy,' thought Pierre, 'and yet at one time I really liked him very much.' (1973: 517)

Characteristically, Tolstoy does not name the 'unpleasant feeling': it is inchoate, barely conscious; and Pierre, self-protectively, misconstrues it as an unwelcome judgment about Boris as a man, rather than about what Boris might do to him and his marriage. That misrecognition, implying a reluctance to act, has serious consequences. Because emotions are *about*

Groundings

the world and what our circumstances mean for us, we do well to heed them. But then Pierre has higher things on his mind; and his formation, composed of character and history, is important too in assessing the meaning and practical import of the episode. The emotion arises, and is modulated, within a broader set of judgments and feelings about life and the world that come with a long and evolving personal history. Bluntly, we could state that Pierre did not realize he felt jealous in confronting a rival; but we would miss out almost everything of psychological and social significance. At the very least, we would misread the plot, the dispositions of actors, and the messages they convey, wittingly or not. Our simple set of universals – the painting-by-numbers guide to the emotions – leaves us hopelessly equipped to navigate the aristocratic Petersburg salons (for that we need Tolstoy); but so, too, would we be lost in the humbler settings of Java and Nias.

Pierre's predicament highlights a number of issues for the ethnographer, issues both practical and theoretical:

- the partial privacy of emotions
- their being subjective *and* objective, in here and out there
- their embodiment
- their relation to judgments and other cognitions
- their immediate context (what elicits them; the intentional object; how they are directed; the target and audience)
- their scope and duration
- their degree of consciousness or recognition
- their naming (or not) and their place within speech acts
- their focalness (or not) in action or thought
- their relation to other emotions
- their place within personal histories and relationships.

The list is not exhaustive. One could, for example, show how Tolstoy subtly conveys the way emotion guides perception. Notice how in the sentence, 'the presence of Boris in his wife's drawing room (and he was almost always there) had a physical effect upon Pierre', the innocent phrase in parenthesis indirectly conveys Pierre's *awareness* of Boris's ubiquity – we are seeing the scene from his point of view – while bracketing (as if disavowing) the suspicion it suggests. The unrecognized emotion is conveyed in the *observation*. Robbe-Grillet's novel *Jealousy* (1965) is entirely constructed in this manner, the roving view of objects and shadows through the slats of a blind (*jalousie*) insinuating, in the absence of a speaking narrator, a monomaniac passion. In the obsessive mind, emotion and perception fuse: jealousy is in the eye of the beholder.

This kind of circumstantial control and psychological penetration, while beyond the reach of ethnography as usually conceived, should alert us to the constitutional complexity of emotion and warn us off a simple label-sticking or a retreat into translation games. We first have to recognize what we are up against; only then can we begin to hazard an approach.

First-person/third-person perspectives

If it is all so complicated, why bother? Why not admit defeat and leave it to the novelists? Indeed, a possible objection to an anthropology of emotion – one frequently levelled at psychological anthropology generally – is the inaccessibility of subjective experience to the outsider. Only we ourselves can know what we feel and perceive, the objection goes. True enough, the privacy of emotions has to do with their partial interiority. But this is not to say that only I know my emotions or that they lead a secret life independent of circumstance and history. The sense I make of my feelings depends on the emotion concepts I have learned and the paradigmatic settings associated with them (Goldie 2000: 33), all of which are shared within a certain world – what the historian Barbara Rosenwein (2006) calls an emotional community. The private is framed by the public; more concretely, by the *social*. Others may, in fact, know better than I do that I am acting out of jealousy. I may be unconscious of

Groundings

my motivating emotions or would prefer not to recognize them. I may lack the self-control to mask them. Conversely, if I am a good actor I may convey emotions without feeling them, or come to feel them while feigning them, surprising myself as I deceive others (Pugmire 1998: 118–121). Interiority is not an obstacle to comprehension but an aspect of a shared experience over which no one, including the subject herself, has a privileged vantage. There is no final say over what an emotion means, no last word on the matter: rather, many words, interweaving among differently placed actors, the emotions responding, shaping and guiding, colouring the scene now this way, now that.

Given the inherently dramatic nature of emotions – *dramatic* in the strict sense – a purely internal, subjective view would be as misleading as a purely external, third-person one. In the passion play there is no offstage, no emotional private language. To grasp this point is to reject the overstated positions of the sceptic ('we can never really know another's emotions'), the relativist ('we are all unknowably different'), and the empiricist ('we are measurably similar, we have a common natural history'). The ingredients of an emotion episode – gesture, expression, voice, words, situation, setting, relationship, and history – are all observable or recountable, even if we do not vibrate on the same wavelength and remain, like the Javanese in their parlour, sympathetic but cool.

As for the feeling – the invisible element too casually equated with emotion – we cannot exactly know what the other feels (or indeed *whether* they feel) though empathy can take us half-way (see Chapter 10). What is more certain is that the unfolding elements of the drama – as we construe it – bring us to an understanding. The play's the thing.

The ethnographic challenge to a cross-cultural conception of emotion

As we have seen, emotions are observable, scrutable, meaningful: fair game for the ethnographer. They are not private events, sealed off from the involved or the curious. But are they of a piece? Maybe 'emotion', as such, is a chimera like one of those randomly defined classes in a Borges fable. What justifies our treating horror and joy as similar sorts of phenomena? Consider their diversity: some emotions come with distinctive facial expressions (anger), some without (regret); some respond instantly to an external stimulus (surprise), others follow introspection (remorse); some prompt action (disgust), others imply inaction (boredom); some have an evolutionary pay-off (fear, love), others lack reproductive advantage (nostalgia). Given this heterogeneity, it is hardly surprising that a superordinate category of emotion has not been reported from many of the places where anthropologists have worked. For the cognitive psychologist James Russell (1991), this is the principal challenge posed by ethnography. If a domain of emotion is unrecognized or unnamed, the comparative project of recording and contrasting exotic emotion terms appears threatened. For what is to count as an emotion? The very idea of an emotional domain – routinely invoked in anthropology – can lead us to misjudge similarly named behaviours as equivalent. As the Javanese vignette in the Introduction shows, it is not always clear whether a reported instance of 'shame' (for example) refers to a feeling, a form of etiquette, or an unemotional evaluation of a situation. Still, *emotion* is the word we are stuck with – or have to find ways of getting around. And if the historical question is why the category should have arisen in Europe, the scientific and philosophical question is whether its cultural origin vitiates its utility. Can it be that our folk concept just happens to capture a human universal? Or are scientific definitions – more precise and explicit than ordinary usage – notably different? Are they culture-free?

A glance at the literature shows that, without being committed to a firm definition of the object of study or a shared view of its reality, theorists in the social sciences, the affective sciences, and philosophy can nevertheless agree on a rough area of discussion they call

Groundings

'emotion'. In such collections as Ekman and Davidson (1994), Goldie (2010) and Manstead et al. (2004), leading thinkers on emotion appear to accept the usefulness of the English word to categorize certain socially embedded psychobiological processes, without agreeing about how such processes cohere, or how much causal or definitional prominence should be given to such components as arousal, feeling, appraisal, action tendencies, and facial expression. For some theorists 'emotion' denotes a class of distinctive phenomena conveniently labeled by the English word; for others it lacks any essential referent. After a lifetime of experimental work, the psychologist Nico Frijda concluded that, though '"emotion" represents a meaningful and necessary concept' (2008: 68), it does not designate a uniformly constituted domain. Instead, '"emotion" can perhaps best be taken to designate any process in which the various components [appraisal, feeling, etc.] are intimately connected' (2008: 73). For Frijda, the emotion concept 'therefore serves as a shorthand for, or pointer to, intrapersonal processes and mechanisms' (ibid., 69). The task of the emotion researcher is thus justified without needing to presume that emotions are *natural* kinds – a question on which the jury is still out (Barrett 2006; Scarantino 2012) – or, indeed, one kind of thing at all.

A different compromise position between scepticism and realism (the view that emotions are constituted independently of how we understand them) can be found in James Averill's (1994) suggestion that emotion is a polythetic class, that is, a class composed of overlapping sets of members belonging in some loose grouping, not by virtue of exclusive identity, but by sporadic family resemblances. Rodney Needham (1975), from whom I have taken this definition, was the first to explore the implications of polythetic classification for anthropology, pointing out that many of the analytical categories used by anthropologists (religion, kinship, marriage) have turned out, on critical inspection, to be polythetic; which meant that generalizations based on the assumption

32

that kinship – Needham's field – was a homogeneous category were false. This led him to declare that there was no such thing as kinship. Later authors took the point, but were more accommodating. Rather than abandoning the kinship concept altogether, one respected its polythetic configuration and looked for regularities at a lower level, within a fuzzily bounded field, while remaining alert to connections across the boundary with, say, politics. What matters, in this perspective, is not the identification of an objective domain – emotion – but the productive enquiry into how thoughts, feelings, and situations cluster in recognizable and culturally definable patterns. This non-prescriptive, let-see-what-emerges approach is what emotion sceptics like Richard Shweder (1994) and Anna Wierzbicka (1999) are advocating. Why else write a book called *Emotions Across Languages and Cultures* when, avowedly, the English word 'emotion' does not 'carve nature at its joints' (Wierzbicka 1999: 3)?

Leave aside for the moment the possibility, unconsidered by Needham, that reality is not indifferent to how we divide it up, that classification interferes as it orders; on a practical level the idea that emotion categories are polythetically defined is liberating. It grants the ethnographer licence to look anywhere, to find connections and significances in unlikely places – outside the realm we normally associate with the psychological, for example. Standing back from the cabinet of ethnographic curiosities, we might then agree with Shweder that 'emotion is a complex synthetic notion; and particular emotions (e.g., sadness, envy, guilt, and love) are derivatives of various combinations of wants, beliefs, feelings, and values' (2004: 83). The anthropologist's job, on this view, would be to investigate such combinations without a prior commitment to that notional whole, 'emotion'. In similar terms, the linguist Anna Wierzbicka proposes investigating 'questions focusing on what people think, feel, want, know, say, and do; what happens in their bodies; how the thoughts, feelings, wants, and bodily events are linked . . . and what role the feelings . . . play in the stream of

Groundings

life' (1999: 24).[1] This proposal, which encompasses a great deal while taking little for granted, offers a robust basis for ethnographic research. Those who see emotion as having some theory-independent reality or integrity (various contributors to Manstead, Frijda & Fischer 2004; Mulligan & Scherer 2012) might wonder at the rationale of a comparative project whose organizing concept is in doubt. But given the possible yield – the discovery of ways of acting, thinking and feeling unimaginable in the lab – the challenge is worth taking on. And the risk, surely, falls to both sides of the debate.

Fortunately for dialogue, in any case, both relativists and realists (to oversimplify positions) are interested in how appraisals, feelings, words and actions are variably linked, however those linkages may be conceived. Shweder (1994, 2004) is prepared to suggest that the linkages might not point to something that 'we' would call emotion. To assume otherwise is to prejudge the case and rule out the possibility that in other cultural settings appraisals, feelings, and behaviour might not hang together in ways familiar to us. He argues that we must be open to the possibility – attested by ethnography (Levy 1973) – that serious loss may be experienced as fatigue or illness rather than 'emotionalized' as 'sadness'. This would not be altogether surprising given that, as Lutz writes of the people of Ifaluk, Micronesia (and as many ethnographers testify), 'emotion, thought, and body are seen in ethnotheory as intimately linked through their roles in illness' (Lutz 1988: 100; Sobo 1996). However, a *non*-emotional response to loss would depend on the possibility that cultural practices do not merely shape experience but can override putatively universal processes. 'Emotionalizing', on this view, would consist in consciously dwelling on the personal dimension of loss, thinking about the feeling, or thinking about the loss in a

---

[1] Wierzbicka's project is to identify conceptual primes – simple concepts like 'think', 'feel' and 'say' found in all linguistic traditions which can be combined to define more complex culture-specific concepts like 'emotion' or 'nostalgia'.

Emotions in the Field

particular involving way. It would be an empirical question which kinds of experience are emotionalized or not in a given cultural setting.

The headman's defeat and the case of the poisoned buffalo

Shweder is onto something here, and his deconstructive method is useful for the fieldworker. It helps to make sense of two puzzling episodes in my Javanese fieldwork. In the first, the headman of Bayu, my host village, was humiliated by critics in the mosque on the occasion of the Prophet's birthday (see Beatty 2009 for the full story). A visiting preacher had denounced the secularism and laxity over which the headman had presided. Islamists in the audience had clapped and cheered, breaking convention and offending the other villagers, lax and pious alike. Stuck at the back on a sofa beside the VIPs, the headman could do nothing. No one spoke up in his defence and, without a platform (he was not listed on the order of service), he was unable to outface the mockers. When a second speaker called on the congregation to rise in praise of the Prophet, he remained seated at the back. And when he finally rose – with my encouragement: I feared his isolation would make things worse – moments later he sank back in a faint. 'Dizzy', he croaked, and collapsed. That was the start of his mysterious illness.

What was going on? In the headman's place we might have experienced shame, humiliation, and anger; but he, apparently, did not. He had grasped the threat to his position and reputation, but he did not fully emotionalize his response. Although I cannot precisely know the string of thoughts and feelings leading up to his collapse, seated next to him at the back I was party to his deliberations as he whispered to me and passed me notes, which were all about *tactics*. The telegraphic commentary was quite different from the self-reports of 'angry', 'ashamed', and 'not comfortable', which usually justify or announce an action. The headman was paralyzed by hesitation – whether to strike or

Groundings

submit. Hamlet's dilemma. A Javanese adage I often heard when conflict loomed goes: '*Aja kalah, ngalah!*' ('Better concede than be defeated!') It is futile to oppose brute force, stupidity, or craziness; better to yield, as a tree bends in the wind, and survive. My friend explicitly deliberated in this way, weighing the odds ('Shall I speak?' 'Ah! Let them have their head!'), but evidently felt the attack as overwhelming. He could neither accept defeat nor shrug in face-saving concession, his usual recourse. So how did he construe the assault? In some way, he did not allow it to translate into emotion; that is, he did not appraise the event or the feelings evoked in terms that entailed the locally predictable emotions. If, as Lazarus (1991) argues, an emotion is a felt appraisal of a situation seen in terms of expectations and motivation, or 'core relational themes' (disgrace → shame; insult → anger); or if emotions entail 'action tendencies', as Frijda (1986) proposes, the headman seems to have cut short the process, disengaging, refusing to play. To put this in English terms (and setting aside the question of their cross-cultural validity), his defeat was experienced less as a shaming *disgrace* or angering *affront* than as something like a physical blow. so it materialized as he collapsed beside me. Accordingly, his slow recovery, which I observed at close quarters over many weeks, was not effected through emotional introspection or catharsis (an unpicking of causes, a conscious feeling of implications); nor through hot revenge or a public expiation of shame. Instead, he outflanked his critics in a long and calculated campaign. Victory was the cure.

I think also of the ploughman – a casual friend, not an intimate like the headman – who one afternoon received me in his house shortly after finding his buffalo, his sole means of livelihood, poisoned in the stable. As we chatted and smoked clove cigarettes, his even composure and broad smile gave nothing away. It was only later that I learned about the buffalo and the tormenting details – the poison pellets found in the hay stall; the hurried sale of the dying beast as cheap meat in the next town; the dealer who had happened by the reeking stable. Was *he* the

Emotions in the Field

poisoner? Or was it the owner of an adjoining field, sick of the buffalo trampling her border? What other designs did the malefactor have? As the ploughman later explained, these calculations ran through his mind as he dealt with the fallout. By evening, when the news had broken, he was entertaining a stream of well-wishers and by then he had formulated his response: how it was his *due*, a blow destined to make him 'aware'; how relieved he was that his daughter had been spared the attack (though he could no longer provide for her wedding); how he had felt much worse when his adopted son joined the army. Peasant fortitude laced with philosophy; that, and a canny avoidance of open speculation – who knows, the culprit might still be smoked out!

But it was the earlier stolidness that puzzled me. You might call it the limiting case of Javanese display rules, which demand a bland appearance, a steady composure. You might call it iron self-control – but the lack of tension, the sheer ordinariness of the encounter ruled that out. You might call it extreme obtuseness on my part; but I had known him for two years as a neighbour and felt relaxed in his company; I was familiar with his faces and voices. As reconstructed later, the links between event, evaluation, feeling, and expression were nothing I could comprehend. Whatever he had felt on discovering the massive, foam-flecked body in the straw – shock, fear, and anger, perhaps despair? – you would have expected some residue in the immediate aftermath. His appraisal of what had happened, what it meant to him and his family, cannot so drastically have changed. In his classic writings on Java, Clifford Geertz makes much of *iklas*, an Arabic-derived term that denotes the moral sentiment of acceptance, 'a kind of willed affectlessness, a detached and static state of "not caring"' (Geertz 1973a: 153). But *iklas* comes later, during the long night's reckoning; it is a sentiment made for repose. As with the headman's fall from grace, something in the sequence of an emotion episode or in the sparking of ingredients appears to have been short-circuited or overcome: exhibiting less, implying more than what might have been

Groundings

expected. What the ploughman had very quickly achieved was a kind of disengagement, a refusal to feel. Caring, but not feeling.

As these perplexing examples show, Javanese emotion episodes are not always readily translatable into the patterns of Western psychology: the scripts for responses are not just different, as we might expect; they tap into experiences and temperaments with quite different developmental backgrounds and capacities, and they belong to histories not easily reduced to formula. Such episodes cannot be replicated under experimental conditions. Emerging in narrative context, they are invisible to science.

Or very nearly so. But if emotional dramas cannot be staged in the lab, that is no reason to exclude scientific theories from the field. In deconstructing emotion episodes, or attempting to recover them within broader narratives, it may be helpful here to refer to a longstanding debate in emotion studies. What can we learn about emotions by training different lenses on our ethnographic specimens? What do they reveal about the awkward cases?

Feeling theory v. appraisal theory

– He turned away, his heart still knocking in its cage, as if it were trying to transmit a message, a warning, in a code he didn't understand.

Graham Greene, *The Confidential Agent*

As briefly mentioned in the Introduction, in contrast to appraisal theorists, who give causal and temporal priority to the cognition of the event over the feeling it elicits, Jamesians – named after pioneering psychologist William James – see emotions as an awareness of bodily changes that follow the initial stimulus. You encounter a bear, your heart pounds, your hair prickles, your muscles tense, and you flee; but *fear* is the feeling of the bodily changes, not a conscious mental appraisal of danger that feeds into feeling. In James's capitalized

Emotions in the Field

formula, which seemed to flout common sense, 'My thesis on the contrary is that the bodily changes follow directly the PERCEPTION of the exciting fact, and that our feeling of the same changes as they occur IS the emotion' (1884: 189–190). In an influential updating of James that takes into account a century of scientific discussion *pro* and *contra*, the neuroscientist Antonio Damasio (1999, 2003) argues that feelings are mappings of the state of the body in changing circumstances (which might include thirst, danger, and sexual opportunity). A feeling, as a 'representation' of disturbed bodily states (2003: 130), prompts a search for meaning in the internal or external environment, a context that makes sense of what has already been subliminally cognized and felt and which requires action. 'Joy and sorrow and other feelings are largely ideas of the body in the process of maneuvering itself into states of optimal survival' (2003: 140). If we have survived as a species from the Pleistocene through the Ice Age and into the Health-and-Safety Era, it is thanks to evolved rapid reactions, not pondered wisdom. A wide range of evidence outside the Jamesian tradition seems to support this view. In a landmark experiment which showed that subjects favoured visual stimuli they had previously seen without knowing they had done so (the stimuli were too quick to to be consciously registered), Zajonc concluded that 'to arouse affect, objects need to be cognized very little – in fact, minimally' (1980: 154). In a famous slogan, 'preferences need no inferences'. Yet complex emotions like guilt and love do, in fact, need a good deal of anterior processing. The question of precedence largely depends on where you draw the line in bounding an emotion episode; it depends also on what qualifies as an appraisal, minimal or maximal. Hard to feel guilty before you have worked out who is to blame.

In Shweder's hypothesis, which in this respect is Jamesian, the emotion is an interpretation of the *feeling* rather than an interpretation of the eliciting event. Emotions are 'complex narrative structures that give shape and meaning to somatic and affective experiences' (Shweder 1994:

Groundings

37). How true is this of a given sequence? My Javanese cases are equivocal; but so too is introspective knowledge. Sometimes we scan our feelings as a touchstone of what really matters to us, as if asking them to tell us what *they* know: 'Do I really love her?' 'How *much* do I want that job?' 'Should I stay or should I go?' The sense that our feelings are particular to us ('the job bores me') and therefore closer to what we really are than our detached thoughts, which have a certain discardable impersonality ('the job is worth having'), justifies such intuitions. More often, however, the touchstone is the affecting *situation*: 'Was that really meant as an insult? Should I be angry?' Without a context – a construction of the eliciting situation – you cannot interpret a feeling; it cannot come into being.

Feeling theorists like to hit appraisal theorists with James's thought-experiment in which he tries to imagine fear, rage, and grief minus their physical attributes. James puts the case with characteristic force:

What kind of emotion of fear would be left, if the feelings neither of quickened heart-beats nor of shallow breathing, neither of trembling lips nor weakened limbs, neither of goose flesh nor of visceral stirrings, were present, it is quite impossible to think.... In like manner of grief: what would it be without its tears, its suffocation of the heart, its pang in the breast-bone? A feelingless cognition that certain circumstances are deplorable, and nothing more. Every passion in turn tells the same story. A purely disembodied human emotion is a nonentity. (1884: 194)

And so it is. And yet all those agitations without a recognized context are equally unimaginable. Palpitations and visceral stirrings without perceived danger would not be fear but a medical emergency. Feelings, perhaps, but not *affective* feelings, not emotions. Hence the need for a 'two-factor theory' – or something more than two – that gives due place to cognition and bodily agitation in their multiple interactions (Cornelius 1996). In fact, the effort to sharply distinguish the bodily from the cognitive, or the inner from the outer, feels untrue to

40

experience. As Wittgenstein puts it, in what amounts to a rejoinder to James: 'I should almost like to say: One no more feels sorrow in one's body than one feels seeing in one's eyes' (1967: 88).

The ethnographic conundrums

I want to come back to the ethnographic puzzles and the challenge they pose for a theory of emotion. Fieldwork turns up examples that contradict our expectations of how emotions work, prompting doubts about whether they qualify as emotions, and therefore whether there *are* such things – cross-culturally and unambiguously – as emotions (as opposed to diverse combinations of appraisals, feelings, etc.). As ever, the exceptions present the greatest difficulty. I have mentioned two instances of my own already. A well-known example that bears revisiting is that of Robert Levy's Tahitian informant, a man abandoned by his wife, who 'interpreted his feelings about separation as some sort of vague sickness' (Levy 1973: 304). To be precise, he was tormented by thoughts of his wife and child but seemed not to connect them with his 'feeling "not good" and "without energy"'. A sense that something was wrong, out of the ordinary, brought him to Levy for medicine. And it is this puzzle that arouses Levy's interest. Wouldn't you expect to feel sad in losing your family? On Shweder's view, we should not apply the concepts of 'sadness' or 'emotion' here – nor does Levy – because the feeling has not been emotionalized. In another Tahitian example, a man seen crying at the grave of his wife is assumed by witnesses to be feeling remorse for his infidelities rather than – as we should suppose – sadness for his recent loss (Levy 1973: 298, 301). This is a different kind of evidence from the self-reported malaise of the deserted husband. Nevertheless, in all such cases, the ethnographer argues, Tahitians 'hypocognize' sadness (ibid. 227). Lacking an equivalent word, perhaps lacking the concept altogether, and without the cultural formulas and expectations of prolonged grief, they have no means of packaging their

Groundings

feelings and thoughts as anything like sadness and do not recognize or expect persisting sadness in others. Troublesome feelings following loss are interpreted, instead, as possession by the departed spirit (Levy 1973: 299; 1984). For Levy, this implies misrecognition of the primary apprehension, a culturally induced cognitive mistake rather than a simple absence of what would be, to us, the predictable emotion. Like Shweder, Levy makes the interpretation contingent on the feeling. (The abandoned husband obsesses about his loss. So we cannot say that the *event* or the *core relational theme* are underrated, only the bad feeling.)

Despite the wealth of cultural information presented in *Tahitians*, these much-discussed examples are reported in scant terms, with minimal concrete observation, and mixed with hypothetical cases. We know nothing of the background of the individuals, the quality of their relationships, the history of separations, or how normal the individuals are. (In my example from Tolstoy, the backstory permits us to divine Pierre's jealousy as unrecognized but dimly felt, at once disturbing and motivating, rather than categorically 'hypocognized', which would be unlikely in the Russian case.) The absence of idiosyncratic particulars, and the recourse to general cultural factors and folk psychology, make it hard to compare among Tahitian cases and across cultures. I cannot easily apply Levy's analysis to my Javanese friends whose reactions, in any case, are not typical, even of the men themselves. To make sense of them you need a good deal of biographical background and narrative context. Levy's Tahitians are presented as both typical and fully explained by immediate context; yet only in the *general* terms of cultural logic do the examples carry conviction. On a human level, as persons with particular relations and histories, they remain enigmatic, merely exotic. We cannot help wondering whether the sharpening of the argument, the distillation of a generalization, exaggerates the difference. Is there, as in Ifaluk and Java, a close association between emotion and illness that might explain why a man haunted by his wife's departure should experience 'vague illness' and lethargy? Or are there untold stories that explain the underrating of the feelings associated with loss? Something is missing but we should not assume it is missing from the Tahitians.

If I have laboured an old example, it is because Levy's ethnography has featured in many discussions of emotion, besides serving as the model for subsequent 'person-centered ethnography' (Hollan 2001). *Tahitians* remains unsurpassed in its comprehensiveness, a classic of psychological anthropology, but the problems with its presentation of emotion have not been properly identified or overcome. And there is a further lesson. If, as is often the case with cross-cultural comparison, compression, selection, and narrative omission enhance difference, so does the inverse stereotyping of 'Euro-American culture', the usual point of departure. *We* emotionalize, *they* somatize. We feel sadness, they feel fatigue. Yet anyone who has attended a modern English funeral cannot be shocked by Tahiti. The collective determination to put on a good face, the cheerful tributes celebrating the life of the deceased, the lack of solemnity before tragedy would all have seemed unaccountable fifty years ago. And we learn from the latest edition of the American psychiatrists' Bible, the *Diagnostic and Statistical Manual of Mental Disorders*, that grief lasting more than a few weeks is to be classed as pathological. We are all becoming 'Tahitians'.

Description v. explanation

If emotion cannot readily be placed or defined – or reliably identified, as in these enigmatic cases – why should its anthropological investigation have any scientific value? We cannot explain a thing if we do not know what it is – where it begins and ends, what counts as an example and what does not. In this respect a focus on emotion highlights a more general problem with anthropological analysis, where the terms of comparison (religion, clanship, etc.) are imprecise in their reference – a problem compounded by the difficulties of classification ('family

Groundings

resemblances'), and the embeddedness of all social phenomena. As the methods manuals are apt to lament, anthropology scores high on validity, low on reliability: its findings are irreproachably authentic but hard to generalize; its 'experiments', like life itself, unrepeatable.

Fleeting, entangled in circumstance, emotions are especially resistant to abstraction. All of which makes the line between description and explanation hard to draw. Most anthropologists would agree that it is not enough merely to describe; but how far can you depart from the particulars without losing the object of analysis; and how far does description, in any case, smuggle in explanation? Or to put it the other way around, to what extent is explanation merely a form of redescription? A definite answer cannot be given without taking up some concrete position – the fixed perch I am determined to avoid. That tension between the quest for universals, which characterizes an important strand of psychological anthropology, and the drive for fidelity to experience that moves the working ethnographer instead compels a compromise: a respect for diverse, even opposed, views of a given case and a recognition of the multidimensionality intrinsic to an emotion episode. A singular explanation of emotion – whether evolutionary, biological, structural, or cultural – has no place in this approach. Indeed, many otherwise cogent presentations are marred by messianic claims to possession of the whole truth. Good reports are weakened by overstatement: that emotions are *nothing but* political ploys, evolutionary strategies, or social commentaries. In the field, nothing is ever nothing but. An account of what emotion does in a given setting should not be read as an account of what it is (the functionalist fallacy). Nor should an account of what an emotion means be assumed to exhaust its functions (the idealist fallacy).

With so many options, one admits to feeling torn. But if my argument so far makes any sense, the proper choice is between alternative ethnographic objectives (A politics of emotion? A perspective on memory? A study of emotive language?) rather than, pre-emptively,

44

between rival views of what emotion might be. The ethnographic maxim must always be to cast the net wide – wide enough to catch the Russians, Javanese, *and* Tahitians – and to present our cases in enough narrative detail to make sense of the egregious exception, the odd fish. An ethnography worth its salt will overflow the bounds of analysis, approaching in abundance and intricacy realist fiction and the historian's data-rich reconstruction.

Conclusion

In this chapter I have focused on practical and theoretical problems involved in recognising and identifying emotions in the field. Close focus reveals not only the diverse constitution of different kinds of emotions, but the problem of how emotions are bounded and located. I have set out the argument for a polythetic view in which no single element is necessary or sufficient. The approach taken is inclusive but also sceptical. In opting for 'emotional episodes' rather than emotions-as-entities, we open up ethnography to unexpected junctures of thought, feeling, and action and widen the scope of comparison. We also gain insights into the odd cases, the anomalies that confound theory. But a strong sense of mystery remains.

Recognition, location, definition, scope: the issues seem so fraught with difficulty it would be easy to feel paralysed before them. And paralysis, of a kind, is what typically afflicts the intending ethnographer. For this there is only one remedy: plunge in.

TWO

Nias
Emotions Dramatized

An ethnographic approach

Ethnography takes us into different emotional worlds, revealing other modes of relating and ways of being. A cliché, no doubt; something for the blurb. What does it actually mean? Anyone who has travelled knows that the feel of a place, the social rhythm, the warmth or chill of relations, the embodied etiquette, the enthusiasms and taboos on or off display – in a word, the ethos – are different from one place to another. We register these differences; we make adjustments, storing up anecdotes, sometimes getting into trouble. There is something to write home about.

What interests the anthropologist, however, is the conceptual and experiential roots of those perplexing differences, the interlocking of salient emotions with social systems that the casual visitor barely suspects. For which we need more than an inventory of ethos or habits of the heart. There is a case to be made, by example, for an *ethnographic* approach to the emotional life. Intensive forays into other worlds yield something altogether different from the hypothetical scenarios used in philosophy or the statistical specimens of psychology. Fieldwork brings to light unsuspected aspects of emotion, novel linkages of word, action, and feeling that challenge standard views of emotion and expand the range of discussion, enlarging our sense of human possibility.

This chapter on Nias, and Chapter 3 on Java, are ethnographically hefty; but their weight is needed to anchor later chapters. They are the grounding of what follows. Ethnography always contains a surplus of detail relative to the theoretical frame; but the detail affords the reader a vicarious experience of a different emotional world and the writer ammunition for later theorizing. To glance ahead to the themes of later chapters: in analyzing the structure of emotional episodes, cultural frames of understanding, modes of empathy, and the role of language in constituting emotion, we need more than snapshots and vignettes. And in developing the case for a narrative perspective on emotion (Chapters 4–7), we need firm foundations.

And so to the field. In the following extended example – a wedding negotiation – the focus is on language use, but the aim is not to reduce emotion to language (a *nothing but* explanation), rather to explore one particular aspect of emotion in an unusually explicit instance. I could have started anywhere, but it helps to begin with a stark – even extreme – example, and a case I know at first hand. The people of Nias, the Niha, are specialists in the rhetoric of emotion, virtuosi of emotional blackmail. The cultural emphasis that lends Nias its agonistic ethos, its taste for melodrama (*Oxford Dictionary of English*: 'a sensational dramatic piece with exaggerated characters and exciting events intended to appeal to the emotions'), offers a rare opportunity of witnessing unscripted emotions onstage. We can put ourselves among the audience without making too many assumptions and without the need to read minds or know much about personal histories.

First some background. Eighty miles off the coast of Sumatra in the Indian Ocean, next stop Africa, Nias is one of the least developed islands in Indonesia. A tribal, kinship-based society, living by shifting cultivation and pig husbandry, Nias converted to Christianity (mainly Protestant) between 1915 and 1930. In what is still mainly an oral, non-literate culture, the Bible is practically the only book: a source of oaths, killer proverbs, and prophetic clues rather than doctrine or moral guidance. The hill people of the interior are among the poorest in Indonesia, but they marry expensively, a contradiction certain to generate passions and

Groundings

passionate words. Bridewealth – pigs and gold transferred to the bride's relatives – compensate for the gift of life, represented by the bride's fertility and her labour power, both of which are praised in songs and labelled in the marriage payments. Her male relatives, for their part, exercise a mystical control over her husband who, in both senses, owes them for life.

What's at stake: the emotional calculus

Poor the Niha may be, but bridewealth is huge – up to a hundred pigs for a high-status bride. Wedding negotiations resemble affairs of state in dragging over months, with talks about talks, spin doctors, fence-mending, and damage-limitation. The early stages – which in diplomatic jargon would be called 'constructive' – are led by skilled orators whose job is to agree broad terms: how many groups linked by marriage will be involved, the number of payments, and the schedule of delivery. If that sounds hard-nosed and practical, in the torrent of words it is not easy for an outsider to have much sense of what is going on. In contrast, later talks of the diplomatically 'free and frank' kind – involve ordinary speakers and are simpler, with a blunt readiness to name sums. Pruned of metaphor and euphemism, the linking of 'emotion' to numbers emerges more starkly.

A Niha melodrama

In the following extract, compiled from tape recordings, debate revolves around the bridewealth sums so far delivered and the inadequate reception given to the groom.

The two parties are gathered in the bride's house, a wooden clan dwelling raised on columns, with a gallery like a longhouse and apartments for seven or eight families to the rear. Men and women from the groom's village – the visitors – pack the window bench that runs the length of the building. The bride's people – the home side – are seated around them; some huddle on the floor, others loiter in dark doorways. There is a continual coming and going, as youths thread through the crowd carrying firewood or bearing hunks of raw meat. Above the hubbub of the speeches, grunts and squeals rise from below where pigs are corralled for slaughter. The air is rank with smoke from the hearth out back, the vinegary smell of bodies and betel-chews, and the greasy remains of a feast.

Following a strict order, each speaker addresses a member of his own side, who echoes his phrases with whoops and cries to add point and emphasis. Speeches last up to half an hour, with a good deal of strutting and bluster. But we pick up the thread towards the end when the formalities and frills have been dropped. The chief negotiator for the bride's lineage is her father's brother, a tough, bear-like man with a goitre. The bride's father – thin and peevish, with bulging hyperthyroid eyes – keeps in the background, issuing occasional signals from the dim room behind. This ill-sorted pair – notorious poisoners – do not make an attractive prospect as allies (marriage creates a lifelong alliance), and the groom's father has long resisted his son's wishes. But two things have changed his mind. The groom's mother has been caught in an affair with a schoolteacher, a scandal that lowers the groom's stock and threatens his marriage prospects. No less dismaying, letters have been discovered between the youth and the girl. Such things cannot be mentioned without knives being drawn. But a mutual distaste between the parties, a fear of letting things slide, and unspoken suspicions hover in the background and can be read into allusions to the principals' 'feelings'. With much to lose on either side, fear of failure is ever-present.

As the debate goes back and forth, the rhetoric of emotion (signalled in bold typeface) is ramped up. We pick up when the bride's uncle has just concluded a rambling, ungracious speech, the gist of which is: *You've been welcomed generously, so why not cough up?* In the brief pause that follows, his sharp words hang in the air. Their tone will

Groundings

determine the response from the groom's side, which is carping, a touch ironic, but formally respectful. The attempt is to deflect the demands by shaming the bride's men and implying that bridewealth has not been properly solicited with countergifts; also to stress the possibility of withdrawal. The spokesman is a tall, rather fierce man with a penetrating voice. He gets up from the window bench and hails a respondent on the far side of the hall, commanding the space between.

GROOM'S SIDE: Hear this, brother! ('*I heeeaar you!*' returns the echo). The bride's party salute us today as 'in-laws', which I won't quarrel with because it assumes a **happy** outcome, as if we were already **of one heart**; yet there was no dance of welcome, no welcoming gift save for a piglet. If I accepted it I'd be **ashamed**, mocked by my own children ... But we shall be like a buffalo tethered by the nose [i.e. dangerous but restrained] – we'll submit, **soft-hearted** to your proposals. We'll even let our **hearts be prodded** [encouraged]; then our hosts will give us **joy** [and yield up the bride]. So let it be as though they'd danced!

BRIDE'S SIDE: We waited to see what you'd bring and saw there was very little, a mere twelve pigs, yet we **felt only pleasure** in your arrival. (*Truuuue!* cries his respondent.) So when you say, 'Let it be as though we'd danced' [i.e. complaining of your reception], we feel **two-hearted**. Why? Your words give and take back. In such a speech the beginning **pleases** but then a sprite enters: we knew before you had reached the staircase there was **something in your hearts**. We are **startled** by your reproach, **shrivelled-hearted**. As to our demands, don't be too quick to **resentment** ['painful heart']. When I demanded 500 for the trousseau, maybe that was **rash** of me. But we too have our **feelings**. ('*We dooooo!*' comes the echo) With so little to go around, not all of us are **content**. Some of us will get left out, and what then? Will our **hearts not be squeezed**? We accept your twelve pigs as an instalment, not the final sum.

GROOM'S SIDE: People will say, 'It's all been settled; what are they waiting for? Let the bride be handed over.' What we haven't brought today, we'll see about in the future. No more talk of instalments. You know why we're here. If the groom's father hadn't come they'd be saying **anxiously**, 'Where is he? Where's Pa today; why only the lad?'

This last phrase was uttered with wheedling sarcasm. But in a sudden theatrical shift, the groom's speaker stiffens and thrusts out an arm, his voice shaking with indignation.

GROOM'S SIDE: Well, he's here! Yet his welcome was not exactly **big-hearted**; and if *you* aren't **angry** ['hot hearted'] with *us,* our reception invites **anger**! ('*I witness!*' shouts the respondent.)

The bride's uncle counter-attacks, but leaves room for compromise:

BRIDE'S SIDE: There are thirty of you here today who all expect to fill your bellies: you'd be **angry** otherwise. But what of *my* people: how will *they* **feel** to be cut out of the bridewealth? ('*Hooooow!*') But listen here: if you come up with what's required, we'll be **agreeable** ['of one heart']; if not, we won't go so far as to say, *May the headhunters get you!* We remain **cautious**, as there's cunning ['thoughts'] in all this talk. As for my brother, he has his **own feelings**. Whether he speaks is up to him. That's my reply! ('*Yessss!*')

Always the unhappiest man, with most to gain or lose, the bride's father rarely intervenes, but his 'feelings' are a constant factor. His inarticulate heart is what everyone dances around. They speak for him, because if he spoke things would rapidly come to an end. A compromise nevertheless

Groundings

seems possible, a meeting of hearts. An old man with an ornamental stick resumes for the groom's side, now stressing the feelings on *both* sides.

GROOM'S SIDE: We're not **happy** if the bride's father gets short-measured. No more than if I'm left out: me, on the lip of the grave! [laughter] But there are things in your speeches that **hurt us**. (Someone interjects: *'It's all in their hearts, grandpa! They've concealed bad feelings.'*) Let's straighten what's crooked, so that we are all **happy** ['clear-hearted'] with the bridewealth. What's here is here! [he raps the floor with his stick to indicate the captive pigs, who grunt on cue]. If it's not enough, you must divide it among fewer men. You may say, *I'm all worked up* ['My heart is growing'], but that's how it stands!

It seems like stalemate. But at a signal from the bride's father one of his cousins is urged to sum up – an adjusting of sentiments rather than figures.

BRIDE'S SIDE: Upstream or downstream, it's the custom to lay out the leaves and tally the kinsmen [in bridewealth reckoning]. We clansmen are **happy** to see our names down there, even if they don't stand for much. But we're also **mortified**, *our* **hearts scorched** to hear your words. Yet we should know what's in each other's **hearts**. Indeed, none can forbid you your say. If, on that fateful day, we didn't put a name to our **wishes**, didn't spell out the debt, that was because of our **confidence**, our **certainty** [i.e. we assumed the sums were agreed and understood]. Now we are **doubtful**; the girl's father no longer **content**. And so much is owing: Not much less than twenty pigs! Where on earth will they come from? Isn't that what each of us is now thinking? It makes the bones rattle! (*Trruuuue!*) But such sums cannot be **regretted**. **Love** is great in the name of bridewealth, is it not? Whatever you can afford, brother-in-law; that's the way of the world. But if you are short, you will surely **feel crushed**.

This final speech appeals as much to values as to emotions. In the trade of blackmail and bluster, bluff and counterbluff, speeches advertise feelings; but feelings, implicitly, are causes in themselves, motivations linked to ultimate values. Bridewealth is about generosity, the token of 'love'; you cannot regret the expenditure as a waste. And to fail in this regard is not merely to look cheap but to feel crushed, an emotion of self-reckoning. You wouldn't want to pay little, would you? What counts, the speaker implies, is not compliance to some formula, but the generosity and 'love' that becomes an honourable wife-taker. So we won't insist on a particular sum ('whatever you can afford, brother-in-law'). For your part, look beyond the tally to what *really* counts and you will surely find the wherewithal.

Mise en Scène

The appeals throughout (abbreviated here) are to custom, as are the rebuttals. Says one side, in effect: 'There's a right way to do things; we shouldn't have to spell it out.' Says the other: 'But you *should* have; and now you can't complain.' These are the opposed *reasons*. But the rhetorical tactics are emotional. Rather than argue in a legalistic manner, with refutations and proofs, people sum up their position or mark where the debate has got to by referring to their hearts, each claim to frustration or resentment pegging their progress and forcing the other onto the back foot. We cannot speak of emotion here as mood music, *distinct* from reason; rather the emotions contain reasons. Each is a claim of a certain kind that demands a fitting response, usually a concession. One speaker reacts to the emotional posture of the other. At

Groundings

the same time, each knows the other, like himself, is putting on a show, making a case. Emotions are performed and proclaimed. Does that invalidate their authenticity? The philosopher Robert Solomon (1980) argues that you cannot really be classed as angry if you are using a display of anger to gain advantage: that is acting, not anger. But Erroll Bedford (1984) makes the point that we can never really know what someone else is feeling, so our judgments of what counts as anger should not presuppose a feeling; rather, they refer to a certain kind of behaviour. Emotions are often performative – intended to influence, persuade, or repel. We learn how to feel anger by observing its behavioural contexts, how it is manifested and pragmatically used. For Bedford the meaning precedes and shapes the feeling. Feeling angry is just a way of saying 'feeling as people do when they are *being* angry'.

To take a slightly different point of view, being angry, according to Solomon, is holding a certain judgment of a situation, for example that you have offended me. If I do not think you have offended me I cannot really be angry, however much I *seem* angry. Pretence, in these terms, refers not to a discrepant inner feeling but to a discrepant judgment. In the Niha debates, we might think that speakers have crossed the line into pretence, but in fact no one ever questions the sincerity of a claimed emotion. It matters little whether your heart is in the right place. What they question is the *judgment* – of offence, stinginess, or generosity – in effect arguing that the proclaimed emotion is unjustified.

Part of the difficulty of assessing the nature of the emotions on display is that the orators speak for others as well as themselves; they are voicing a collective judgment ('our hearts'). This is another reason why sincerity is not relevant. Niha emotion talk is a moral discourse not an outpouring of self-expression. But it is more than words: the voiced emotions enact judgments and stir feelings.

To understand how this works, consider the dynamics of oratory. A named emotion refers on several levels: it describes a state of the heart ('clear', 'squeezed'); it refers to a group ('*our* hearts'); and it defines a situation as negative or positive, as emotions generally do. In turn it has a target. The speaker addresses a respondent on his own side, but the target is the opposed group, who observe the parade of emotions from the sidelines. As a speech rolls on, the speaker paints the situation in changing colours, shifting the mood and the effect on the audience. The respondent's job is to heighten the effect through commentary and echo. If the speaker is bad, the operatic echo can sound ironical or even parodic (*Goood sense!*). But the whoops and calls, which overlap the speaker's voice, sometimes drowning it, usually have a thrilling effect; for which reason, a good soloist chooses his rhythm section with care. The audience, ruminative, critical, remains silent but for the rustling of betelnut bags. Each man is heard through until his closing flourish, *That's my word!*

Note that the mode of address is indirect, keeping tempers in check. No one expresses anger or contempt directly at the opposition. Moreover, indirection permits the vaunted emotions to be reclassified in order to press home the advantage or mollify the opposition. This is not unlike the form of political rhetoric found in the New Hebrides called 'disentangling' (White 2005). In debates among the A'ara, if you can get anger reclassified as sadness or regret you have made progress towards reconciliation.

The historian William Reddy (1997) has coined the term *emotives* to refer to the performative aspect of emotion speech. The bandying back and forth of 'anger' and 'love' in my example is not a matter of description but manipulation; and its effects depend on something like the linguistic performatives analyzed by Austin and Searle, according to which the doing is in the saying, as in 'I sentence you to ten years' or 'I promise you I'll come'. In promises, vows, and renunciations, words become deeds. In naming an emotion in the flow of discourse, according to Reddy, you set in train a recursive process of re-evaluation in which feelings are formulated, revised, and launched upon the world. Of course, merely by saying 'I love you', you don't create the emotion in

Groundings

yourself; but you certainly *do* something; and your self-assessment undergoes a modulation whose output changes the feeling, the evaluation and so on. You can discover your love or hate, quicken it, or feel it vanish in the utterance. Likewise, with your audience. Hence *emotives.*

One further characteristic of rhetorical emotions may be noted: that the encoded judgment is personalized (Calhoun 2004: 116–117). An analytical comment on the meagreness of a gift might invite detached rebuttal, but expressed as *resentment* it demands action for its implied threat. We might feel miffed at our gifthorse being looked in the mouth, but if the rider is resentful as well as critical we might get trampled. On the other hand, the packaging of criticism in feeling may soften the effect by relativizing the judgment. 'I feel hurt at your negligence' leaves room for negotiation and compensation (perhaps I have misunderstood, perhaps I am playing for sympathy) where a bald neutral criticism is final.

The tell-tale heart

Let's come back to the idioms used in the speeches. Many of the coinages refer to the heart, *tödö* (modified in compounds as *dödö).* In Indonesian and Malay, it is the liver, *hati* – usually Englished as 'heart' – which is the seat of emotion; but Niha say, and mean, heart. This was Sundermann's German translation (*Herz*) in the first Nias dictionary (1905); and although Indonesian speakers and some recent lexicographers translate *tödö* as 'liver', that inert organ (properly, *ate* in Niasan) lacks the pumped-up plasticity implied by the idioms.[1]

---

[1] Lase's Niasan-Indonesian dictionary (2011) translates *tödö* as 1 *jantung* (heart); 2 *hati* (liver), reserving emotion idioms under 2. In turn, a standard Indonesian–English dictionary (Echols and Shadily 1989) translates *hati* as 1 liver 2 the seat of emotions (each instance of which is translated 'heart'). The contemporary supplement (Schmidgall-Tellings & Stevens 1981) translates *hati* 1 mind, mood,

The heart is more than a source of throbbing sensation, serving in some phrases as the organ of thought. *Ba dödögu*, 'in my heart', means 'I think (that)'. The heart thinks, feels and speaks. Opening gambits often begin with *imane tödögu: My heart says.* A myth still recounted tells how, when the First Man died, his heart was preserved in a flask. From the flask Hia's heart continued to nag his descendants. Irked by the constant reproaches, his daughter-in-law threw the flask into the river where it was washed down to the sea and across the waves, which explains why knowledge and wealth departed the island. Like the 'Tell-tale Heart' of Edgar Allan Poe's story, the detached heart serves as judge and conscience (for which there is no distinct word; Sundermann gives *Gewissen*, 'conscience', as a secondary meaning of *tödö*). One might go further and suggest that the myth objectifies conscience, locating it outside the self. Indeed, the deeper promptings of the heart are experienced as alien and overwhelming. In the Great Repentance, a Protestant conversion movement that swept the island in 1916, penitents were driven by powerful unconscious urges to act out their sins in trance.

Heart-speech is nothing if not moralistic. But is it metaphorical or literal? According to the linguist Anna Wierzbicka (1999), emotion phrases which include a body part – and most languages have them – are best translated as *I feel X* or *Y*. They do not, or need not, refer to an exotic folk psychology, and they should not be understood metaphorically. If they are metaphors, they are dead metaphors, like our phrase 'she was broken-hearted'. The difficulty for the interpreter of Niha idioms is that most of them do not correspond to anything in the European lexicon. There is no obvious psychological equivalent. You cannot fall

---

disposition 2 heart (in cards). Lea Brown's 'A grammar of Nias Selatan' [South Nias] prefers 'liver' while conceding (476) that 'This example [people with medical heart trouble] seems to indicate that people think of *tödö* as "heart" these days.' Possibly Central Nias, less open to Indonesian/Malay, has held on longer to the older meaning known to Sundermann and the missionaries.

Groundings

back on *I feel X* or *Y*. Who is to say what feeling corresponds to having a heart that is swollen, spotted or scorched?

Consider some examples, starting with those that seem transparent. *Aukhu dödö*, 'hot-hearted', means, roughly, 'angry'; *ohahau dödö*, 'clear-hearted', means 'contented' or 'happy'; *afatö dödö*, 'broken-hearted', means 'disappointed'. These terms refer to emotions by any definition. But other heart-combinations refer to non-emotional cognitive processes. *Aboto ba dödö*, 'broken *in* heart', means 'understand'; *era dödö*, 'count heart' = 'think' or 'reckon'; *elungu dödö*, 'lost-hearted' = mistaken; *törö dödö*, 'pass through or by the heart' = remember. Not all cognitions, however, refer to the heart. To 'know' is *ila* ('see'). And some heart idioms are neither emotional nor to do with thought processes, such as *owökhi dödö* = 'thirsty', *erege dödö* = 'tired'. As Donald Rumsfeld, the captious former American defence chief, might have said, there are cardiac and non-cardiac emotions, cardiac and non-cardiac cognitions, cardiac non-cognitions and non-cardiac non-cognitions.

Before coming to the more arcane phrases (Rumsfeld notwithstanding, we began simply enough), I should mention that some ordinary emotions, of the kind usually deemed universal, are denoted by a single word, not by idioms. Thus 'afraid' is '*ata'u*', cognate with Indonesian *takut* and Ifaluk *metagu*; 'want' or 'love' is '*omasi*'; 'disgust' is '*ogoro*'; 'furious' is *afönu*. These simple terms are much commoner in regular speech than the debating-chamber *cris de coeur*. They give no clues to the meaning of flourishes like 'our hearts are squeezed' or 'he is rotten-hearted'. It was expressions like these that puzzled missionary Sundermann when he began work on his dictionary. In an earlier publication contemporary with the pathbreaking work of James (1884) and Darwin (1872), he compiled a long list of heart idioms, leaving some translations blank and giving up at no. 88 (Sundermann 1887). Most of the terms had no equivalent, though German was equally rich in heart idioms. (Ots, writing of Chinese medicine, refers to a German idiomatic dictionary of 1870 that lists 573 heart terms [Ots 1994: 135].) Nias was not that exceptional in the range of its heart-speech, only in the puzzling way it was deployed. It was hard to imagine the purport of phrases like 'feeling like your heart has swallowed a ball of cat's fur' or 'having a heart with a curly hair in it'. If anything, they suggest a Javanese-style reflexivity or Proustian subtlety unfitted to the rough, heart-on-sleeve melodrama of wedding debates. Are the Niha connoisseurs of misery, professors of pain, as Sundermann suspected? To be sure, the vast majority of their heart-terms are negative in valence. But most emotion vocabularies, especially in societies where oratory is practised, score highly on negatives, for the obvious reason that emotion terms point to problems needing resolution. About happiness there is not much to be said. If emotions are prompts to action (Frijda 2004), so too is emotion speech.

Word and feeling

Sundermann gets stuck because he takes the heart out of context. And as with many such emotion lists, he makes a number of problematic assumptions: that the words refer to distinct feelings; that the words are *names*; and that they have a transcultural psychological reality and therefore a German equivalent.

If an emotion word is a label for a feeling, it could be argued, there are as many feelings as labels (see Chapter 9). This is a common belief, fitting with the realism of common sense in which words name things; but it also applies to a range of respectable theoretical positions, including the brand of cultural relativism summed up in Harré's (1986:10) statement that 'there are historically and culturally diverse emotion vocabularies. I claim that it follows that there are culturally diverse emotions.' It might be objected here that the complex events we call emotions are not the same as feelings; that the emotion 'love', and the word that denotes it, include a number of feelings, while, conversely, different emotions – regret, remorse, shame – might share a certain

Groundings

feeling (Ben-Ze'ev 2010). Harré's relativist point might therefore apply to emotions but not to feelings. Nonetheless, at the level of experience, in which the different components of an emotion are unified, a label-feeling equation implies that a set of near-synonyms like 'exasperated', 'annoyed', and 'irritated' discriminates distinctive experiences. On this view, lack of the right words does not quite imply lack of the specific feelings; but the act of naming and contrasting may help in the reporting and regulation of feelings – how we monitor and respond to them; and it may play a part in their socialization. One could be trained to feel in a certain way (H. Geertz 1974; Ochs 1988). Fine discriminations would have a social value and practical use as well as marking a gain in psychological knowledge. New situations, if widely shared and often enough repeated, might in turn give rise to new words and feelings. A rich vocabulary promotes the 'granularity' of emotions.

It could be the case, however, that linguistic fine-tuning is purely conceptual and situational while the feeling tones among a set of similar emotions, so far as we can tell, are constant. In a variant of Wittgenstein's (1953) Private Language Argument, Bedford rejects introspection as a criterion of interpretation because, he suggests, we are notoriously bad at identifying our emotions. Nor are emotion words to be taken as *names* for interior states, which would presuppose 'a richness and clarity in the "inner life" of feeling that it does not possess'; rather, they are social interventions, acts of approving, blaming, and judging. 'Their principal functions are judicial, not informative, and when they are informative, it is often not merely psychological information that they give' (1984 [1957]: 275). It would be a mistake, therefore, to make unreliable differences in feeling the criterion of meaning. As Solomon puts it in a useful summary, 'Bedford suggested that the difference between shame and embarrassment, for example, is not some shade of difference between internal *qualia*, but the differences between descriptions of an awkward situation in terms of responsibility or innocence' (Solomon 2008: 11).

Nias

It is obvious how this behavioural (which is not to say behaviour*ist*) approach might help with baffling cases like Nias. In their speeches, Niha appear to offer feelings as *causes*, in effect diverting from circumstances, which are much more readily pinned down. (You can't deny that I am angry, though you might refute my reasons for being so.) But they are not offering a theory of emotion. And we need not take them at their word: after all, as the bride's uncle cautions, 'there's cunning in all this talk'. Like Bedford (1984: 276–277), we might say that such appeals are not to an occult interior state as the *cause* of behaviour, which is 'unilluminating and only one step from saying that the action is unaccountable'. Instead, the emotion phrase (1) implies or refers to a social context or relationship (of obligation, solidarity, refusal); or (2) acts as a justification for an action. And this is how it is understood by its target audience. The squeezed heart is not a description of a mental or bodily state but part of an argument with a goal or tendency; it has a definite rhetorical force. Which, again, is why authenticity is not at issue.

Bedford's general position, though not the details of his argument, would now be considered orthodoxy in anthropology: 'Emotion concepts ... are not purely psychological: they presuppose concepts of social relationships and institutions, and concepts belonging to systems of judgement, moral, aesthetic and legal. In using emotion words we are able, therefore, to relate behaviour to the complex background in which it is enacted, and so to make human action intelligible' (Bedford 1984/ 1957: 277–278). Bedford's influential thesis, which Harré counts as an early instance of constructionism, is intended to apply generally to emotion talk; it is not designed to solve empirical cross-cultural puzzles. But it has a convenient application in the field, not only because it gets over problems of privacy and reference but also because it opens up the whole question of whether people in other cultural settings might take a perspective on emotion very different from our own – one less concerned with feelings than valuations, for example.

Groundings

In fact, Niha heart-terms are used mostly in political speeches and the debates centred on feasts of merit and weddings: occasions concerned with exchange, negotiation, and ranking. In these set-piece confrontations, states of the heart do not register psychological nuances but serve as tools of persuasion. (I do not follow Bedford in eliding the psychological and pragmatic: emotion talk often *is* explanatory, reflexive and communicative, as we shall see with the case of Java.) With a few notable exceptions, in daily life a simpler set of readily understood words is used, including those single-word terms like *ata'u*, afraid, and *aila*, shame.

So how do the heart phrases work if they do not refer to actual feelings or individual psychology? It might be said that they *comment* on supposed feelings rather than naming them. Rather than assaying emotions, Proustwise, Niha idioms allude presumptively to situations; *presumptively,* because they make a claim about a situation that others might disagree with (or why make it?). Your heart is *squeezed* when you are pressed from both sides. For example, the bride's father might say his heart is squeezed because men of his lineage are pushing him to ask for more (to increase their share), while men of the groom's lineage are resisting the demand. The purpose of saying your heart is squeezed is either to get people to back off or to avoid giving in to one side or the other. This is not very different from 'having a trapped heart', when one is caught between two contrary imperatives. The heart in these cases becomes a stand-in for the person, the actor.

Because heart-speech defines – or rather *redefines* – the situation, and does so contentiously, it becomes a matter of strategic importance whose hearts we are talking about. The use of personal and possessive pronouns and suffixes linked to emotion terms is highly manipulative, obliging a response in the opponent. Recall our picture of the speaker and audience. The ideal situation and the goal of debate is one in which 'our hearts are one', *fahasara dödö*. This term is translatable as 'solidarity', 'agreement' or 'unanimity'. But whereas the English word 'unanimity' implies a common, perhaps partisan, view ('The opposition was unanimous'), 'one-heartedness' implies solidarity among all parties. Speeches are often punctuated by the remark, 'it all comes back to one-heartedness', with the implication that it is the others who are blocking this goal.

As in other Indonesian languages, there is a distinction between two forms of first person plural: *ya'ita*, 'we-inclusive, all of us', or *ya'aga*, 'we-exclusive', my group but not yours. The inclusive form has a levelling implication, erasing distinctions of seniority, but also an implication of entitlement, as in 'what are we eating?' which you ask when you enter someone's house and smell cooking. (My visitors often asked this question.) By contrast, to say 'you' can be distancing. So, people would amicably ask me, 'What's it like where *we* live?' meaning, 'where *you* live in Inggris'. To use the we-inclusive form when speaking of hearts implies a shared emotion, a shared view of the situation, and thus a resolution of the conflict, which can be either presumptuous or conciliatory; it can imply giving or taking. Alert to any such claim or concession, the listeners respond with their own preferred pronominal forms.

A focal emotion

Among the scores of emotion terms, one stands out. This is *afökhö dödö* 'painful-hearted'. The Indonesian translation is *sakit hati*, meaning 'offended' or 'harbouring resentment'. However, the Niha term has a wider extension covering spite, resentment, envy, malice, and ill will. It can refer to the act of spite as well as the sentiment. When the chief of Orahua was dying, three explanations were offered: in neglecting the clan house he had offended the ancestors and earned their curse; God was punishing him for his sins; or, as his brother maintained, 'The chief is ill because of the spite of men. Resentment is the cause.' That is, the *emotion* of resentment/envy issued in *acts* of spite, the maledictions and black magic of his enemies.

Groundings

As the social psychologist Gerrod Parrott (2001) explains in a fascinating dissection of related emotions, resentment tends to imply a perceived injustice or offence, a sense of getting less than one's due, whereas envy is unjustifiable in objective terms, and therefore reprehensible, typically covert, and often unrecognised by the envious themselves. The envious man wants what the other has, or wants to destroy what they have; in his envy he feels himself inferior, whereas the resentful may justifiably point to other's unfair advantage – at least so he thinks: others may see him as merely envious. In Nias, where one term does for both emotions, either sense may be implied (or differently construed in the same speech act). The chief was undoubtedly envied by many, but also resented for his high-handed ways, his brutal put-downs, and his undeserved perks. Yet he was also admired, even by those who envied and resented him. (Parrott places admiration on the benign end of the envy spectrum.) In the intense world of the tribal village, relationships are manifold and deep-rooted, multi-generational, certainly complicated enough – like those in any family – to require mixed feelings. You might hate him (we all did); but, as one of his bitter rivals conceded in a generous funeral lament, hadn't the chief brought fame to the village through his gargantuan feasts? Who else could have defended local sovereignty and kept out the Devil (the law) for thirty years? Who could replace him?

Another example illustrates both the explanatory and pragmatic uses of 'painful heart' in ordinary speech while remaining ambiguous on appraisal logic. On my way back from bathing in the river one day I came across Ina Zinga,[2] a sack of harvest rice balanced on her head, haranguing her next-door neighbour. 'Someone has scored two of my papaya trees out of spite for my plants. They want to kill me', she wailed at Ina Le'a, then pointedly told her what everyone knew: 'If someone

---

[2] Adults are called by teknonym. Ina Zinga = Mother of Zinga, Ama Zinga = Father of Zinga (a married couple). Ina Le'a = Mother of Le'a.

stabs your plants at harvest time it means only one thing: they intend it for you!' People 'resented/envied' her *and* her plants, she said, exploring every inflection of the emotion, and now she herself 'had been made resentful' (but evidently not envious). Her visible rancour was not simply informative; her owning to resentment – not an estimable emotion – was a warning to Ina Le'a, implying *she* was among the suspects. Ina Le'a's expression, in turn, was one of unease rather than sympathy.

Ina Zinga was our next-door neighbour. I was a friend of her husband Ama Zinga, and I often witnessed family predicaments. Sometimes, as in the following episode, I was their cause.

An anthropologist depends on gossip. Without it there is no way to understand local dynamics: the 'official' version of things is ethnographically useless. Much gossip can be gleaned through ordinary human fellowship, cultivated goodwill, and calculated acts of generosity; but the canny fieldworker pretends to knowledge she does not possess and must play off one source against another, baiting her words to A with titbits from B, but with the constant risk of miscalculation. One day I caught Ama Zinga – whom I depended on for many things – cutting me out of a prize bit of information (the background to a knife fight), which I had, in fact, already heard about. I sensed he had glimpsed an advantage in our dealings, being the first and only person in the village to realize that quarrels and intrigues had both professional as well as personal interest to me, and could therefore be a source of profitable exchange. If the idea got around that the stuff of everyday life was as valuable to me as History or Custom – something to be meted out for advantage by experts – fieldwork would become impossible. Later that day, while wondering what leverage I could apply, I had a visit from Ina Le'a. Sitting in our kitchen, she spotted a big shiny storage tin that happened to be empty. Could she have it for her hulled rice? She crept home with it the back way, through a ditch and past clucking chickens, knowing that the Zingas had first call on our household goods and that Ina Zinga,

Groundings

should she hear, would be madly jealous. Within minutes their young daughter burst in demanding a similar tin, which we did not have. When the girl ran home I could hear an explosion of anger. Later that day I called in with a peace offering. Ina Zinga had a rag tied round her head like a bandage as she sometime did after losing her temper. But Ama Zinga was his normal friendly gloomy self. I felt sorry for the mother and daughter, going about their chores with quiet, closed faces, and ashamed of my petty revenge. (But could I have refused Ina Le'a? I reasoned, in mitigation.) There was no mention of the incident, but when I got up to leave, the girl said: 'So what about the tin?' I shrugged and the father said: 'Never mind, another time, eh?'

One of the phrases I had heard screamed from the Zinga house was *afökhö dödö*; yet the note in Ina Zinga's voice was of anger or, better, indignation. The scenario, and Ina Le'a's fears in creeping home with the tin, suggested the dominant emotion, the framing appraisal, was jealousy. Ina Zinga had been deprived of what she took to be rightfully hers; she had been cut out of her portion, just as Ama Zinga had cut me out of mine. The Zingas were jealous of our friendship and its benefits, but jealousy was not something to admit to. Resentment *was*, implying entitlement and a need for restitution on my side. (One can be justly *afökhö dödö*.) What the episode illustrates – apart from the cat-and-mouse nature of fieldwork in Nias – is the clustering of emotions around the theme of entitlement and dispossession and their dense dramatic complexity.

Frequently mentioned in conversation as well as oratory, resentment *fa'afökho dödö* (n.), or fear of its occurrence, forms the backdrop to everyday life, a shadow behind the otherwise even tone of daily activity. Acts that were blamed on this sentiment while I was in Nias included poisoning someone's fishpond, damaging their crops, releasing their pigs to roam, fouling their backyard, and attacking their livestock. Acts of *alleged* spite included putting poison in food and betelnut. A family that fed me during my last week of fieldwork assured me that they wouldn't poison me because they felt no resentment towards me (they had just boasted of poisoning a dishonest dealer). My host proved the point by sampling the food from my plate, as he insisted on doing every evening, if only to protect his reputation.

Afökho dödö is the opposite of 'one-heartedness' and, at least in its malevolent form, is the epitome of selfishness and anti-social sentiment. When I arrived in the village and had to make a speech at my inaugural feast, I wrote out a text that I asked the village secretary to translate into *li Niha*. Rewriting my ingratiating sentiments, he ended with the following lines, which I memorized like a poem and declaimed to the crowd as they awaited their pork:

We chose Orahua for its good custom, its great chief and knowledgeable men. The world should hear of it so they can learn your ways. But there is no difference between how you do things and how we do them. We call things by different names, but there is no *resentment* between us. So be patient ('broad-hearted'). Here you will find only meagre fare, a dirty glass of hot water and nothing to put in it. We beg your indulgence, our faults are great. *Ya'ahovu*! (Blessings!)

My speechwriter's emotives worked. The disavowal of resentment *created* solidarity, one-heartedness. Our differences did not spell envy: underneath we were the same. And as if I had grasped a simple truth, an elder took my elbow and croaked: 'Under heaven we are all God's pigs, though you're a white one and I'm a black one.'

Afökho dödö is a sentimental key to Nias, just as Love was the password to mid-century Hollywood. The question is why? With resources fairly even, prosperity depends on skill, effort, and luck. You can farm only as much land as you can clear. So, the better-off villagers are those with the most labour power, the most hands. With no social classes, status differences are determined by ceremonial exchange. Prestige is won in grandiose feasting, but there is no formal hierarchy that could justify wealth differences, no concept of blue blood to insulate the rich from envy. Your better-off neighbour could be you; so you resent him, as he fears you. Interlocking emotions, reflecting different life chances and situational appraisals, are built into the system. For fear of envy, anything valuable must be hidden. Extra food is consumed out of sight, in the fields or at home, sometimes in the dark. Seen or smelled, it must be shared. Among lineage fellows, sharing of festive costs is mandatory. Against the strutting one-upmanship of the feast, kinship requires redistribution. Because the private consumption of wealth is impossible, and the claims of others hard to resist, people go to great lengths to hide what they own. A herd of forty pigs might be farmed out among a dozen scattered individuals, while the owner lives in grinding poverty. When he has enough assets to hold a feast, he recalls the pigs and kills them all, distributing meat among his guests and winning a title. In this sense, wealth can never be enjoyed; it exists only at the moment of its destruction and conversion into prestige. Envy and resentment are constant factors (though the 'painful heart' be singular), the sentiments underpinning the system.

We can briefly refer here to another Southeast Asian people. Christian Postert (2012) shows how a similar focal emotion, called 'broken liver', performs the same kind of role among the Hmong of Laos. 'Gift giving and exchange in Hmong highland villages have a discernible emotional tone that invokes particular social rules regarding emotion. If social reciprocity is felt to be dysbalanced, corrective emotions are usually provoked. Emotional behaviour serves to legitimate claims of solidarity.' Postert takes these emotions – which he calls depressed mood and sadness – to be 'real', rather than performative or claimed.

In Nias, resentment guarantees neighbourly solidarity. It is the reverse side of the tapestry. Beneath the good citizen's shirt beats a 'painful heart'. Behind the friendly smile or the gift of meat lurks fear of spite.

The Great Repentance

So far, so functional. A coveted tin, a poisoned betel chew, a hunk of meat: the objects of 'painful heart' could hardly be more mundane or better fitted to the social calculus. But there is another kind of resentment, one that projects ordinary disgruntlement onto the cosmic plane. A sense of unjust deprivation is commonly voiced in Nias, an aggrieved *weltschmerz* amounting to universal resentment. (I think of Ama Zinga with his doggy eyes, staring blankly at the village square; his wry smiles at the priest's empty promises.) This moral sentiment, unnamed in the language but richly articulated, is close to what Nietzsche called *ressentiment*. I believe it originated with the first mass conversions to Christianity a century ago, though it probably derived from local concepts of exchange that were closely tied to salvation and that still have some force. In Old Nias, safe passage across a rickety spiritual bridge to the ancestral Valhalla depended on a clean balance sheet, freedom from festive debt. Debtors tumbled into the chasm below to be devoured by ferocious dogs. Dying chiefs would lacerate themselves in remorse if no pigs could be found to pay off creditors. As a witness to the death of the old chief of Orahua, I was sometimes asked whether he had slashed himself or beaten his breast.

In the new dispensation – inaugurated 1916 AD (a decade later in Orahua) – things were hardly easier. Sins were conceived as debts to God, to be paid off by penance. On Sundays, each convert carried a little quiver of leaves to church to be counted off by the native priest, one for each sin. The tug of conscience was (and is) expressed by a term that evokes the insistent creditor: *isugi dödöda*, 'it duns our heart'. Fond of proverbs, good with numbers, Niha – now *niha keriso*, Christians – learned a new maxim: *The wages of sin is death*. Nobody quotes rest of the sentence – *but the gift of God is eternal life through Jesus Christ our Lord* – perhaps because it seems less obviously true. To Niha, for good reasons, the negatives were always more credible. (As one man said to me, flattening his palms against an invisible wall: 'Hell is as close as heaven is far!') The problem was that Christian morality had quickly proved impossible. Then, as now, Niha hearts were squeezed between contradictory imperatives: (1) to be good in the new way, as *niha keriso*

Groundings

(Christians), which meant acting against your interests and dooming your family to poverty and the curse of neglected ancestors; or (2) to satisfy kinsmen and ancestors in the old way, which meant social exclusion as a *niha baero*, an 'outsider', a heathen. Either way you were damned.

Nietzsche saw Christian morality as *motivated* by ressentiment, the cry of the oppressed. But in Nias ressentiment as a moral stance – a response to cosmic injustice – *followed* conversion. The plaint of the Godforsaken, the perennial outsiders, the losers, it continues to permeate the way people see their place in the world. It can be heard in the grim statement, made matter-of-factly to collective nods, that 'we here, at the very end of the earth, are the pig's tail'. Or in the despair of those left behind in deepening poverty as young people migrate to plantations on the Sumatran mainland. This is a new twist. Globalization, like Christendom, has brought new ways to be an outsider, new opportunities for ressentiment.

How did this come about? German Lutheran missionaries were busy on the island from 1865 but toiled fruitlessly until Dutch conquest at the beginning of the twentieth century. Pacification led to the suppression of the ancestor cult, headhunting, slavery, and human sacrifice. Denied the good things of life and unable to account for the collapse of their world, people burned their ancestor effigies in huge fires, smashed megaliths, defrocked shamans, and turned in droves from their chiefs. The movement spread rapidly across the north of the island, reaching the central highlands a decade later. By 1916, Year Zero in the new order, the missionaries found themselves – miraculously, as it seemed – confronted with thousands of would-be converts. But conversion to what? The crisis took the form of a collective self-revulsion known as the Great Repentance, *Fangesa Sebua* (*fangesa dödö* = 'repentance of the heart'). This cataclysmic event was a total inversion of the order of things: a revaluation of values, to use another Nietzschean phrase. All that was good became bad, and not merely bad but loathsome, horrifying. For the first time in their history Niha confronted the totality of their culture. Like Leontes in *The Winter's Tale*, they had 'drunk and seen the spider'. As former penitents would tell me with distant amazement, 'We saw our past actions as those of animals'. At prayer meetings they babbled in tongues, at mass confessions they wept hysterically. And as the Great Repentance spread across the island, like a mutating virus it took on new forms, each phase named after its primary symptom (see Beatty 2012 for a full account). First came the Crying, then the Shivering, then the Jumping, finally the Laughing, when whole congregations would shake with laughter.

The staging, as always, was melodramatic. But unlike the emotional oratory of feasts and weddings, Repentance sessions were wordless. Confession took the form of acting out past crimes as penitents fell into trance and re-enacted murder and adultery in pantomime before their shocked audiences. The penitent was in the grip of overwhelming emotion (the older word *passion* seems appropriate), experienced as an overpowering heat that threw them writhing to the ground, like someone stricken by a fit, and then lifted them upward – onstage, as it were – in a medieval *tableau vivant* of sin. In these re-enactments they were helpless. Only the evangelist's blessing – a cool hand on the head – would release them.

What were these emotions? Missionaries – witnesses and agents of the first Repentance, movers if not shakers – wrote of Pentecostal fires, of fear and loathing (Anon 1917; Kriele 1927). My own sources, speaking in 1986 of events forty, fifty, and sixty years earlier (there were periodic revivals, aftershocks of the earthquake), recalled feelings of terror and release. I asked one old man – an early convert, later a backslider – about the Jumping, a movement of the 1950s.

Ah, that was new to us! There was an apostle who came from Gomo [a village in the centre]. His daughter later married our chief. He jumped in church. We in the congregation laughed. We had never seen such things.

Groundings

He jumped all round the floor, bouncing and stamping. People mocked. After that we had a prayer meeting and spoke to God, saying, 'Listen God, that's not our way.' But it happened to us too. [*Was it deliberate?*] No, it just hit you. [*What was in your mind when it happened?*] Prayer, recollection of sins. We jumped, we trembled. Our hearts were hot. Our hearts were flooded with sin, startling us. We'd weep with fear of hell. 'I'm done for, with my sins, Lord!' I'd feel hot, then cold, then I'd collapse. They'd pick me up and I'd start jumping. Finally, an apostle would lay a hand on my head and I'd be calm. If my heart was dark I'd say to the apostle, 'Pray that my heart be clear.' In front of the congregation he'd pray for me and show me the way, and my heart would be clear.

This is conversion as dramatized emotion. Later revivals were no less turbulent. A younger man remembered the Shivering that came to the village in the 1960s. 'You shivered as your sins became vivid to you during prayer meetings. The shivering swept over congregation like grass in the wind', he said, clenching his fists like a penitent. 'The shaking was due to the heat in your heart, the heat caused by the work of the Holy Spirit within you. The words that came out of your mouth were the new language; like *your* language they had no meaning. Only God could understand them.' A missionary who came to witness had forbidden the sessions, but they carried on. They carried on, said the man (a pious Christian), until the sense of sin was too deep to need the shaking or the shivering.

Spread by contagion and instigated by collective prayer, these upheavals – physical before they were mental – were a product of crowd commotion, a raw excitement conformable to what the occasion produced: laughter, shivering or weeping. Is it better to speak, then, of unconscious emotion, or perhaps 'affect' in the sense used in Cultural Studies of a pre-reflective energy discharged between colliding bodies? An obvious reference is Freud's 'return of the repressed', with the native priest a barefoot psychoanalyst exhuming dark crimes and buried memories. But the Repentance was no talking cure, and the lack of words was crucial. Even where speech burst out it was the babble of glossolalia, signifying nothing. Some said: 'It was the Holy Spirit speaking.' God's talk, like that of the Europeans, was powerful but meaningless.

The contrast with formal rhetoric is striking. We have seen in the bridewealth speeches a manipulative naming of emotions, an attaching of word to feeling, and feeling to claim. In the Great Repentance, emotions – fear, disgust, and horror, a sense of the uncanny, followed by the ecstasy of release – were inarticulate, spontaneous, contagious, and unrestrained. They spread wordlessly through the congregation, achieving the 'one-heartedness' that is the standard object of rhetoric. Briefly, but memorably, shared affect created what Victor Turner called *communitas*, an unstructured equality of fellow feeling. 'You were happy; like a child in your tears', said one old evangelist to me, his eyes moistening.

But the lack of articulation meant that, once formulated, the emotion evaporated without effect. The outbreaks never accumulated, never led to anything co-ordinated like a nativistic rebellion or a new religion. Instead, a cultural and social defeat. Unlike the heart-speech of debate, the inchoate emotions of the Repentance made no claims. Part of the failure was due to the fact that the movement was purely negative: a rejection of the past with nothing positive to put in its place. Converts embraced Christianity without understanding. The Nietzschean model of ressentiment leading to the 'slave morality' of Christianity is therefore a poor fit. The revaluation of values – the discovery of Niha identity as sinful, the self polluted – did not lead to the adoption of Christian compassion or brotherly love. Instead, what people became conscious of was their marginality within Christendom, their exclusion from salvation and from the fruits of civilization, the world of goods that colonial masters enjoyed. In this respect, their confused envy of colonial cargo drifted into a different kind of sentiment tinged with despair: what Parrott (2001: 312) calls 'global resentment', distinct from personalized

Groundings

'agent-focused resentment'. 'We are God's stepchildren', as one man said to me bitterly. 'We can never have what you have, we shall never inherit the kingdom of heaven.' As in other colonized societies, relative deprivation fuelled religious change; but a persisting sense of injustice created by this very change led to a deeper resentment, an impotent rage against the world. Even today, this despair finds temporary consolation in the island's many evangelical schisms that practise speaking in tongues. A home remedy for a chronic, indeed cosmic, ailment.

*

In exploring the life of emotions in Niha society we have seen how hearts figure in the system of exchange, how they stir debate, how they were caught up in colonial transformations. To construct the argument, I have had to draw together aspects of emotion that an experimental scientist would keep apart: idioms, behaviour, existential stances, feelings and performance. But the manifold nature of emotion makes compartmentalization suspect. There is no controlling for reality. What we get from Nias is a beguiling picture, boldly coloured but vaguely bordered, to be set against other examples in other fields. If that sounds like a Benedictine *Patterns of Culture* argument in the making, I shall disappoint (Benedict 1934). For what we are talking about is not constructed vignettes derived from generalized observations and psychological assumptions, but the life of emotions in action, in specific circumstances, formed under discernible pressures, material and ideological.

What emerges in the theatre of debate, as in the crucible of conversion, is a dramatistic emotional skill and a kind of stubborn obtuseness (as we should see it), whether willed or innocent: in fact, all that makes Nias fascinating and compelling. To put this more positively, what I am getting at is the outward, agonistic thrust of Niha emotionality, which combines with an urge to pursue a course to the bitter end and, emotionally, take it to the limit. In writing about my Niha companions,

I am haunted by a line from Shakepeare's *Timon of Athens*: 'The middle of humanity thou never newest, but the extremity of both ends.' Ethnographically, emotionally, humanly, the anthropologist is at full stretch.

In Java, we shall find the opposite case: the tendency to look inwards ('interiority' a key concept), a preference for the golden mean, and an analytical interest in emotion, combined with a studious effort to remove its disruptive effects – not always successful.

THREE

Java
Emotions Analyzed

Ethnography – as shown – takes us into different emotional worlds. It does more than explore difference and inform theory: it poses a personal challenge. To move from Nias to Java, half-way across the sprawling Indonesian archipelago, is to discover another realm of human possibility, one that calls upon something different, perhaps untapped, in ourselves that participant-observation nurtures and tests – and which the reader is invited to share. In Chapter 2, language was our point of entry and exit: we began with oratory and ended with the wordless babble of the Great Repentance. In the present chapter, language is no less important, but the articulation of emotion in Java is very different, more reflexive and analytical. Emotion has a much greater role in self-monitoring and in thinking about morality and social orientation.

Words and worlds

Consider the contrast. Niha veterans lament that the time of deeds has passed. The heroic days of raiding are over; now is the time of words. There have always been speeches, but now – the old-timers like to complain – there are *only* speeches. Yet words can be a form of action, a thinking aloud that changes minds and turns situations. And emotions feed the circuit: presented, paraded, reverberating in hearts, acting on the world. They 'hit the mark', as Niha say, redefining the state of play, rearranging the players. Doubtless, not all of the emotional weapons in the orator's armoury are *bona fide*: assume a good deal of sabre-rattling. But they are effective whether or not their owners' hearts are really scorched or pierced.

In Java, words and deeds are differently linked, sometimes at several removes. Instead of hearts on sleeves, expect caution, philosophical doubt, a bland smile. The meaning of things is not obvious, it must be sifted, tested against experience. 'Do you know that, or do you only *think* you know it?' said one elderly friend as I showed off what I had learned in another village. The truth of an utterance is justified not by theoretical or esoteric knowledge but by a felt rightness, a fittingness (*cocok*, key word in Java) that clinches the point and has its roots in inarticulate experience. 'Don't take my word for it, I might be wrong', said the sage on another occasion. 'Accept it if you really feel it [*nganthi kerasa*] – otherwise not.'

A philosophical psychology

The force of that statement, typical of Javanese philosophical-mystical discussion, depends partly on its earthy wisdom, partly on a deep connection between the concepts of sense, meaning, feeling, and consciousness, which all have a common root in *rasa* (feeling, meaning).

Feeling and meaning are not opposed; the sharp apprehension of realities, including interior states, is, if anything, more reliable than the logic of words. And the matching of word with affect or sense impression is the touchstone of truth-telling – at least, in the cultural orientation known as *kejawèn* (Javanism), which stresses the Indic and native over the Islamic elements of Javanese syncretism (Beatty 1999). Javanist valuation of feeling (in its cognitive aspect) contrasts with its devaluation among pious Javanese Muslims. In the orthodox Muslim tradition, which is an important part of the Javanese mix, *akal* (reason)

Groundings

trumps *nepsu* (passion). But passion, a Javanist retorts, is itself a misapprehension, a misdirection of *rasa*.

Much has been written about this complex word. One Javanese–English dictionary (Robson & Wibisono 2002) gives the meaning of *rasa* as 1 taste 2 sensation 3 meaning, sense. Another (Horne 1974): 1 taste 2 physical feeling 3 emotional feeling; with derivatives that include 'think over', 'empathize', 'talk about', 'idea', 'sensitivity', 'thought' and 'inner feelings of the heart'. The word has an Indian origin. For a thousand years before the coming of Islam, which spread slowly across the island from the fourteenth century, Java was Buddhist and then Hindu, sometimes a combination of the two. Contemporary Java, where most people identify as Muslim, is a fluid mix of unequal traditions, with much regional variation. In mysticism and the courtly arts, which are steeped in both Sufism and Indian thought, *rasa* is the faculty of intuitive feeling (Stange 1984: 119), conventionally located in the solar plexus. Rasa is also synonymous with indwelling divine life, and it is in *rasa* that outer and inner, person and God are united (Geertz 1960: 238–240; Gonda 1952: 158; Zoetmulder 1995: 182–184).

A highly specialized take on emotion and perception, you might think; but the strength of Javanism in much of Central and East Java until the Islamic resurgence of the last couple of decades meant that, to varying degrees, many – in some places most – ordinary villagers shared this mystical orientation, with an admixture of ritualism and a strong communitarian ethic. In Bayu, a village of 2,000 souls which I have known for twenty-five years, until very recently a quarter of the adult population belonged to a pantheist mystical association, and as many again could be counted sympathetic to their orientation. In the tolerant, ecumenical settings of neighbourhood feasts and late-night visiting it was the mystics rather than their orthodox counterparts who gently dominated after-dinner chat and whose views quietly commanded respect. Over and above doctrinal differences, most villagers, mystical, orthodox, and indifferent, subscribed to a broadly Javanist attitude towards emotions and their place in the scheme of things, one that stressed self-control, self-knowledge, moderation and poise (Beatty 2009).

Java/Nias

Nias and Java emerge as polar types – at least they can easily be made to appear so. To be sure, I am contrasting here different sorts of speech context, the worked-up oratory of one with the coffee-table conversation of the other: not quite the same thing; and not the same as spontaneous emotions either. But immediate feelings are, so to speak, mediated; spontaneity is trained. Differences at the level of performance and discourse are likely to imply differences in the ordinary flow of emotions in action and the nature of experience: words frame, impede, express, reflect, distort, evoke, and enable. In juxtaposing Javanese reflexivity with Niha histrionics, subtlety with spectacle, I am amplifying, or at least sharpening, but not much. I could not reverse the terms.

Consider this scrap of monologue recorded in the bamboo house of a retired headman. He was talking about the meaning of a well-known poem to a group of villagers – card-carrying mystics and fellow travellers. In the verse, which draws on a Javanese version of the Ramayana story, the monkey Anoman (Hanuman), sent by Rama to the forest to look for Sinta, climbs a tree and looks down to see a beautiful woman. What is relevant here is not so much the content as the interpretive resources brought to bear.

So 'looking down, seeing a woman' [he quotes] indicates *desire*; but what's meant by the verse is not what's really intended; because when one 'looks down' [in meditation] one sees only the tip of the nose, right? Anything else is visible only in *rasa*. To find the true meaning we must always go beyond. Because, according to the wish of the poet, what's indicated isn't necessarily in agreement with the words. It's a paradox, a verbal disguise. The sense and the purport are not the same. Even if one is clever, the significance of the words is not certain.

Groundings

The former headman, now a rice farmer, had completed only primary school but he knew the Hinduized mythology inside-out and could move nimbly through the layered philosophy of the shadow play, the vehicle for myths and epics in Java. Though Nias's violent past and Lutheran present make for a good deal of moral agonizing, it is a safe bet that no Niha ever looked so closely at semantics. (Yet I recall a warning from an elder keen to disillusion me over a promise: 'Here, Mister, what's said is only a shadow of the intention.' He, at least, would have appreciated Java.) For all its rhetorical richness, the language of Nias does not enable such refinements – or such casuistry, as the plainer-speaking pious Javanese Muslims like to call it.

Emotion in a complex tradition

Java's long history bears a legacy of interwoven linguistic traditions – Old and Modern Javanese, Malay/Indonesian, Arabic and Sanskrit, plus a smattering of Dutch. This linguistic syncretism, fertile in concepts and continually changing, is evident in the umbrella terms for emotion – for which there is no single word – and in the *meta* categories of psychology. Most commonly, one 'feels' or 'senses', *ngrasa* (from Sanskrit *rasa*, via Old Javanese). But provoked, one might be *emosi* (Indonesian, from the Dutch *emotie*), i.e. stirred by strong emotion. Depending on temperament, one is prey to certain passions, *nepsu* (from the Arabic). And one has *perasaan*, an Indonesian compound of *rasa,* meaning 'feeling' or 'sentiment'. Emotion words and categories are taken up from different languages and social settings – school slang, the marketplace, the mosque, local radio and popular culture, television, and Twitter. Mobile phones were unknown when I began in 1992, but by the time of my last visit young people had become enthusiastic texters of emojis. During evening power cuts, they sit outside in the dark, their phones glowing, as they ping smileys across the village.

There are always local inflections.[1] My examples come from the Banyuwangi region on the eastern tip of Java, which has its own distinctive dialect of Javanese called Osing. Among the villagers of Bayu, *perasaan* tends to be used not as a general term for emotion or feeling but more narrowly for 'fellow feeling' or 'empathy'; though they reserve a different term, *tepa slira,* for the moral-psychological *act* of empathy. *Tepa slira* refers to a situation or stance ('putting oneself in the other's place'), not a mental state. As we shall see, however, *situation* in Java – perhaps more than anywhere – tends to imply *feeling*. Emotion has spatial and relational dimensions, and vice versa.

Like Japanese, Javanese, has a number of distinct speech styles or levels that label objects, actions, and pronouns in contrasting ways, depending on the relative status of interlocutors or the person referenced (Errington 1988). Speech levels also constrain emotional expression. High Javanese (*krama*) is a formal impersonal register, sparing with sentiment, in contrast to the salty, affect-rich Low Javanese (*ngoko*), which voices interactions between familiars.

Regional variants, such as the Osing dialect of Banyuwangi, which retains many Old Javanese words as well as borrowings from neighbouring Bali, further complicate the picture; as do slang and the regional languages heard in markets and ports. Throw into the mix a fondness for word play and folk etymology, plus a range of scripts – Javanese, Arabic and Roman ('Latin') – and you have a number of ways of linking word, concept, and feeling and of representing those links. This is not Babel, as the newcomer fears, but a linguistic cornucopia. To speak in Java is to be conscious at every turn of verbal choices and near

---

[1] Heider notes regional differences in the meaning of emotion words in Indonesian, spoken as a second language (2011: 7). In his questionnaire on emotion classification, he uses *perasaan* as an equivalent umbrella term to 'emotion', such that *marah* (anger) and *malu* (shame) are instances of *perasaan*. However, he notes that among Minangkabau of Sumatra 'there was little support for a clear category of *perasaan* or "emotion"' (2011: 113).

Groundings

equivalents, of social boundaries, horizontal and vertical, often vague, that have to be negotiated with care. The easy Niha assumption that everyone will understand who is included in *we* or *our* (or excluded by *you* or *my*), and the unsubtle manipulations that depend on it, would not apply in Java. One reason, perhaps, why ordinary Javanese are not orators or storytellers.

In contrasting these two emotional worlds I am reminded of an essay by Robert Levy (1994) on what he calls person-centred anthropology. Levy's central point is that the different ways of being a person in Nepal and Tahiti (for which read: Java and Nias) go much deeper than ethnic personality and cultural dress, implying different ways of feeling and thinking, different notions of freedom, destiny, and morality, diverse philosophies and insertions of self in cosmos (or, in Java, cosmos in self: the microcosm). Levy suggests that the question *What kind of person are you?* – a real question in Nepal with multiple answers, depending on caste, sect, education, and ethnicity – would be puzzling, even meaning-less, in the simpler setting of rural Tahiti or other tribal societies where, in the neat phrase of Stanner, ethnographer of Aboriginal Australia, life is a one-possibility thing. In Java, too, that more-than-personal question is real, indeed urgent, with a range of divisive replies, cultural, religious, and existential. When I underwent initiation into Sangkan Paran, an atheistic–pantheistic mystical sect congenial to Anglo-Saxon scepticism, the first question I heard, wrapped in my funeral shroud, was *What kind of person are you?* My preceptors had given me the correct reply (and its occult meaning): 'I am a man of old who follows the rules of now.' More pertinently, they had coached me in how to *feel* that the answer was 'really true, not just something known with your head'. When a Muslim dies, the mosque official puts the very same question to the departed spirit in a funeral catechism. So it goes for mystics and orthodox alike. But the correct graveside response – voiced for the dead – is the deceased's given name, a plain *Ismail* or *Sri*. No need for paradox or symbol.

What kind of person are you? In Java there are different ways of answering Levy's question, different ways of thinking and feeling the response. But the question is not just – or even primarily – theoretical. The difficulty of knowing how to act, how to relate to others, takes a good deal of savoir-faire in a community of ploughmen, irrigation officials, peanut vendors, harvest brokers, money-lenders, transvestite singers, atheists, actors, clerks, musicians, clowns, mystics, prostitutes, pantheists, healers, dancers, spirit mediums, mosque officials, hajis, builders, carpenters, cattle dealers, midwives, monotheists, make-up artists, herbalists, mechanics, matchmakers, diviners, wedding organizers, and, of course, rice farmers and landless labourers. Nobody ever tells you. It is something you must absorb and, necessarily, feel. The problem is not simply how to be this or that kind of person, but how to be whatever you are with others who are not.

Feeling your way: Emotions, persons, and places

In ordinary conversation pretty much everywhere people cite emotions as reasons for doing or desisting: 'she was eager to go', 'I didn't feel like it', 'they left in a huff', 'he dropped it in disgust'. Emotions are prompts to action: that is their job. And in Java, too, people explain themselves emotionally. 'Why didn't you go?' 'Scared'; 'reluctant'; 'embarrassed'. The cognitive content of the reported emotion might be a complex judgement of situation and role, tailored to the interlocutor; but the emotion word sufficiently sums it up. The judgment need not actually have taken an emotional form for the report to be accepted at face value: the word encodes the reasoning that prompts the action. Yet in practice certain emotions do, in fact, take on a constructive, directive role in social relations. Feelings of reluctance, ambivalence, embarrassment, and shame are not merely reactive or motivating, but orienting and informing. Perhaps this is the case everywhere; but if so, Java offers a particularly vivid illustration. For in the crowded but loosely-structured

Groundings

villages of Banyuwangi, emotions serve as social antennae, feelers put out to guide the actor through the social labyrinth.

Why should this embodied skill be useful, even necessary? Without clear demarcations of class, clan, or caste; without broader groupings above the household, such as abound in neighbouring Bali, with its temple groups, irrigation societies, and status groups; without the formal ties of marriage alliance that govern tribal societies like Nias or Tanimbar at opposite ends of the archipelago, what holds things together? With no direction home, what gives shape and purpose? In the absence of explicit rules and institutional regulation other factors must come into play. Values are a help of course; but values, by definition, are general and what the *flâneur* needs is something more finely tuned, alert to differences and responsive to social cues, a navigational tool not just a map or set of instructions. In rural Banyuwangi what gets you safely around is something uniquely discriminating and particular: emotions. The villager literally feels her way through the social maze.

There's a broader argument to be had here about the structural role of emotion in society (a fundamental one in sociology that goes back to Durkheim), but let us concentrate for the moment on practicalities. How, if you are one of those harvest brokers or gong players, do you make your way?

Without much fuss, as it happens. As other ethnographers have noted, village life in Java moves with a studied casualness, a sort of willed randomness that gains gentle impetus from a characteristic dislike of cliques. In his book, *Javanese Villagers*, Robert Jay even claimed that 'sheer physical proximity' was the fundamental principle of association (Jay 1969: 216). Who do you talk to? Whoever happens to be passing by. Who gets pulled in to assist at household rituals? Whoever is at a loose end in neighbouring yards. With its diaries, appointments and programmed socializing, the life of Western middle-class urbanites is about as far from this easygoing non-pattern as could be imagined. But even in Indonesian terms, life in the Javanese village would rate as informal. For months I had the impression that there were no purposeful visits outside of Lebaran, the week-long feast that ends the annual fast. Not that people avoid house calls; rather, their coming and going is barely remarked as others make way for them or drift off without acknowledgment. Mostly one just happens by: no need to announce one's arrival or excuse oneself on leaving. With few rules or customs pointing the way, what guides the stroller, saves her from mishap and misstep, is something felt.

The focus of these transient gatherings, as Jay observed, is less often a house than some open neutral space in front of a store or next to a well-trodden path that guarantees a constant flow of people in and out of the ensemble. Women with babies stand outside talking or calling across to other women spreading out rice to dry. Passers-by are asked where they are going or half-heartedly invited in. You drift over for a word and move on. Unlike neighbouring Bali, with its walled compounds and guard dogs, where the boundary between inside and outside divides domestic from public space; unlike, too, the sprawling Javanese settlements further west, houses in Banyuwangi are packed close together and their boundaries are weak. The split-bamboo walls are lifted out for weddings and circumcisions, like the walls of a doll's house. Even the front room, conceptually, is not quite inside: it is the inner enclosed room, which is called *jerumyah*, 'within the house'. This is where the family sleeps and where the rice goddess Dewi Sri is kept, tucked in a flap of the wall.

The front room is semi-public: it opens onto the path and to casual callers. And fitting this blurring of public and private spaces, the arrangement of furniture allows degrees of presence, monitored by feeling and expressed in posture. The man of the house sits at a small marbletopped coffee table, facing out, attentive and complaisant. A caller who stays a while sits facing him. Others who drop by out of curiosity or idleness sit on the *planca*, a platform the size of a double

Groundings

bed, looking on, contributing a comment or joining in a laugh, but not fully participating. If a female caller arrives, a male onlooker will move to the coffee table to allow her to sit on the platform. The woman of the house then disappears to the kitchen to prepare more coffee. An equable tone is maintained by these mutual adjustments.

Nobody is admitted with anything less than gracious acceptance, which is to say, they take their place, minimally acknowledged, with a sense of total right to be there – or to leave with a nod when they feel like it. Even if you are discussing some private matter, a business deal or quarrel, a caller simply settles down unfazed. I once dropped in on a man dispensing advice to a friend who wanted a divorce from his unfaithful wife. Vaguely following the patter (*whose* fault, how often, etc.), I was not allowed to leave but remained slightly to the side while they continued quietly until their voices lifted, smiles were assembled, and coffee brought us together.

Modern concrete houses, which now make up a third of the village, have factory furniture – sofas and armchairs – uncongenial to this sort of graded presence. There is no equivalent to the *planca* and no possibility of hovering or discreetly shifting position as new callers arrive: you are either in or out. Worse still, males and females are obliged to sit together, which for Javanese feels awkward. ('Feeling awkward' is a reason for changing course or moving on.) The usual solution is either to have two sets of furniture – which means two competing conversations – or to turn the kitchen into a parlour and leave the stiff front room for show.

The easy coming and going that I have described enacts the pre-eminent value in village life, which is *rukun*, social harmony (H. Geertz 1961: 149; Jay 1969: 66). *Rukun* begins with the household – or rather with the well-adjusted, spiritually-balanced householder in regular touch with the ancestors and guardian spirits – and radiates outwards to the 'neighbours left and right', the ward, the village, and the nation. *Rukun* models the integration of microcosm and macrocosm.

Java

The mystics have a formula for it, as they do for most things: *rukun* in the person (the 'neighbours of the soul'), in the house, in the village, and in the state.

It all sounds very inclusive and orderly; but this integrative principle operates successfully because people do not range far beyond the neighbourhood unless to call on a restricted circle of kin and associates scattered about the village. A sense of social decorum – what feels right and *where* – marks boundaries otherwise left vague. The dogma of the house being open to all and sundry depends on tact in not treating it too seriously. Here certain social sentiments – emotional attitudes that partake of normative values – play a crucial part, as do the feelings associated with them. A sensitivity to invisible lines and an awareness of degrees of solidarity and difference within the neighbourhood are expressed as feelings of 'reluctance' (*sungkan*), 'embarrassment' (*isin*), 'respect' (*aji, wedi*), and so on. Having tagged along with callers and idlers, noting here a confident step, there a tentative withdrawal, I am certain these feelings are often felt as well as announced, if not always in synchrony. As Fred Myers writes of a very different society, an Australian Aboriginal group, 'the emotions define and orient Pintupi in their social world' (Myers 1986: 126). In the Javanese case, that orientation is at once conceptual, emotional, and spatial. In the absence of groups, clans, or factions, it is a sense of social tact – embodied in shame, reluctance and so forth – that guides one through bamboo alleys and around dusty yards to those places one feels *pernah*, a key word denoting the feeling of being 'at home' or 'comfortable in a situation'.

It is *pernah* that decides where newly-weds or the elderly-infirm reside. Informally fostered or 'borrowed' children – the bustling life of the neighbourhood – settle and establish relations of pseudo-kinship where they feel most *pernah*. There is a constant coming and going of these half-tame creatures – said to be 'not yet people' – as they find their berth or opt for a change. Some prefer to eat at a neighbour's and sleep

Groundings

at their parents'. Others spend a few weeks with an aunt. One child of three would only fall asleep in the arms of an elderly neighbour before being carried back home every night. Inconvenienced parents can only shrug, for a child's wishes cannot easily be gainsaid. I have seen a borrowed baby dangled before its anxious mother while yelping for safety, then pulled back into a smothering bosom with the excuse: 'Doesn't want to' or 'not *pernah*'. Our own infant daughter was the pliant, sometimes resistant, object of these tender battles (but Mexican motherhood prevailed, my wife Mercedes taking refuge in the proverb, *Madre sólo hay una*, 'there's only one mother'). For a month, the headman's newborn grandson alternated between two homes as rival grannies waged a coddling war, always justified in terms of *pernah* (the baby's mother, who had failed to establish suckling, was ruthlessly excluded). Even in the powerless, the concept recognizes or proclaims a certain autonomy.

Being *pernah* or not is sufficient reason for remaining somewhere or getting out of a situation, be it job, marriage, or house. Whether a man moves in with his wife's family or she with his depends on *pernah*. They do not have to say why. *Not* being *pernah* registers the undesirability of a situation – an incompatibility of persons and places – without having to specify or make criticisms. This useful sentiment lacks the moral implications of *isin* ('shame', 'embarrassment') and *wedi* ('fear', 'respect'), since no one is being held up to a standard and no one is *obliged* to feel *pernah*. But nevertheless it is a desirable state that others should try to engender. You should always make a guest feel *pernah* by the exercise of good manners and hospitality. (The restless chair-shifting is part of this process.) In the Osing dialect the word *pernah* also refers to family relationship, position on a genealogical map (Hasan Ali 2002). 'How are you *pernah* with that person?' means 'How are you related?' It may be a homonym of the homely feeling but in any case, *in practice*, emotion, location, and relation are interlinked. Someone who acts selfishly, without regard to others, is said to be *pernahe dewek*, which literally means, 'their own location' ('up themselves', as we should say), or perhaps 'self-related', a social contradiction.

Pernah seeks and registers equilibrium in a fluid social environment, whereas 'reluctance' and 'fear/respect' mark separation, hanging-back or withdrawal, typically associated with certain kin relationships, e.g. between in-laws or a father and son. Thus, social distance and movement in space are alike governed by a set of conventionalized feelings. One could put this the other way round: such feelings are expressed, and evidently experienced, as a physical reticence or expansiveness (as we might say, 'He shrank from the ghost.'). And if you do the highly unnatural thing of asking people about *isin*, *sungkan*, and *pernah*, they define them in terms of where you can or cannot go, or whose house you would be happy to enter on a particular occasion; they define social emotions in terms of moral constraints on movement in space.

Here is part of a conversation I had with a villager.

Let's suppose [he explained] I was passing your house and just dropped in, without announcing myself: I just walk in. I didn't know you were holding a *slametan* [neighbourhood feast]. So I'm *isin* ('ashamed/embarrassed'). Difficult to turn back, but difficult to stay. That's what you'd call *kemisinan* (inadvertently shamed, caught out). It's not a question of wrong (*salah*), but *isin*, 'shame/embarrassment'. And it arises from a false step. *Isin* means being out of step with others, doing something that jars with the arrangements or rules of others or yourself.

We note several things: (1) a distinction, underlined in Javanese thinking, between inherent badness or wrongness (that of a thief or adulterer) and a social infraction; (2) the attachment of shame and related emotions to such infractions; (3) the connection with being in the right place at the right time; (4) the emphasis on social harmony, which means being in step with others. Significantly, the speaker chooses for his illustration a *slametan*, precisely the ritual that creates community,

Groundings

defines the household's place within it, and establishes the sentiments conducive to *slamet*, 'well-being', from which the ritual takes its name.

Another villager, a construction worker less given to philosophizing, produced a similar example, suggesting the predicament is a common one. The night before a big event, you happen to pass a house hosting a donor's meal and are politely called in. Your pocket is empty and ordinarily you would not be among the expected contributors, so you are caught between two impossibilities: declining or dining (for free, as it were). 'The embarrassment comes from the inappropriate action', he explained, 'not from doing anything wrong.' So what would *you* do? I ask. 'Make an excuse, say a blessing and move on. If I sat down to eat, everyone would feel a bit awkward, not just me.' We have all experienced something similar; but the constant to-ing and fro-ing of life in the crowded, sociable Javanese village makes the predicament a regular hazard. They have had to come up with a way of dealing with it.

Spatial feelings are not always situationally relative. Certain feelings – of awe (*wedi*) or eeriness (*angker*) – belong in specific places: haunted spots, graveyards, shrines, old mosques. In imagination and experience, Java is an emotional terrain, a landscape honeycombed with caves, crags, and grottoes where the pilgrim or rover comes in contact with the Otherworld. Such places have what the cognitive psychologist James Russell (2003) calls an 'affective quality'. But in ordinary social interaction, feelings and orientation are not linked to a concrete sense of place (symbolic zones, no-go areas) as they are in more formally rigid societies; rather, they are relative to the situation and dependent on the presence and disposition of others. You find your bearings in a fluid social field rather than within a fixed and stable locality. Again, the contrast with Bali and with many other Indonesian societies is striking. Compare Geertz & Geertz (1975: 138): 'the intimate connection between physical space and social groupings is a general characteristic of Bali'. Or Boon (1977: 100): 'If pressed to define the central Indonesian notion of *adat* [custom] in its specifically Balinese context, one might say it is dharma attached to space.'

Whether claimed or attributed, *pernah* has rhetorical and performative force. A culture-specific emotion tailored to Javanese conditions, it alters a situation, stabilizes a relation. Yet unlike homegrown concepts that are *merely* rhetorical or only indirectly linked to feeling (like the Niha 'cat's fur feeling'), *pernah* has an experiential dimension; it is felt not just postulated. Indeed, Banyuwangi-Javanese would be lost without it. For *pernah*, along with the other relational emotions, enables the villager to do the rounds with poise and equanimity, knowing whom to drop in on, when to pass by with a nod, and how to avoid an awkward encounter. These educated emotions provide a means of feeling your way through an intricate social system with few rules or markers. They are felt cognitions, apprehensions of whether you are welcome, untimely, appropriately clad, in or out of place. Confronted with a room full of people and doubts over whether to enter, retreat, or sit discreetly to one side, you must feel the right thing in order to do the right thing.

What is crucial about these positional emotions is that there is no fixed point of view; the affective quality of persons and settings changes with every twist of the social kaleidoscope, as actors switch roles – now parent, now child, now neighbour, now rival – tapping into past experiences and assuming new configurations. In a cultural setting unusual for its conceptual and moral relativism, emotions must be trusted for the knowledge and social competence they embody. Indeed, a person lacking such emotional intelligence is said to be 'not yet Javanese'.

In the labyrinth

I have suggested that the ethic of keeping open house is qualified by people's sense of propriety and social sensitivity, glossed as

Groundings

'embarrassment' and 'reluctance', which set limits to their movements. Since people do not generally talk about such things, having no need to, one can easily be unaware of them. One's initial sense of nobody visiting, since everything is so informal, soon gives way to a sense of everybody visiting, of a decorous free-for-all. But this, too, is misleading.

A woman's range, in particular, is quite restricted; and if block A overlaps B and B overlaps C, it would be unusual and awkward, outside of feasts, for a woman in A to call into C. One day there was a commotion in a nearby house cluster when a wild civet cat ran through the village pursued by children. With our usual lack of Javanese cool, we dashed over to see what was happening, but our neighbour, equally curious, hung back. She confided that she had never visited some of the houses that were less than a stone's throw away and could not make this the first occasion. *Isin* was her simple word of explanation. She would be 'embarrassed' to go.

Another young woman who had recently married out of the neighbourhood, though only a hundred yards away, felt unable to ask for help when she went suddenly into labour. She staggered in painful silence along the path home to her mother, hoping no one would see. It was not that her new neighbours would have refused her, or would have been indifferent to her plight; rather, she would have felt compromised in her display of weakness before people with whom she did not yet feel *pernah*.

A woman who marries into a different part of the village, perhaps a quarter of a mile away, ceases to have frequent contact with the neighbourhood in which she grew up. This is almost true of men, though more diverse occupations and a tendency to roam increase their circulation. The casual and purposeless nature of social calls, the drifting in and out, is only possible among neighbours or people living on your normal routes through the village. Those who marry into other villages can lose touch with kin. Again, feelings of reluctance and embarrassment are said to constrain them in venturing out.

The Javanese case illustrates and develops a line taken by Robert Solomon in a reworking of his much-discussed formulation of emotions as *judgments*, the point of departure for most cognitivist accounts in philosophy (Solomon 1993, 2004). Judgments, he argues, have been wrongly assumed by his critics to be purely intellectual, lacking a relation to body or feeling. But the kinds of unreflective judgments made in emotions are often more like the kinesthetic judgments that we make in moving about the physical world (2004: 82). They are 'judgments of the body' (87). In Solomon's rethinking, emotions are 'engagements in the world' (83), not merely intellectual responses, perceptions or appraisals. (We might say they are *felt* judgments.) The nature of the engagement varies with the emotion, anger being active, urging action, while grief is passive.

The concept of *pernah* nicely captures this judgment/engagement formula and locates it precisely, which is to say flexibly, within a fluctuating pattern. As a social sentiment and an expressed reason or motive, *pernah* is both real and tactical. It contributes fundamentally to *rukun*, social harmony, and satisfies a desire not to rock the boat. Being *pernah* implies keeping things as they are, neither disturbing nor feeling disturbed; *not* being *pernah* implies tactfully withdrawing. It has an aesthetic aspect too – the smooth, unruffled and predictable being valued over the sudden, harsh, loud or flashy. Comportment, to which *pernah* is integral, is aimed at achieving an *alus* (refined) and spiritually calm style of interaction.

Because emotions register relevant changes in circumstances, monitoring their desirability, it has been argued that 'emotional meaning is mainly comparative' (Ben-Ze'ev 2010: 44; Frijda 2001: 66). In hoping, regretting, feeling reluctant, or getting angry we weigh possibilities against expectations, feeling the consequences of what to do or what might have been. For good reasons, the Javanese conceptual repertoire deftly exploits this aspect of emotion. If good fences make good neighbours, so too do good emotions.

Groundings

The conceptualizing of social emotions

Most of this goes without saying. In daily use, *isin* ('embarrassed'), *pernah* ('comfortable in a situation'), and *sungkan* ('reluctant') are intuitively applied, a matter of educated dispositions and the accumulated experience of living in a diverse, highly sociable setting. Which is not to say that such emotions are beyond formulation or inaccessible to reflection. Javanese are good at finding words for feelings – a fruit of that syncretic heritage that stimulates reflection on alternatives. Without giving an extended example, it is hard to convey just how carefully people talk about emotion (when they choose to); so before further examples accrue, I want to go back to that earlier conversation about the reluctant guest.

My life coach on that occasion was a dignified man in his late fifties. Never without the plain black garb and Panama hat of an old-fashioned farmer, Rayis had had only a few years of formal schooling, but he could read in all three scripts – Javanese, Arabic, and 'Latin' – and had preserved the right to think for himself. He belonged to the Sangkan Paran mystical association, but he had mostly worked things out for himself; indeed, an axiom of the group is that one should never accept an idea on authority. We had been talking about the differences between *isin*, *sungkan*, and *wedi*, three emotions that Hildred Geertz, in a classic paper (1974), saw as being at the core of Javanese sociality. Geertz's focus was socialization. Rayis was more interested in conceptual links and psychology. If that sounds more like a graduate seminar than the small talk of fieldwork, Java is gratifying in serving up generous portions of big talk with the ubiquitous coffee.

In his example of the neighbourhood feast, Rayis had linked *isin* (shame or embarrassment) to decorum and to spatial awareness, a sense of being out of place. 'You feel *isin* because you feel something is inappropriate.' Shame, in this case, did not imply wrongdoing. So what, I ask – wanting to turn the discussion from *place* – would you feel if you

94

were caught doing something wrong, say stealing something? 'I'd feel *wedi*. Because I have done something wrong (*salah*), broken a rule.' *Wedi,* the translation equivalent of 'fear' (sometimes 'respect'), contains here an element of what we should call guilt, consciousness of fault, but it refers to one's relation to others, the risk of discovery rather than personal wrongness. Why not feel *isin*, shame? I ask. 'I'd only feel *isin* about the act if it's generally known; but that's secondary', he replies. '*Isin* derives from a rule or action that is inappropriate, rather than wrong.'

Rayis then gives another example of *isin*: the feeling of awkwardness or reluctance between a father-in-law and his son-in-law. But this is obviously different from the embarrassment or shame due to an inappropriate action. As if aware of the contrasting sense, Rayis adds, unprompted: 'I say *isin*, but in this case it doesn't have quite the same meaning. What *isin* really means here is *being polite*, showing respect. You see, my son-in-law wouldn't want to sit down next to me here; he'd sit over there on the platform-bed; especially if a guest came in. He'd move away, out of [a sense of] *isin*.'

So in regulating kinship, *isin* is likewise related to place and decorum, and to a respecting of levels. In kinship as in etiquette, *isin* is about being in the right place *vis-à-vis* others. Once again a clear analytical sense emerges of how emotions interlock with each other and with actions and persons. A sense of shame or reluctance (or what this practically entails) alerts the actor to the impropriety of a situation; which is one reason why, as Ward Keeler writes, 'the acquisition of isin is thought by Javanese to be the crucial element in a child's emotional development' (Keeler 1983: 158).

Shame, embarrassment, fear, and *pernah* are social emotions through and through. They locate persons in places and in interaction, allowing for face-saving adjustments and minimizing confrontations. They have a structuring role in a flexible social system. And they depend on an awareness of others' discomfort: a fine-tuned empathy cultivated in the

Groundings

practice of *tepa slira*, standing in the other's shoes. In Solomon's sense, they are engagements with the world; but they also structure that world. In making this claim, I am not falling in with the view that emotions are subjective colourings, Sartre's magical transformations of the world. Unlike subjective fantasy or wishful thinking, they have real effects, controlling the ebb and flow, shaping a sense of place, monitoring relative status, arranging what Hildred Geertz calls the social minuet.

Geertz's pioneering essay on 'social emotions' struggled with definitions and with the psychological status of the terms considered – were *isin*, *sungkan*, and *wedi* feelings, attitudes, or values? How did they overlap? Like Geertz, I too puzzled over the slipperiness of this cluster of words and their near-interchangeability. It was only when reading Frijda's great theoretical synthesis, *The Emotions* (1986), that I understood why. In a discussion of types of expressive behaviour, Frijda makes a distinction between 'relational behaviour' and 'interactive expressions' (whose primary function is to influence the behaviour of others). He explains the former category as follows:

The notion of relational behavior easily applies to variations in attitude for which appropriate emotion words are often hard to find, but which continuously modulate social interactions: variations in acceptance, interest, reticence, bashfulness, and the like. The terms themselves refer to variations in approach and sensory reception activities and their being toned down by simultaneous withdrawal or unreadiness features. . . . Relational behavior. . . consists of behavior that establishes, maintains, or disrupts the relationship with the environment by changing spatial relationships and sensory and actional readiness. (Frijda 1986: 24–25)

Applying Frijda's distinction to our Indonesian examples, we might say that Javanese villagers have developed, to a very high level, sensitivity to, and cultural formulation of, 'relational behaviour' – and in a manner highly functional in their loosely structured social system. Rayis's explanations and spatial examples (dropping in, withdrawing, *rukun*) correspond closely to Frijda's more abstract analysis and seem designed to illustrate it. Frijda would have felt *pernah* in Java.

In contrast, the people of Nias – specialists in oratory, aggressive persuaders – cultivate 'interactive expressions', eschewing reflexivity in the quest for influence. The inwardness of Javanese experience, their cosmology and philosophy (*kebatinan*: the science of 'inwardness'), correspond to the self-monitoring, structuring poise of their inter-actions; while Niha heart-on-sleeve histrionics fulfils an opposite function.

What is at issue here, then, is not the hyper- or hypocognition of specific emotions (as in Tahitian 'sadness' or Utku 'anger'; Levy 1984, Briggs 1970), nor a selective use of the emotional keyboard (the black notes, the upper register, C-sharp minor), but the cultivation and hypertrophy of entire dimensions of behaviour that are regulated by emotions. Here we have an advance – psychologically credible and ethnographically grounded – on purely functional or aesthetic accounts of cultural variation in ethos or emotional styles.

Emotions tamed: Socialization and self-control

Whether in its peasant-animist form or in its mystical-philosophical flowering, Javanism is very much about self-mastery and control of emotion's disrupting effects on the self and others. The popular shadow plays, with their refined, effete princes and bloodthirsty, guffawing villains, present cautionary tales of greed, lust, anger, and envy, with some of the puppets even colour-coded for mood or temperament: red-faced Bima radiating courage and turbulence, golden Arjuna refined love, the monkey Anoman white for purity. A passion play. But ortho-dox Islam, as practised in Java, shares a similar concern with moderat-ing the passions. Fasting, spiritual austerities, and the disciplining of mind and body are practices undertaken with a quiet determination unconnected to overt religiosity. The violent religious passions of the

Groundings

Middle East are something people observe on TV with detached horror, quietly shaking their heads in dismay. Until recently, such zealotry was remote, alien, almost unimaginable outside war. The few village zealots were seen by ordinary Muslims as *fanatik* – not to be taken seriously, though in need of cautious handling. Piety, at least the respectable kind, goes with moderation and a lack of show. Many people give as reasons for their religious observances not a love of God or a sense of vocation, but a desire for order and calm. Javanese virtues. And this common ground, which finds expression in a shared ethos, an equable tone in social life, enables people of different religious stripe who might other- wise dislike one another to get along.

It begins in childhood. Children of all backgrounds are encouraged to mix, give in to younger playmates, and never to assert themselves. The model is the sibling set in which the younger are indulged by the older. Among neighbourhood children – the little bands that roam yards and run freely from house to house – the stubborn and selfish find themselves shunned by their playmates. In time, piqued by the laughter of others, they learn to moderate their tempers. Older children prefer to cut off communication with peers rather than quarrel, a practice so common that almost any group of playmates is likely to include a pair who are not on speaking terms. This pattern, called (in Osing dialect) *sing nyapa*, 'not saying hello', is quite formal, even rigid. It involves avoidance *within* a relationship, blanking while associating, not feeling bad when there is reason to do so. *Sing nyapa* prevents feelings deepening and disagreements ramifying – hostilities are not transitive – minimizing disruption to the group. In adulthood, when quarrels are potentially more dangerous and there is more at stake, those childhood tiffs and snubs prove useful training. Any neighbourhood contains two or three pairs who are known not to be on speaking terms and are respected as such, others serving as intermediaries when communication is vital. The method is so reliable that it becomes a problem – a matter of regret – of how to escape from it once the antagonism has died.

In a way quite inconceivable in Nias, Javanese work on their feelings, inspect them, polish them, and put them away. Whereas Niha live their emotions onstage, Javanese stage them so as not to feel them, or not to suffer them. Who wants to end up like the puppet villains, crushed in their ambitions or eaten by ravening ogres (i.e. consumed by their own passions)? Still, nobody is the least surprised when people lose control, sometimes spectacularly. Daily life in the village may run smoothly enough – in over two years' fieldwork I rarely heard voices raised in anger – but Java has had its intermittent bloodbaths, its political convulsions, famously its Year of Living Dangerously. Not for nothing the Malay world has given us the word *amok*. Self-control comes at a price.

Emotions in two societies

I have sketched two very different kinds of society, two different emotional worlds. Nias is egalitarian but meritocratic. Achievement is praiseworthy, fiercely sought, but resentment acts as a drag on the overreacher. In the zero-sum game of life, your gain is another's loss. Only a few get to heaven. Rural Java, mildly egalitarian (mildly most things), suppresses individuality and smoothes out differences. Standing out is bad manners. Except in its undercurrent of aggressive joking (nose-tweaking, public taunting in song) and in its wildly confrontational games (whip fighting, musical contests at which one orchestra tries to outplay its rival *at the same time*), Banyuwangi lacks open competition and the lust for glory. Bad behaviour onstage reminds us why we value good behaviour off.

Functionally, discursively, and conceptually, emotions thread through these systems in contrasting ways. Niasan hearts – stand-ins for persons and factions rather than private feelings – are ever on display, battered tokens in the give and take of life. It is because private feelings are unknowable that heart-speech is so important. Emotions are, literally, all about public life. But as each man (rarely woman)

Groundings

pursues personal advancement – his own heart squeezed, his rival's puffed with envy – the ideal of 'one-heartedness' remains elusive, a prize not of this earth. The faint-hearted give in to world-despair.

In Java you start with the presumption of equal hearts. In the philosophical perspective, all humans are alike in their feelings; ultimately, all are one, just as everything shares in the oneness of life. In a standard folk etymology known to every schoolchild, *manungsa*, human being, 'means' *manunggal ing rasa*: 'one in feeling-intuition'. It resonates with Shylock's plea in *The Merchant of Venice*, and is elaborated in like fashion: 'Hath not a Jew hands, organs, dimensions, senses, affections, passions; fed with the same food, hurt with the same weapons, subject to the same diseases, healed by the same means, warmed and cooled by the same winter and summer as a Christian is? If you prick us do we not bleed? If you tickle us do we not laugh?' (III.i.49–61). Your companions complete the demonstration with a pinch or a poke. And who could deny a simple truth? Personal differences are built upon a common base and are unimportant, even illusory. More arcanely, the goal of mysticism is a filtering out of trivial differences and distractions, a penetration to the core of *rasa*. On this, however, not all would agree: the pious have other goals, and many ordinary villagers do not trouble themselves about such things. But the practices of mutual tolerance, ecumenism, child borrowing, *rukun* (harmony), and the integration of opposed religious ideologies in shared rituals all depend on a mutuality – a finding of the common denominator – that owes much to the Javanist perspective.

*

Shylock was only half right, of course, else there would be no drama. Fieldwork reveals deep similarities but also differences that are more than skin-deep: differences not just in the content of emotion – what we get angry or ashamed about – but also in what we feel and, this being Java, *where* we feel. Let me end with another emotional story, one more legible to the outsider than those of the hesitant headman and the stoical

Java

ploughman (Chapter 1) but still inflected with local meanings and given a distinctive phenomenology by person, history and cultural framing. The story was told to me shortly after the events it describes. Like the gems on a string, named emotions stud the narrative: a collective narrative, as it happens, related – almost enacted – by a poor family of sharecroppers whom I had known for many years and who were filling me in after a long absence.

A twenty-year-old youth, the oldest son of the family, had got into a fight at the rice mill and had injured a rival. The victim's family reported the incident and Nanang, the offender, fled to Bali before the police arrived. Appeals and offers to pay off the victim's family failed, and Nanang was persuaded to come home and face the music. During his twelve days in the local police cell, his mother was so distraught that she could not sleep at home: she was not *pernah*. Instead she slept in a field shelter not far from the police station. The boy got six months in prison – a time of great anxiety to the family – but bribes were paid and he was let out after four. When he came home, two days before the annual feast of Lebaran, they were all *girang,* joyful. They went down to the sea together and cast adrift his prison clothes, throwing away the misfortune and grief. Then they feasted for three days, in their joy spending what little money they had left.

A simple story with the kind of universals that newspaper editors call 'human interest'. The interlocking of emotion and context is instantly comprehensible: anxiety at the impending doom, frustration at the lack of a settlement, joy at the release. But there are distinctive Javanese elements – the locating of specific feelings in places; the horror of dislocation; the mother's lack of *pernah* and her flight to the fields (feeling more 'at home' *away* from home); the casting off of grief; the formalized joy at release. To be sure, the sequence is stamped by the conventions of storytelling (further edited in my summary) and the tidying up of hindsight. Things are always more complicated as they happen. (Husband and wife were, in fact, at odds over a mistress in

Groundings

another village, aggravating the wife's lack of *pernah* and perhaps the boy's aggression: a story behind the story.) But as I felt at the time, the breathless re-enactment, the overlapping confirmatory interruptions – impossible to convey in orderly prose – attested to the sincerity of the narration. How they told it was how they had felt it, or rather how they remembered they had felt it. Yet narrative shape was not purely retrospective. Notice how *pernah* and grief were handled: narrative constructed on the wing, emotion responding to and directing action. In the next chapter we shall explore this contextual narrative-shaping in more detail.

Postscript

Pernah: 'settled, at home'. So says the dictionary. But English does not quite match the Javanese. Not only is the formula cumbersome, depending on a dead metaphor; it papers over a gap between two emotional worlds. A Spanish speaker, my wife Mercedes found my translation inadequate to convey what *pernah* meant. Only an English person could make 'feeling at home' a distinctive emotion, she said; home having a special sentimental significance in English life. *Pernah* does not actually evoke home or imply it. It lacks the sense of privacy associated with 'home'. (You favour the school or prayer-house where you are most *pernah*.) In fact, home is sometimes a place where you are *not pernah*, as our neighbour was one day when she stepped out of the gloom with her little son. 'Where are you going?' asked Mercedes. 'Out for a while, I'm not *pernah* in the house with no one around.' 'Not at home at home', the English would have to say; or 'not comfortable' (which lacks the requisite sense of place). In Spanish there was a better term – *a gusto* – that, like *pernah*, applied to circumstances where you felt a sense of well-being, and that usually implied being with others – a congenial office or place of recreation, a chance meeting, even home. The contrast in semantic meaning, as well as in connotation, highlights

Java

differences in cultural constraints on what constitutes well-being. In Anglo cultures (stereotypically), the home is a refuge, if not a castle. Exile means 'homesickness'. In venturing out into the social world, home is where you start from. For the American poet Robert Frost, 'Home is the place where, when you have to go there/They have to take you in.' But for Javanese villagers, the house is functional, sparse, a place to sleep and eat; you feel more *pernah*, more *a gusto*, in the sociable kitchen at the back, seated on a bench in the yard, or in the company of neighbours. When the headman of Bayu was recovering from his defeat by Islamists in the mosque, he used to lie on a bamboo bench in the yard adjoining our houses; at first curled up, withdrawn but not isolated; later stretched out, listlessly smoking, slowly reawakening to the world going on around him. And there his aged mother would bring him soup. The house was no longer *pernah*.

Part II

Narrative

FOUR

The Case for Narrative

A woman stands outside a tent on a plain, dust blowing in her face. She looks ahead but her gaze is unfocused, her mouth half-open. Something important has happened; but the look shows expectation as well as reaction (the tears are half-checked). Her eyes are narrowed, her face taut. Whatever she sees is not the simple object of her emotion. We recognize apprehension, perhaps fear or regret. Trained in other expressions, we might have difficulty with Kazakh faces and with unfamiliar voice-tones, yet the story that has brought us to this point supplies what we need to know. The woman's husband, a gruff shepherd, has just had a fierce quarrel with her brother, who demands a greater share in the running of things. Back from service in the Soviet navy, his knowledge meaningless on the steppe, the brother cannot have a herd of his own until he gets a wife; and on the windswept plain there is only one other family, whose daughter Tulpan (for whom the film is named), refuses his proposal. She is the unattainable, never-seen bride of his dreams, mistress of the homestead he has drawn in fantasy on the lining of his sailor-suit collar. But now he must knuckle down and submit to his tough brother-in-law, perhaps remaining forever unmarried, or leave the isolated yurt for a distant half-mythical city. Loyal to both men, standing between them, the sister suddenly confronts the crisis and it tears her soul. Love for her brother, disappointment on his behalf, resentment of her husband, fears for the future, the apprehension of

107

Narrative

loss. All seem plainly legible as she stares at the retreating figure of her brother, while her husband, too big for his puny horse, rides off in the other direction in search of a lost sheep.

Our response, our being moved, is superficially in our reading of her face, our sympathy a felt evaluation of her expression. So what do we read? It's not a matter of 'basic emotions' (too few), 'human nature' (too vague), or 'universal expressions' (too vacant), but something altogether sharper and more detailed: the contexts, persons, and histories that produce the emotions. This is the power of narrative.

The director of *Tulpan*, a Russian documentary maker named Sergey Dvortsevoy, devised his quasi-ethnographic drama as a 'fiction film' because – he explains in an interview in the extras – you cannot put such scenes in a documentary without overexposing the subjects and betraying their private lives. Documentary hides the important, often intimate moments. The truth is in the fiction. But fiction does not exactly mean making it up. Dvortsevoy's commitment to the unstaged actuality is revealed in an unbroken ten-minute sequence of a sheep giving birth – surely the most unlikely, unappetizing climax ever put in a film. Having stalked off in a huff after the row, bent on the city over the horizon, the sailor comes upon a sick ewe, lost on the swirling plain. He approaches the groaning beast tentatively, probing at arm's length; then, bracing himself, hauls out the limp black mucous-covered body of a baby lamb. With an incredible tenderness he crouches over the trembling creature, resuscitates it by mouth, and urges it towards its mother. He is born as a shepherd. Exhausted, he lies back in the dust, stunned by relief, happiness, awe. Again, the emotions are wordless, minimally gestured in face and posture; but we understand.

In giving place to this surprisingly powerful scene – which is acted but real, opportunistic in the way of true ethnography – the director had to reassemble parts of the story: the reality was too strong, too significant, to be truncated or intercut with made-up scenes. The twin births of sheep and shepherd were his artistic reward. In the interview he

The Case for Narrative

stresses the universality and stark simplicity of the lifeworld he was attempting to capture, but also its cultural specificity, the tenderness behind the harshness of daily life, the feel for a unique landscape, the special beauty of the particular. In all this emotions play a crucial role; but their evocation and explanatory power depend on the precision of narrative. This is what good ethnography can do.

Why narrative matters

The importance of narrative is threefold: in the construction, understanding, and reporting of emotions.

(1) Narrative is implicated, firstly, in the **construction** and shape of an emotion episode (or, as emotion sceptics might say, 'in those culturally variable collocations of situated thoughts, feelings and bodily stirrings that English speakers call emotions'). In getting angry, we perceive an offence, take umbrage, attribute blame, tense up, and prepare a response. In feeling ashamed, we commit a blunder, prickle with awareness, blush at the judgment of others, and beat a retreat. Every emotion tells a story. Which is why a latecomer stumbling on rage or laughter hastens to find the cause – the backstory – the better to follow the dénouement.

Consider a short sequence from the *Tulpan* outline: the sailor's consternation on coming across the lost sheep. His consternation is a product of his striking out for the unknown, the lost sheep that thwarts his plan, the puzzle of what to do next, and the pressure, knowing nothing, to do something. Consternation is revealed to have an 'intentional structure' (Frijda 1986: 98–101) composed of interlinked expectations, frustrations, and resolutions. ('Intentional' is meant here in the ordinary sense of 'bearing an intention', not in the philosophical sense of having an object.) Or consider the longer sequence, marked by shifting emotions: the sailor's wary approach to the sheep, his

109

Narrative

determination to complete the grim task, his relief at the outcome, his joy at what this means for his future and his newfound vocation. The emotions fit together in an unfolding story, embedded within the larger story of life on the steppe. The sequence as a whole and any of its moments depend on what went before and what might come after, not merely in a succession of unrelated points or even a cause–effect chain, but as a thickening strand of meaning, feeling, reappraisal, anticipation, and implication. Though wordless, the sequence is inherently narrative-like in structure.

(2) To **understand** the sequence or any of its linked emotions – to figure out the tissue of connection and implication – is to grasp that structure. A narrative understanding of a narrative construction. (Chapter 6 develops this point.)

(3) Likewise, to **report** it is to find words or images to carry the construction through all its phases. A snapshot will not do. (See Chapter 7 on 'writing emotion'.

Composition, construal, and recounting thus all involve narrative. These three complementary perspectives on the same events, though analytically distinguishable, are not easy to tease apart. My emphasis in this chapter, however, is mainly on the first, the composition or construction of emotion.

Emotions, as we have seen, are made up of components (events, appraisals, feelings, expressions, actions) corresponding to 'intentional structures' that enable us to distinguish, for example, envy from jealousy. Envy entails thinking that someone else possesses something that we ourselves desire; jealousy, a fear of dispossession by the other, a dread that letting be will mean letting go. Iago is envious, Othello jealous. It is interesting but probably not crucial for their distinctive phenomenology – what it is like to *be* jealous or envious – that envy and jealousy are lexically distinguished. In some languages they are not; in contemporary English, especially among the young, the terms are often confused ('she was jealous of my dress'), though the underlying model of thoughts, feelings, and persons (envy two, jealousy three) remains clear. Minimal behavioural scripts for jealousy and envy are probably found everywhere. Why? Because loving, getting, wanting and losing figure among any group of human beings, cradle to grave – beyond which the envious dead come back to haunt us.

In linking narrative to emotion, I am tapping into an ancient line of thought that goes back to Aristotle, whose interest was in the emotive power of *plot*. In an influential modern formulation, the psychologist Richard Lazarus (1991) used the term 'core relational themes' to denote the meanings attached to the relation between person and environment that characterize and motivate particular emotions. Recognizable across cultures, a putative universal, a core relational theme is 'a meaningful plot or scenario' (Lazarus 1994: 309): in the case of anger, 'a demeaning offense against me and mine'; in sadness, the experience of 'an irrevocable loss'; in guilt, a moral transgression. Likewise, cultural psychologist Richard Shweder (1994: 37) refers to the 'narrative structure that gives shape and meaning to the emotion', that is, the script or 'story-like interpretive scheme' that assembles appraisals, feelings, and actions in a particular way as 'anger', 'sadness' and so forth. In philosophy, Peter Goldie (2000: 144) relates emotions to the 'narrative part of a person's life', that is the interleaving of past, present, and future in a tissue of expectations and concerns.

Is narrative structure imposed or intrinsic?

In all these discussions a narrative-like structure is seen as intrinsic to the emotion as an event that unfolds through time and among persons pursuing particular goals. Emotions differ, of course, in their duration. Surprise is brief, love is long. Most theorists, seeking clarity, go for the brief, isolable emotions. Staccato not legato. Yet those of greater weight in our lives, the joined-up emotions, have a more complex narrative structure; they are the hinges on which our lives turn (Zweig's *Beware of Pity* [1939] is a stunning example).

Among emotion theorists, Goldie is unusual in allowing considerable time-depth and personal resonance to what I shall call *narrativity* ('the quality or condition of presenting a narrative' [*Oxford Dictionary of English*]), a concept that usefully spans construction and representation. Emotions are not just flashpoints in the daily round, 'upheavals of thought', in Nussbaum's phrase; they may frame entire sequences of behaviour and shape experience over the long run. Emotions have a vintage, they are not – or not merely – products of the moment. The question is: are we imagining shapes, like dragonish clouds, where none exists? No one regards emotions as anything less than complex affairs; the issue is how they hang together; by necessity or contingency, intention or retrospect? Is it advantageous (adds the hedging ethnographer) to avoid being prescriptive? Suppose that, in discerning structure, it is not a matter of 'either/or' but of 'more or less'.

There is a useful, if recherché, parallel with a controversy in historiography. In advancing the case for a narrative approach to emotion we can learn something from the historians' debates about whether narrative shape inheres in events or is imposed retrospectively on mere succession. In doing so, we need not accept the contenders' all-or-nothing options. On the sceptical wing, Louis Mink maintained that 'narrative form in history, as in fiction, is an artifice, the product of individual imagination' (Mink 2001: 218). We can recognize the force of his point without accepting that temporal–causal shape is entirely alien to history-as-lived. (When has reality excluded imagination? What form of words, verbal or written, present tense or past historic, is *not* artifice?) Similarly, we can accept, in part, Hayden White's (2001: 224) claim that 'historical situations do not have built into them intrinsic meaning in the way that literary texts do', not because historical situations as they happen are meaningless but because the meanings of text and experience are of a different order. The narrating of history responds to the

The Case for Narrative

intentionality of human action, the fact that people act with a purpose in mind and with ideas and feelings about the world they engage. Narrativity would only be *alien* to events were they to be lived by thoughtless beings without intentions or emotions (cf. Kearney 2002; White 1981).

On the realist wing, David Carr's defence of narrative history – I quote his conclusions, not his reasoning – resonates strongly with ethnography: 'Narrative has not merely an epistemological but also an ontological value. That is, it is not only a 'cognitive instrument' as Mink claimed – a primary way of seeking, organizing and expressing our knowledge of a part of reality. It is constitutive of our very being, it is our way of existing, of constituting ourselves' (Carr 2001: 198). Further support for the narrativity case – that our understanding responds to *inherent structure* – comes from the seminal work of cognitive psychologist Jerome Bruner. In *Actual Minds, Possible Worlds* (1986) and *Acts of Meaning* (1990), Bruner sets out the case for narrative as one of two fundamental modes of understanding, the other being the logical-scientific approach that deals in causal explanation, abstraction, and generalization. Narrative, he argues, is better suited to the exploration of meaningful action than the external perspective of positivist science that treats meaning as an 'overlay' of 'behaviour'. Bruner opts for a cultural relativism in tune with American interpretive anthropology of the time, which Clifford Geertz (his preferred anthropologist) had opposed to positivist 'explanation'. There is a nice analogy. In the bad old days:

The causes of human behaviour were assumed to lie in [the] biological substrate. What I want to argue instead is that culture and the quest for meaning within culture are the proper causes of human action. The biological substrate, the so-called universals of human nature, is not a cause of action but, at most, a *constraint* upon it or a *condition* for it. The engine in the car does not 'cause' us to drive to the supermarket for the week's shopping, any more than our biological reproductive system 'causes' us with very high odds to marry somebody from our own social class, ethnic

Narrative

group, and so on. Granted that without engine-powered cars we would not drive to supermarkets, nor perhaps would there be marriage in the absence of reproductive systems. (Bruner 1990: 20–21; original emphasis)

Few anthropologists today would see culture as a cause. But the larger point holds. We can best understand social interactions through narrative because sociality is shot through with intentions and meanings. More radically, Bruner contends, like Carr, that 'narrative structure is even inherent in the praxis of social interaction before it achieves linguistic expression' (1990: 77).

We might put Bruner's position as follows. The tale needs no teller; it is written into the stream of life, the way we act and think. I would add 'and *feel*'; but, curiously, Bruner does not extend his analysis to emotions *per se*, even though emotion episodes would, presumably, count as 'acts of meaning', his principal focus. To be be sure, not all emotions qualify as *actions* (regret does little), though most involve action tendencies – the urge to approach or withdraw, strike, or embrace. Nonetheless, in his discussion of the elements of narrative proper (stories, anecdotes, fiction), Bruner identifies criteria that apply readily to the construction of emotion:

Narrative requires ... four crucial grammatical constituents if it is to be effectively carried out. It requires, first, a means for emphasizing human action or *'agentivity'* – action directed toward goals controlled by agents. It requires, secondly, that a *sequential order* be established and maintained – that events and states be 'linearized' in a standard way. Narrative, thirdly, also requires a sensitivity to what is canonical [i.e. usual] and *what violates canonicality* in human interaction. Finally, narrative requires something approximating a *narrator's perspective*: it cannot in the jargon of narratology, be 'voiceless'. (1990: 77; my italics)

Adapting Bruner for my purposes, how might these four features of narrative apply to the constitution of emotion (distinct from its retelling or narration)?

114

(1) *Agentivity* corresponds to a focus in appraisal on the cause or source of the eliciting event, for example in the attribution of blame in anger or guilt, the kindness that leads to gratitude, the threat implied in fear.

(2) *Sequential order* corresponds to the time-bound property of emotions as initiated by changes in circumstances and marked by phases in the unfolding of the episode. This is a critical difference between an emotion and a mood.

(3) *Violations of the canonical* – reversals of fortune, breaches in the quiet surface of everyday life – are what trigger prototypical emotions like rage and disgust. Emotions are prompted by changes in the relation of self to environment that impinge on our concerns (Frijda 1986, Lazarus 1991).

(4) *Narrator's perspective* corresponds to the egocentric perspective of emotional appraisal, the me-focus that identifies changes relevant to one's well-being. In narrative theory this property is called focalization.

More recent attempts to set criteria for narrative could equally be applied to emotion. David Herman proposes that prototypical narratives represent: '(i) a structured time-course of particularized events which introduces (ii) disruption or disequilibrium into storytellers' and interpreters' mental model of the world evoked by the narrative ... conveying (iii) what it's like to live through that disruption, that is, the "qualia" (or felt subjective awareness) of real or imagined consciousness undergoing the disruptive experience' (2007: 9). In like manner, classical narratologists like Todorov (and before him Propp) have focussed on the disruption that spurs the narration: 'Todorov argued that narratives prototypically follow a trajectory leading from an initial state of equilibrium, through a phase of disequilibrium, to an endpoint at which equilibrium is restored (on a different footing) because of intermediary events' (Herman 2007: 10). Which would be a pretty good definition of

Narrative

an emotion! As we have seen, independently of narratologists, emotion theorists point to the eliciting event, the appraisal of harm or benefit, the subjective feelings or qualia, the transformation of consciousness and bodily state, and the restorative or consummating action.

These striking parallels do not justify a blunt claim that emotions *are* narratives – they do not *represent* anything, even if they communicate a 'story'. The claim is rather that emotions resemble narratives in structure – a resemblance underplayed by most writers on these matters despite frequent recourse to literary examples (Oatley 2012 a key exception). Given the common factors in how emotions and narratives are put together it is hardly surprising that literature – the realist novel, but also drama and narrative non-fiction – offers some of the sharpest insights into the construction of emotion, as well as lessons for the ethnographer, that conflicted figure whom Edmund Leach saw as novelist manqué. Nor is it surprising that the narrative arts deal mainly in emotion. They work with the same ingredients.

In Chapter 6 I present some literary examples. But let us first consider what anthropology can do. My focus here will be on the *composition* of emotion rather than on the way we understand and report, though obviously these perspectives overlap, as will their illustrations.

Narrative and social dramas: Restoring the detail

The novelist and the ethnographer find common cause in a special concern with particulars, the odds and ends that get left behind in theoretical discussion as excess baggage. Without a firm grasp of the actuality there is no safe step to cross-cultural comparison, let alone grand theory. In developing arguments, the well-worked example scores over the matrix of variables, the flow chart, or the summary formula. Such is the lesson of fieldwork. Yet disciplinary history is haunted by a sense of incompleteness, the shadow of things left out (more on this in Chapter 7). Which perhaps explains why each new theoretical

The Case for Narrative

movement tends to bring a recovery, or at least a recognition, of what its predecessor ignored. Paradigms get abandoned *not* when their conceptual flaws are exposed but when discards find a place in a new kind of theory, or when shots from afar are seen to bear too high a cost in collateral damage. Emotions are the first casualties of anthropological theorizing. How then to put them back in?

In his masterwork, *The Emotions,* Frijda calls the price of generalization 'information loss', for which reason he favours 'descriptive analysis' over 'reduction to basic dimensions' (1986: 186). One direct way of recovering the information – more favoured by contemporary philosophers than psychologists – is through introspection. To observe our own unfolding emotions, catch them on the wing, is to glimpse what escapes the booth in the lab. But as Frijda cautions, 'introspection is an act of consciousness that has awareness as its object, and not the object that was intended in the first place' (187). To think about your emotions while having them, to scan your anger instead of your offender, is to lose the relation between subject and object, 'the relationship with the world' which is definitive of the experience of emotion.

For the anthropologist, too, introspection of emotion ('reflexivity') cannot recover what generalization misses. (Frijda's point bears on the problem of using our own emotions as an ethnographic resource.) Yet pure description is not enough. To advance knowledge, rather than merely to pique curiosity, what we need is a theoretical handle on the vicissitudes of emotions in action. But where can we find it? One proven means of investigating the dynamics of social processes is the 'extended case method' developed by the Manchester school of anthropology. Mid-century ethnographers – notably Max Gluckman and Victor Turner – followed factional disputes and witchcraft trials through all their twists and turns to show how structural tensions between generations, leadership contenders, and organizational principles could be explored through 'social dramas' (Turner 1957, 1981). Rather than looking for structural contradictions in a static framework, as in

Narrative

standard functionalism, you followed tensions as they emerged in action, diagnosing the stress points, for example, between matrilineal descent and patriarchal authority. From contrarieties issued conflicts that unfolded in predictable ways: the pattern in the flux. The success of the method owed much to the manifold form of relationships in the small-scale communities observed by anthropologists of the time. People were connected and divided – but always *related* – at many levels, through kinship, political alliance, witchcraft accusations, land tenure, religion. Breaches at one level were spanned at another. Patrilineal foes were matrilineal friends. Like the subplots of a TV soap, with its quarrelsome small-town cast, the social drama develops through these breakings and mendings.

But does the extended case method work with emotion? The tentative answer is yes. Tentative because – somewhat surprisingly – it has seldom been tried, and because anthropology has new priorities in a globalizing world where interconnection flourishes at higher levels (cyberspace, the imagined community). The method can extend only so far.

Somebody who did try is A. L. Epstein, whose *In the Midst of Life* (1992) remains one of only a handful of ethnographic studies with an emotional focus. Epstein's rather old-fashioned book was ignored in the emerging 'anthropology of emotion' of the 1990s. It came out when more exciting approaches – social constructionism, ethnopsychology, person-centred anthropology – were in vogue. And it drew (unnecessarily) on a biological theory of emotion at a time when, in the social sciences, the word *biology* required scare quotes, as if the natural sciences were a Western folk theory. (The scientist in question, Silvan Tomkins, has had a strange afterlife in the cultural-critical venture known as 'affect theory', discussed in Chapter 8.)

Epstein's ethnography of the Tolai people of the New Hebrides focuses, as did his Manchester colleagues, on local disputes. But his aim is to explore the distinctive cultural shape and social ramifications

The Case for Narrative

of what he calls, following Tomkins, 'affect', a term he uses synonymously with 'emotion':

> My hope is ... to show through the evidence of dispute material some of the *kinds of emotion that are generated within particular relationships* and at the same time to illustrate the emotional tone of these relationships. In addition, I believe that the use of material of this kind has a further value of its own: first, insofar as any dispute is concerned with contested aims, in *exposing the emotional roots* as distinct from the legal basis of those claims; and, second, in demonstrating how *appeal to the emotions can play a central and regular part in dispute-management* itself.
>
> (Epstein 1992: 117; italics added)

What was new about this? The first objective recalled functionalism, in which stereotyped sentiments defined structured relationships. It also recalled the Culture and Personality work of Bateson and Mead, whose indefatigable mission, wherever they alighted, was to test the emotional temperature, the ethos of the community, and to uncover 'emotional roots' in patterns of child rearing. Epstein's last-named objective was more firmly contemporary. Although working to very different agendas, other students of emotion in Oceania were also exploring the pragmatics of emotion discourses (Lutz 1988; White 1992). Feeling was saying was doing.

So the aims were not original, nor was the method. But the lasting interest of the study lies in its descriptions. In them we recover some of the effectual detail that functionalism had scorned in quest of principle: the life of the social organism, where functionalists had seen only structure. Emotions emerge, more roundedly, as vital ever-changing aspects of relationships: motivating, commentating on, and directing social action. As Epstein demonstrates, it is not enough to report the shame-based modesty that inhibits a Tolai brother and sister, to show the affective tug of matrilineal authority, or to make emotion a mere function of the social order. You have to trace how appropriate

Narrative

sentiments emerge in action and how emotions with different developmental origins and countervailing tendencies come into play. You have to attend to their *narrative* structure. In one case study, a man beats and shames his wife when she helps her brother in his taro garden. He is jealous of her attention but also resentful of the stronger productive ties between brother and sister in the matrilineal group and of his own exclusion as an affine (1992: 117–123). The public assault – he tears off her clothes in front of the brother – offends the sibling sex-taboo, colouring the quarrel and reaching into deeper emotional territory. At a tribal moot, the brother cautiously disavows anger (his feelings assuaged by compensation) and keeps up a show of affinal respect; but third parties reproach the husband for lack of *varmari*, a word meaning 'love' and 'care'. It is this long-term sentiment that characterizes the married relation and that lends it stability in the face of competing matrilineal claims. In another case, a dying wife appeals to her husband to care properly for the children and remember 'our love' – the word, the sentiment, carrying moral force and existential value beyond conventional duty (123).

What strikes us about these vignettes is not that they confirm or defy stereotype (*So what?* we should ask), but that emotions are the very substance of the encounters. They have a narrative shape it is the ethnographer's task to reveal. In being owned by the participants – as actors in a 'social drama' rather than ciphers of structure – emotions transcend simple scripts. They feed off and respond to social structure constructively, rather than merely serving it. And they become the focus of reflection and debate. What are the right emotions in this situation, for this or that person? How can hearts be suitably stirred or calmed? In social dramas, as Turner noted, 'whether juridical or ritual processes of redress are invoked against mounting crises, the result is an increase in what one might call social or plural *reflexivity*, the ways in which a group tries to scrutinize, portray, understand, and then act on itself' (1981: 152; original emphasis). Turner's eye was steadily on structural

The Case for Narrative

principles and their affective underpinnings; but in Tolai social dramas, as in Java and Nias, the reflexive focus is on the play of living emotion and on deliberate acts of emotion work. The dramas seem to say: Sort out the emotions and the rest will fall into place.

At least, that is how it looks, how it feels, and how it pans out. (For a fuller example, see my *After the Ancestors*, chapter 16.) Niha heart-speech is a virtuoso riff on this theme, a relentless plucking of heart strings, while Javanese efforts aim at smoothing out emotions to *avoid* social dramas. When trouble looms and the unavoidable erupts, again it is emotions – shame, *pernah*, anger – that are the point of interest, the issues to be worked through. To get them right, to make up or calm down, is to rearrange persons and situations, to tweak the narrative constituents, to restore the status quo. 'It is not technical skill or special brilliance that the Arapesh demand either in men or in women', wrote Margaret Mead; 'it is rather correct emotions, a character that finds in co-operative and cherishing activity its most perfect expression' (Mead 1935: 142).

Epstein brings this process of emotional adjustment into view, as well as indicating what cannot be brought to light. For his larger point, which takes time to make – and patience in the reader – is that in the 'multistranded relations' of kin-based communities, surface disturbances have deep and obscure roots. 'An observer following the case sees clearly enough that the parties are deeply aggrieved, but what is upsetting them may not always be immediately plain nor easy to disentangle' (128). A passionate dispute over some trivial offence will often have its origins 'in the complex and frequently conflicting feelings generated within a given set of culturally defined relationships' (130). The healing process of local justice must engage those deeper feelings and their sources.

We do not all live in tribal communities, to be sure; but what we bring to an encounter from our scattered relationships and clinging pasts must affect how we respond to the present challenge, whether as actors or

Narrative

observers. Our emotions have a historical dimension, as psychoanalysis has always insisted. The hitch these days is in the unavailability of the data and the relative thinness of the encounter, not in the invisible nexus of causes and meanings (a perennial problem). So, at least, it must seem to the virtual ethnographer, the student of globalization, and the corporate anthropologist. Either way, in the tribal village or the dark web, the writer who skimps narrative, like the theorist who deals in snapshots or simulations, makes light of the emotional freight.

Epstein takes the extended case method as far as it will go, and then a bit further. The problem is that once you start pulling on a strand it can be hard to stop – a predicament endemic to ethnography because fieldwork always begins *in medias res*.

There can have been few domestic disputes that came before the village forum that did not have a long and complex history or did not build on old resentments. But little of this background was likely to emerge in the course of the hearing itself. Much of it of course was well known to many of the villagers who made up the audience, and into it the present claims and counter-claims of the protagonists could now be slotted. (158)

The *real* story is always some way back in the past. The emotions on parade, whether long-prepared, situational, individual, or collective, have more than a structural and incidental context; they have roots, which is why Epstein finds himself constantly surprised by bursts of anger and upwellings of grief. Each dispute taps into older disputes, reviving hard feelings, slights and slurs that go back decades. A woman brings a case against her maternal grandmother for driving away her brothers and speaking ill of their dead mother (1992: 153–162). As accusations multiply and insults fly, a history of bridewealth contributions paid, diverted, and denied opens up a chronicle of opportunism and neglect. But the facts reassembled for judgment suddenly give way before long-buried grief that has all parties, even the mediator, weeping.

The Case for Narrative

And when Epstein pulls on *this* strand it leads in a quite different direction, losing itself in a tangle of emotionally-charged dealings with *tambu*, the shell money which Tolai handle, hoard and release with 'compulsive interest'. As both a medium of exchange and a sacred money (the word is cognate with *taboo*) *tambu* links bridewealth partners and the living with the dead. A deceased relative cannot enter the Abode of Spirits until the accumulated tambu are dispersed, in an odd aggressive splurge, among surviving kin. In Epstein's literally interminable case (those strands), the plaintiff's parents had died before reaching their full estate and before their proper obligations could be discharged; hence the meeting breaks down when emotions linked to the circulation of tambu are triggered. Epstein follows through with a Freudian excursus into tambu-love.

It is like a story told backwards, as deep as memory. And it presents a problem that is not just empirical but theoretical and, beyond that, literary. A concern with the constitution of emotions turns into a problem of selection and reporting. The puzzle is not simply where will it end, but how did it begin? Those aspects of narrativity I earlier applied to emotion – agency, sequence, breach, focalization – are all in evidence as the dramas play out, but the boundaries of each case seem arbitrary.

In one of his prefaces, Henry James remarked that 'really, universally, relations stop nowhere, and the exquisite problem of the artist is eternally but to draw, by a geometry of his own, the circle within which they shall happily *appear* to do so. He is in the perpetual predicament that the continuity of things is the whole matter for him' (1984: 1041). In their selective handling of the data and their modelling of cases, ethnographies are, in this sense, fictional; even – one thinks of *The Nuer* – geometrically exquisite. There is an obvious trade-off between detail and explanatory power. In getting the story right, identifying what is significant, it is easy to let the particulars overwhelm the general; but in limiting detail, we risk losing the reality altogether – Frijda's information loss – and end up explaining nothing. In dealing with emotions, how do you know what is

Narrative

essential and what is contingent, especially when so much is out of reach? In drawing the causal boundary around a complicated case, Epstein settles on material factors – the dues of brideprice and marriage – as his springs and motives; but he does not leave it there. Perhaps the concern with surface and depth should have sounded the alarm. In Epstein's hands it leads not to ethnographic scepticism – How can we know about the past and make good on our ignorance? – but back to a kind of faith. That the powerful feelings surrounding tambu are not self-explanatory we can readily accept; yet for most readers an appeal to the Viennese verities at this point will no longer do: the tropical hut is too far from the brocaded Freudian couch. Assertions that the affective load of tambu derives from 'anal erotism', and that the enormous hoops of shell money displayed at ceremonies are giant anuses or vaginas, are claims unsupported by developmental evidence (193–197) – a bizarre twist in the tale. If the story runs out, as fieldwork stories do, better to recognize the limits of ethnography than fall back on supposition and cliché.

Where does that leave us? The case for narrative established, we have come some way in sketching its *ethnographic* value; but whole regions of emotional life remain elusive – not just the traditional territory of psychoanalysis, the suburbs of the soul, but the historical hinterland and living reality, the life incarnate. The extended case method might provide a mapping of local emotional worlds, but it cannot cope with idiosyncrasy, temperament, and character, or with the invisible branching past, all of which infiltrate emotional encounters. It shows us how emotions are triggered and framed, but nothing about their 'phenomenology', what it means and feels like to be a certain named Tolai facing defeat, triumph, or humiliation. What works for village feuds and tribal moots undershoots with emotion. A thicker narrative is needed, a firmer grip on its personal and biographical constitution. In Chapter 5, I develop an analytical perspective on the biographical dimension of emotional episodes, show what happens when this is ignored, and finish with two extended examples of emotionally vital ethnography.

FIVE

Persons and Particulars

Despite a century of progress on other fronts, a strain toward the generic – the death of emotion – has persisted unchanged in much anthropological writing up to the present. Functionalism, structuralism, constructionism, and person-centred ethnography all drained emotions of content, reducing them to counters in games of signification, domestic politics, and folk theorizing. Fortunately, there are exceptions, ethnographies with a vivid emotional presence. But, revealingly, departures from standard operating procedure are usually justified on other grounds – that a descent to the particular decolonizes the ethnographic subject, affirms common humanity, or authenticates fieldwork. Gains in emotional realism are incidental; rarely are they justified by any theoretical vision.

In advancing the case for narrative, we need to be clear why it is good for emotion, not just good for conscience and readability. In this chapter I focus on persons and particulars, two ingredients of emotional episodes and narrative alike that get casually discarded at the level of theory. I begin with a discussion of biography and point-of-view, without which emotions make no sense. I then present a critique of constructionist studies that take a different view, and end with a close reading of two works that beautifully convey the emotional quality of life in another society.

Narrative

Egocentric and biographical perspectives on emotion

For an ethnographer interested in emotion, among possible objections to generic accounts two are paramount. The first goes as follows. Emotions might be third-person constructions, a product of evolution, structure, and history, but they are *first-person experiences* irreducible to their causes and components. Their particularity is to do with their subjectivity, their *me*-focus (Barrett et al. 2007; Ben-Ze'ev 2010; Goldie 2000, 2012; Roberts 1988; Solomon 1993). Unlike other things that are in some sense socially constructed – norms, values, cultural models – their *sine qua non* is their personal reference. You feel anger because it is you who is insulted, sad because the loss is yours. Others may read the situation in similar terms, recognizing the loss or insult, but they do not experience the emotion; and they cannot understand it without referring it to your concerns. Emotions are particular or they are nothing. An adequate account of emotion has to reckon with this primary fact. It is the first objection to a generalizing format.

The second is that emotions are *biographical*: primed by evolution, to be sure, shaped by culture, constrained by subject position, but given relevance and intensity by individual history. Emotions respond to motives and interpretations laid down in personal experience. As Cheshire Calhoun (2004) argues, an individual might respond to a predicament in various ways, any of which would appear justified and therefore comprehensible to others: the predicament and the emotion have a certain objective framework; but biography tips the scales in favour of, say, anger rather than disappointment. In Calhoun's example (2004: 118–119), an ambitious man who has neglected his wife for his job, and who later discovers her in an affair, might experience anger (at the perceived offence), regret (at harm to the marriage), guilt (it was really *his* fault), or fatalistic despair (one thing led to another). Each emotion highlights an aspect of the predicament, identifies an injury to the self, and triggers an action tendency. But the 'choice' among alternatives, the

Persons and Particulars

prevailing emotion, need not be a matter of 'subject position' in the generic sense; nor is it culturally determinate. Two men of similar profile will react differently depending on their past history, their record of attachments, their experience of betrayal, and their personal values (job over family, peace over confrontation, blame over forgiveness). In these respects, their emotions are, in Calhoun's phrase, 'biographically subjective'.

The range of 'choices' between situationally suitable emotions will differ between societies. In strongly gender-marked societies such as tribal Pakistan or Afghanistan (Grima 2004), in a case of adultery the appropriate emotions would be shame (at a man's impaired honour and failure to control his wife) or a rage for revenge. The object of anger might be the lover or the wife; the offence construed as dispossession or betrayal. But this is just to vary the alternatives, not to deny the biographical pathway, which must vary individually as well as culturally. Between one society and another the scope for variation will depend on the strength of social pressures and the rigidity of institutional arrangements. But as Frijda writes (2004: 164), there are several ways of apprehending a situation. 'Emotions are always the outcome of a balance of multiple appraisals, multiple meanings, and relevance to multiple concerns. What you gain by your fearful flight you may lose in self-respect.' The calculus of concerns depends on biographical as well as situational factors, and the ethnographer who ignores them may misread the emotion and get the larger context wrong. Likewise, the existentialist 'choice' implied in a given emotional response (and the 'bad faith' of passively succumbing to events) refers to this biographical, self-making dimension (Solomon 1980).

A biographical perspective on emotion goes against the grain in anthropology. Generations of students were raised on 'joking relationships', 'sibling solidarity', and 'mother-in-law avoidance': sentiments sounding like music hall jokes that served to distinguish kin relationships by hostility, respect, ambivalence, or indulgence. Once the stock

Narrative

figures of textbooks, softhearted mothers' brothers and timorous sons-in-law reflected rigid social systems and static ways of portraying them; but accounts of generic relationships remain an ethnographic staple, linking contemporary 'person-centred' studies with the impersonal abstractions of functionalism and structuralism.

The formally correct attitudes you learn in the field provide only a bluffer's guide to local protocols, as will any approach to persons through categories. Even supposing relations between a father and son in a certain society are typically cool, the reaction of one to the death of the other will be unpredictable, nonstandard in whatever makes that particular relation humanly interesting. The warmth concealed in the reserve, the gestures of recompense, the relief that accompanies sorrow: these tell the fuller story. And it is this diversity of human types, this specificity of circumstances and histories, that give emotions their distinctive hue, their social significance, their personal fit, their ineluctable grip. Jean Briggs writes of her adoptive Eskimo father: 'it was from Inuttiaq that I learned most about the ways in which the Utku express their feelings toward one another. It was partly his very atypicality that made it possible for me to learn from him what the proper patterns are' (1970: 42).

In the 1930s, Culture and Personality pioneer Edward Sapir had asked his students: 'Where do socialized patterns leave off and the primordial human being begin? We do not know yet where culture ends' (1994: 44). A question that, for urgent practical reasons, was forced upon Briggs in her Arctic oasis. Tracing the line between what culture ordains and what biography produces – what, as an ethnographer, she must respect, and what, as a New Englander and honorary 'daughter', she can resist – Briggs gives a vivid portrait of her intense and assertive 'father', a man both feared and admired, *not* as a cultural exemplar but as one cast against type. 'They feared him for the very reason they admired him: because he never lost his temper. They said a man who *never* lost his temper could kill if he ever did become angry' (47). By attending to

Persons and Particulars

Inuttiaq's unguarded expressions – his ferocious attacks on his dogs, his fantasies of whippings and murders, his violent nightmares, and the 'inner intensity' that communicated itself to others, as well as to Briggs herself – she is able to penetrate his armour of self-control and read the internal struggles behind the neutral tones and curt demurrals, the effort that goes into public performance. To Sapir's question, then, there is no reliable answer; only a patient method that combines doubt with exact observation and a measure of self-knowledge.

The relaxed gender politics and tranquil ethos that prevail in rural Java could not be further from the buttoned-up Utku or the lavish violence of Northwest Pakistan's Pakthun region; but there is no less pressure to conform, and small deviations count all the more. As neighbour and witness to his domestic troubles, I was amazed at the headman's tolerance of his son-in-law's disloyalty when the storm with the mosque activists broke. How could the pious young man, living in the adjoining house built for his wife, take sides against his benefactor, a man he kneeled to every year at Eid al Fitr? Nobody could explain it. And how could the headman maintain the young couple for so long, carrying on household arrangements as if they were newly-weds, when the son-in-law owned a rice mill and an airconditioned Toyota while he himself rode a rattly old Honda. 'What can you do?' he groaned one day. 'It's not fitting, but he doesn't *feel* it! And my wife's fed up doing the cooking for them. (Don't tell her I told you!)' Like most of his dilemmas it was settled with a shrug. But there was a certain satisfaction in his self-sacrifice. To condone the son-in-law was to indulge the daughter, an only child like the headman himself – and like the infant grandson who would, in turn, be spoiled rotten. And what better way to keep an eye on the zealots than to nurture one of them next door? *Father-in-law avoidance*, beloved of textbooks, does not begin to cover it.

A discussion of biography, family dynamics, and emotion raises once again the spectre of psychoanalysis, which professes their intimate

Narrative

relation; but the talking cure does not sit happily with ethnographic fieldwork: it speaks in a different register, conjures fantasies alongside 'facts', and its therapeutic goal is a narrative of a different order from that of ethnography – a pragmatic, often strained, compromise between analyst and analysand (Kirmayer 2000). While psychoanalytically-inclined anthropologists have provided rich accounts of motivation and attachment (Crapanzano 1980; Levy 1973; Mimica 2007; Obeyesekere 1981), the one-to-one clinical encounter and the ethno-psychoanalytic interview are remote from the emplotment of emotion in action. Because they sample one story to tell another, always finding significance elsewhere, they are poor models for a narrative ethnography anchored in a shared cultural setting, a storyworld that is also a real world. You cannot do ethnography on the couch.

Biographical particularity, as I have sketched it, is not quite the same as the first-mentioned kind of specificity, the quality of *self-reference*. It has to do with the fact that nobody else can lead my life: my biography, memories, and psychological formation are my own. These personal circumstances, built over time, sedimented in character and temperament, affect – not to say determine – emotional experience and the course of relations between people. A psychoanalyst would say as much. But for the anthropologist this biographical story is not primarily internal or individual; nor is it amenable to manipulation or translation into other terms or isolable from the living context. What counts here is the embedding of emotion in interwoven lives and 'acts of meaning', not its remembrance in the bubble of an interview.

These two sorts of particularity, the egocentric and the biographical (both of them resistant to a generalizing format), pose different implications for the ethnographer. They represent the inner and outer dimensions of experience: consciousness, on the one hand; lives and histories on the other. They are filtered out by any systems approach that fails to connect the cultural, social, and psychological, and that removes emotion from the stream of history. By this measure, an account framed in terms of cultural categories, scripts, social tensions, display rules, or any other synchronic or schematic analysis, will fall short.

It is not difficult to find examples, but two stand out for their influence and their fertile contributions to interdisciplinary debate. Both are concerned with the construction of emotion, but both omit most of what goes into living emotion: the confluence of character, biography and circumstance that shapes what we feel and do, what emotions *are* for people with blood in their veins.

No man is an island (nor woman either)

Catherine Lutz's *Unnatural Emotions* (1988) – an ethnography of the Ifaluk, denizens of a Pacific atoll – was, in its time, a brilliant provocation, a case for 'cultural constructionism' that turned the tables on Western emotion theory; its aim: 'to deconstruct an overly naturalized and rigidly bounded concept of emotion, to treat emotion as an ideological practice rather than as a thing to be discovered or an essence to be distilled' (4). By showing that Western notions of emotional privacy and individuality did not fit Ifaluk sociality Lutz was able to relativize standard psychological concepts, locating them in a cultural tradition different from but not superior to – or even informative about – a Pacific lifeworld. The presentation was compelling enough to make the book required reading for any emotion researcher who ventured outside the biological fold. Lutz even managed to smuggle into the scientific lexicon two culture-specific emotions, *fago* and *song*. What more could be asked of anthropology? Yet an ethnographer alert to the complexity of living emotions must resist following her. Despite an avowed preference for 'naturalistic observation' (43), Lutz depends for the most part on the analysis of emotion terms excerpted from minimally contextualized episodes, interviews, and word-sorting tests. The past experiences, personal confrontations, non-linguistic behaviour, and unvoiced reflections – not to mention the feelings – that contribute to occurrent

Narrative

emotions lie hidden in a method that prioritizes and isolates verbal performance and stereotypical script-definition.

Unnatural Emotions contains only one emotion episode witnessed by the author that extends over more than a few lines (125–127). The episode concerns a child's death – not the sort of incident that requires much narrative context or attention to the inflections of interpersonal history. Over the course of the book we learn how Ifaluk talk or think about emotion – during interviews, at least; much less about how their emotions interlock in reality, how emotions shape and are shaped by personal histories. Unless we assume that talk about emotion *is* emotion – and the discursive approach comes close to this – we are missing something here.[1]

There is much to admire in *Unnatural Emotions*. In tackling the politics of emotion via 'discourse', Lutz digs below the orderly ethnopsychological surface. Her framing of emotions as ideological practices – ways of exerting or resisting power by the manipulation of emotion terms – seems well fitted to a dramaturgical or narrative ethnography of the sort I am proposing here. Lutz could almost be writing about Niha dramatics when she declares: 'Once de-essentialized, emotion can be viewed as a cultural and interpersonal process of naming, justifying, and persuading people in relationship to each other. Emotional meaning is then a social rather than an individual achievement – an emergent product of social life' (1988: 5). What Lutz shows (and as Bedford had argued thirty years earlier) is that the performative functions of emotion may be exploited as a social resource and elaborated as moral discourse, a tendentious way of framing and reframing relationships. To proclaim yourself *song* ('justifiably angry') about a disrespectful youth or a neighbour's stinginess is less a psychological description than 'an effort to

---

[1] A number of points in this section echo those of Rosenberg (1990) in an astute critique of approaches to emotion through 'discourse'. Rosenberg's particular target is M. Rosaldo's *Knowledge and Passion* (1980).

Persons and Particulars

install a particular interpretation of events as the definition of that situation to be accepted by others' (162). Emotions, thus announced, become social commentary, a mode of politics.

But that is not all emotions do, even in places like Nias where 'hearts' tirelessly strut and fret their hour upon the stage. Emotions are more than words, and more than words invested with power. The error, as I read it in the passage quoted above, is in eliding 'emotion' with 'emotional meaning'. To tease them apart *and* get at their interwoven composition you need a much thicker narrative. Otherwise the pragmatist gambit becomes just another kind of essentialism, a universal claim that (to repeat my formula) feeling is saying is doing.

In sharpening 'East–West' or US–Ifaluk contrasts, the methodological risk is in conflating ideology with experience, which has the instant effect of orientalizing or 'othering'. People are the not the sum of their theories, of principles and concepts extracted under questioning. Keesing puts the general point: 'We radically caricature ourselves by taking ideologies as if they were constitutive of our consciousness – as if our subjectivities were determined by the pronouncements of Enlightenment philosophers or Protestant theologians or factory owners' (1994: 8). As anti-relativists of different stripe have emphasized, you cannot read off life from ideas about life, though each feeds off the other. Folk theories float free of the constraints of practical living (Bloch 2012; Gellner 1985: 93–94). Perhaps, as Lutz asserts, the Ifaluk – despite referring to feelings as 'our insides' – really do live out their lives in public discourse and construct their emotions outside-in. Perhaps Ifaluk concern-relevance, and therefore emotion, is plural – *we* rather than *I* – and subjectivity weakly felt. And perhaps they distinguish their emotions by external scenarios rather than introspection. Or are those Ifaluk features, so contrary to Western individualism and psychological theory (which is not to say Western *experience*), exaggerated by the method? Niha likewise explicate emotions in the abstract plural (*we, one*), and with reference to stereotypic situations. But only if you

Narrative

happen to ask. So too do Javanese, who nevertheless build a whole philosophy on 'interiority'. How else can you characterize an emotion to a curious outsider than with a hypothetical story? The methodology is certainly productive and suggestive (though of *what* remains unclear); but it cannot substitute the firm smack of reality. Or, for that matter, the softer grip of the virtual: the fear of flying, the doom of despair. For these only a full narrative context will do. That may be an impossible ideal, as Lutz seems to imply, with 'taped conversations' rating only second-best (144), but why not try? Like Mead's *Coming of Age in Samoa* (1932), which had earlier advanced the case of relativism, *Unnatural Emotions* omits detailed descriptions of emotion episodes: the ethnographer's advantage sacrificed for argument's sake.

The same could be said of another discourse-based study, as impressive in its own way, Michelle Rosaldo's *Knowledge and Passion*, whose first sixty or so pages scrupulously avoid extended examples, except for an anecdote that upsets the argument by placing the ethnographer herself within the story (1980: 33–35). Rosaldo's fieldwork with the Ilongot, a tribal group in the Philippines, involved several visits over a long period. When she played back an old headhunting song she had taped in the 1960s, before missionization, her Ilongot friends stopped her, stricken by 'nostalgia' and a terrible sense of cultural loss. Headhunting had been part of the staging – in both senses – of grief, the final release from obligations to the dead (though 'intense and disturbing feelings only occasionally knew a headhunter's catharsis' [34]). Barred from the old remedy, converts took to Christianity as an escape from grief, a refusal to mourn now that mourning was outlawed. But the disembodied voices bring it all back. A joyful song becomes a lament for a mutilated world.

One thinks of the Great Repentance in Nias, another headhunting society haunted by its frozen past. Or, in a different tradition, the suppression of Catholic funerary ritual in Elizabethan England that found poignant expression in Hamlet's grief for his unmourned father – whose ghost commands *Remember me!* (Greenblatt 2007).

Persons and Particulars

The tape incident – the best thing in Rosaldo's book – illustrates how fieldwork can itself be a revelatory provocation, not merely a sampling of native life. For the rest, instead of naturalistic episodes illustrating Ilongot emotions, Rosaldo strings together sayings and usages put to her, as Ilongot (in a telling formula) 'explain themselves' (1980: 36). Thick commentary rather than thick description (Rosenberg 1990). Only thus can the author claim that 'their talk of hearts has less to do with histories that give reasons than with the fact that hearts that stand apart are "moved", "turn in upon themselves", "itch",' and so on (Rosaldo 1980: 43), the vocabulary comprising a static folk psychology, not a history of persons. How could it be otherwise when the method *precludes* 'histories' and emphasizes instead the alienness of Ilongot emotions? The constructionist method, it turns out, excludes the very elements that go into the construction of emotion episodes.

One test of any schematic account is a simple but seldom asked question: If I were *that* person or belonged to that set of people, with their background and their take on the world, would the analysis include what seems most significant to me? In a critique of standard ethnographic writing, Anthony Cohen puts it well: 'My objection to the kind of generalization in which we indulged is that it has little or no authenticity in *our* own experience. Therefore I do not see how we can be content with it as an account of *other* people' (1994: 16). The point is echoed in a recent collection that aims to rescue subjective experience from smothering 'discursive regimes' (Biehl et al. 2007). In pursuit of general factors, 'the subjects of ethnography are rarely offered the [proper] depth of personhood as vulnerable, failing, and aspiring human beings – people who demonstrate the same qualities that we ourselves display in relationships' (ibid. 14).

If the narrativity thesis set out in this book be granted, objections to the 'oversocialized image of human life' (ibid.) apply all the more strongly to schematic accounts of emotion. Is my anger fully explained by my structural position as a slighted mother's brother, by its function

Narrative

within a power play, its place in a contrast set of emotion categories, or its expression as a human universal? None of the above. Positioning, expression, strategy, and circumstances frame the context and possibilities; but what gives the context resonance – in effect, what *produces* the emotion as a self-referring biographical event – is its location in time among figures with similarly distinctive but interlaced histories. This is what ethnography has to reckon with.

*

The distinction between the narrative construction, understanding, and reporting of emotion I have been labouring is awkward to maintain in exposition, if not in theory, and hard to illustrate with examples from authors whose purposes and conceptions of emotion are different from my own. In this chapter and Chapter 4, I have focused on what goes into composing an emotion. Before moving on to understanding and reporting in Chapters 6 and 7, I want to set aside the argument for a moment to consider two ethnographies that superbly capture the multidimensionality of emotion – the roots and tendrils as well as the flowers – revealing narratively what eludes a more analytical or reductive approach.

Of ice and men

Jean Briggs's book, *Never in Anger*, is unclassifiable: personal without being confessional, minutely observed yet never trivial, concretely particular yet laced with larger truths. It also seems out of time, indifferent to the theoretical wars of the 1960s, indeed, to the real wars of the 1960s – Vietnam, civil rights, the Cold War (What would her people have called *that*?) – all of which led to much soulsearching over questions of difference and common humanity: anthropological questions given political answers. The book is hard to place, and despite

Persons and Particulars

frequent citation still tends to merit only brief reference – usually, and erroneously, that the Eskimo feel no anger (Pinker 1997: 364). Yet *Never in Anger* is anything but vague or unrealized. To read it is to glimpse, almost to feel, how the world looks and feels to the Utku, a snowbound population of thirty-five souls in a wilderness of 23,000 square miles. Naturally, this world is very different from anything Briggs or her readers can have known; but thanks to her intimate reporting, Utku ways are comprehensible and, more than that, affecting. That they move us is not only because of narrative impact (the book is wonderfully written), but because Briggs shows us exactly what goes into the making of particular Utku emotion episodes – the concerns, stakes, and tribulations. And once we understand those, as fellow creatures we cannot remain unaffected, we are involved. Here, then, is that unlikely thing: an ethnography entirely personal yet thoroughly scientific.

The circumstances need briefly stating. A young PhD student, Briggs lived on a remote shore in the Canadian Arctic with her Utku hosts for some seventeen months, three of which were spent in semi-isolation when the community ostracized her, keeping her alive, fed and warm, but short of words. Her adoptive family could not abide her bad temper (as they saw it) but nor could they confront her or abjure the sentiments of kinship, the duties owed her as a 'daughter'. *Never in Anger* is what E. M. Forster called Lampedusa's *The Leopard*, 'one of the great lonely books'.

The peculiar isolation of the Utku brought a stripped-down, lab-like purity to the investigation, making Briggs's fieldwork as close to a natural experiment as any ever devised. The usual ingredients of life almost anywhere – the stuff of narrative – were either absent or scarcely present: friends, enemies, the comings and goings of outsiders, a tangible past, a built environment (at least, one that did not melt), property, ceremony, antagonisms, sexual rivalry, generational conflict, unexpected happenings, ambitions, successes and failures; in fact, most of the things that emotions feed off. With only a handful of people around, there was not much social structure to speak of, no institutions of law,

Narrative

religion or government, no specialized roles, no social diversity. If you wanted to learn something entirely new about emotion, this would be the place.

Briggs came to her theme by default. She had intended to study shamanism but among the Anglican converts there were no shamans. *Cross that off the list.* Nor would people discuss the forbidden religion. *That too.* They would not permit genealogies to be taken, sexual relationships in the past being too 'unAnglican' to be safely discussed. On an empty stage with few props, what remained were the actors, their dealings with one another, and their daily struggle for survival.

Deprived of standard ethnographic topics and with little to observe except domestic routines, fishing in ice holes, and subzero home maintenance, Briggs found that 'the aspect of Utku life most accessible for study, and the one most salient in terms of my personal experience, was the patterning of emotional expression' (1970: 4). Without the usual provocations, emotions were relatively simple and functional: affection and concern for family members, annoyance at minor frustrations, fear of aggression, curiosity towards the rare outsider. Although Briggs's characters are sharply observed, she offers only minimal background, perhaps because it barely figures in interactions save in reminiscences and anecdotes. Compared with the Tolai, discussed in Chapter 4, emotional episodes among the Utku require little or no backstory. Nearly all those recounted have a tight situational context, sometimes against a mood of tension created by Briggs herself. The difficulties of reading Utku emotions are not due to their complex framing or historical depth but their manner of expression.

All this makes the ethnography highly convincing but difficult to emulate in the cluttered environments where most anthropologists work. To be sure, differences in scale and social complexity need not imply more complex emotions. Even if my life is overcomplicated and I am a psychological enigma, as I would like to think, my anger at a friend's rudeness is simply explained, as is my fear of a rampaging bull.

Persons and Particulars

If simple situations are selected or the focus constricted to a beating heart and goose bumps the cultural gap is narrowed. Draw the circle close around 'emotion' and we are all pretty similar. In the Utku camp, it is as easy to find 'core relational themes' (danger, loss) as anywhere else. But south of the Arctic, you generally need to know more to be able to follow events. Southern anger is recognizable from its symptoms, but without background you have little sense of what is at stake, how the antagonists stand, or what the possible outcomes are. Moreover, a diversity of relationships and modes of relation (hierarchy, gender separation, racism, rivalry) makes for intricate emotions in densely textured episodes. Among the Utku this is rarely the case.

As Briggs quickly discovers, the key (and lock) to the Utku emotional world is self-control. Except in infancy, when tantrums are indulged or provoked in teasing routines, rash behaviour or loss of control, including any expression of strong emotion, is liable to criticism. When Briggs's adoptive father impulsively shoots a bird, her Utku mother finds it 'childish'. When a teenage boy sheds a silent tear as he sends off his aging father to hospital, his sister reports this to the neighbours as 'amusing'. Spouses show no affection in word or gesture, nor do parents with children over five or six. Small children are kissed and dandled, but otherwise people 'rarely touch one another in any way, except as they lie under the same quilts at night' (117). After long perilous absences on hunting trips, men return home to a brief touch of gloved hands. Yet the inner emotional climate of the iglu is warm, affection signalled in countless tiny details of consideration, gentle joking, mild voices, smiles, and looks. Protective concern towards small children is constantly proclaimed (or teasingly withheld), and much can be expressed by a timely cup of tea or a good portion of fish. Within the family there is no lack of love.

More importantly, negative emotions are kept in check, even denied. When she first arrived, Briggs found the Utku 'so well controlled that my untutored eye could not detect their emotions' (42). Even mild

Narrative

displays of annoyance are deplored as childish and seen as a failure of reason (*ihuma*), the faculty that children acquire by the age of five or six. Hostile feelings are not merely hidden, or half-disguised in a laugh, but actively avoided. Even angry brooding, which involves an excess of thought (also *ihuma*), can be dangerous, as harmful to its target as physical violence. 'Among adults there are no situations that justify *ningaq* [aggressive] feelings or behaviour, no people, Utku or other, toward whom it is permissible to express them' (333). In contrast, to laugh and smile, to be 'happy', is to show one means no harm. Happiness, *quvia*, is a moral good; a state one should cultivate and continually advertise.

From their responses to her own behaviour Briggs learns to recognize anger in others, especially in her adoptive father Inuttiaq, a man of strong emotion but rigid self-control. When she refuses to lend him the primus stove used to heat her spare tent he avoids arguing with her, but the next morning, standing outside in the freezing wind, 'snow knife in hand ... [he] announced in a ringing voice: "The tent is ruined!" So tense was the atmosphere at that moment that I was sure he had hacked the tent to pieces with his knife' (269). It has, in fact, been ripped by his dogs, but Inuttiaq's violent urgency, his harsh voice, gives him away as surely as if he has committed the act, as does his sharpness in refusing further use of Briggs's goods: 'It is my will!'

Transformed into controlled displeasure, anger is mostly conveyed indirectly. When Briggs irritably tosses an object requested by her 'mother', it is thrown back to her, a gesture of uncommon rudeness. Inuttiaq responds loudly, ostensibly to his wife but with a lesson for Briggs: 'Was that tossed? ... Like a *kapluna* [white person] in the house!' (294). The rarity of the outburst and its explicit hostility mark it as emotional.

Given that anger is rarely displayed, the obvious question is how we know it is felt; whether, in fact, it amounts to what *we* would call anger. Language use can give us only a few pointers. Briggs gathers the terms

Persons and Particulars

denoting (roughly) annoyance, temper, envy, anger/aggression and hostility, and recounts situations in which they occurred or might occur. In both cases, actual and imaginary, the emotive circumstances – frustration by others, wilful opposition, non-cooperation – will be understandable to any reader, but the reaction will not. An Utku facing obstruction is more likely to laugh (a little too loudly) or to speak in a studiously neutral tone than to respond aggressively. The effort at control conveys the strength of feeling. Seldom are voices raised or shoulders turned. Yet people gossip about others' *ningaq* ('anger') and sulky withdrawal (*qiquq*, 'being clogged up'), they speak of their fear of *ningaq*, they train their children in mastering aggression, and they are embarrassed even to admit there might be a word for 'hate'. Absence of evidence is not evidence of absence.

Briggs suggests that Utku anger is displaced, transformed, or discharged in culturally specific ways rather than allowed expression. Humour is one vehicle, avoidance another, with ostracism the last resort short of murder. Where *we* would shout abuse or clench fists, Utku laugh, fall silent, or turn away. Is this a different way of being angry or a way of not being angry? The temptation is to invoke Ekman's concept of display rules; the laugh then becomes a culturally modified *expression* of anger. But that is to ignore the modification of feeling and the thoughts that govern or accompany the feeling. It is also to ignore the whole circuit of appraisal, action tendency, follow through, and reappraisal; my response to yours.

Ever observant, Briggs looks for slow smiles, the glitter of an eye, a false note in laughter, as precognitions of anger before the display rules kick in; but often there is no leakage, no modulation of the equable tone. Instead, the muting of hostility, the habitual dampening of feeling, and the careful avoidance of conflict lead to a different patterning of response; one that cannot be summarized as anger management or correct manners. The differences run deep. When visiting Canadian fishermen commandeer the group's canoes, Inuttiaq and the other men,

Narrative

unwilling to oppose the greedy and unreasonable *kapluna*, retreat, some taking to their beds in a sudden collective lethargy (281). They could get angry but, like Bartleby, prefer not to. Anger is put to sleep.

The difficult question, as I found in some of my Javanese encounters, is whether the key factors in these transformations are display rules, meta-emotions (emotions about emotions), or highly unusual forms of negative emotions. But perhaps all this puts too much emphasis on emotions as mental states or actions deriving from feelings. What is mainly at issue, for Briggs as for the Utku, is the immediate terms of a relation: specific modes of engagement with others in the handling of a problem (of threat, insult, dispossession). Not getting angry, for the most part, simply means doing things otherwise, taking a different perspective in order to achieve one's goal of compliance, co-operation or repossession, or – negatively – the avoidance of conflict. If that sounds excessively deliberate, when, as we know, emotions are properly spontaneous, we should remember that the hard work of getting on in the confines of the iglu soon makes what is desirable habitual. Growing up Utku, one learns the futility of anger by wearing oneself out in tantrums and in the teasing routines described in Briggs's later work (1998). Once the lesson is learned, one cannot *really* get angry with a child who is acting unreasonably (though one might *act* a little angry), nor, ultimately, with a foolish *kapluna*. Getting angry is something the other person does; it is a third-person condition, never a first-person confession.

Integrating the particular

Briggs's ethnography is exceptional in its empirical richness and narrative precision. It has all that one can hope for in an anthropology of emotion or – better – an emotionally alive anthropology, though for the special reasons given it lacks the microhistorical dimension needed to understand many fieldwork episodes and is altogether a hard act to follow. A more serviceable model, though its focus is not specifically on emotion, is Lila Abu-Lughod's *Writing Women's Worlds: Bedouin Stories* (1993). As different as sand from snow, the two ethnographies have a similar scale. A shortlist of names, equal to that of an average novel, affords a depth of characterization and cumulative incident that makes reported emotions credible to the reader. Both also make use of a narrative point of view located in the ethnographer's personal experience. And both are carefully wrought exercises in composition. The integrity of reported emotions is an achievement of writing, not just of insight and observation.

In her first book, *Veiled Sentiments* (1986), Abu-Lughod hit on a means of connecting shared cultural forms with individual histories and the ordinarily inaccessible realm of feeling by focusing on the use of oral poetry in everyday discourse. '*Ghinnawa*', she writes, 'can be considered the poetry of personal life: individuals recite such poetry in specific social contexts, for the most part private, articulating in it sentiments about their personal situations and closest relationships' (Abu-Lughod 1986:31). And in *Writing Women's Worlds* (1993), Abu-Lughod uses a sequence of stories that subvert generalization to achieve an emotional conviction and realism not normally available to ethnography.

The author calls her method 'narrative ethnography', though it might more accurately be described as a collage of stories told by its subjects: the narratives are positioned within the larger text rather than framing it and the Bedouin narrators, quite clearly, are not engaged in ethnography. That task falls to the author, who with skill and tact, presents the lives of her fieldwork family mostly in their own words and in their own way; not in the seamless chronicle of a life history – which would be false to their sense of themselves and what a life amounts to – but as a series of loosely connected recountings of incidents in the teller's life prompted by questions or recent events ('stories' sounds too made-up, too rehearsed; 'anecdote' too casual for these well-turned yet forthright tellings). A quarrel between the co-wives is the opportunity to revisit earlier

Narrative

quarrels and trace the history of a fractious, many-sided relation of rivalry and mutual dependence. In another set of narratives, a mother and son give variant accounts of the son's injury in a land mine explosion and his rescue in the desert by a crashed pilot. Hers is about mother-love, his about male friendship and heroism; both are manifestly true. Sometimes Abu-Lughod herself takes over, narrating the narrators. She asks one woman how she had helped assist her co-wife in childbirth.

She demonstrated the squatting position a mother should take while giving birth and told how she had held Gateefa from behind while her sister-in-law had held her from the front. Suddenly wiping away some tears, she described to us how Gateefa had cried and prayed to God to protect her daughters, sure that she was dying. The two co-wives, sitting cross-legged on the freshly laid bedding, their knees almost touching, and the tiny swaddled infant lying between them, looked long at each other. In that moment I saw something about these two women that I had not grasped before, although I had known them for many years. Despite their difficulties with each other – and they had many – there was between them a closeness and dependency, perhaps as women who give birth (indeed, other women remarked that day, 'Men experience nothing compared to women – do they think giving birth is easy? It is as hard as war'), perhaps as women bound together by sharing a household, daily life, and a history. Fourteen years of shared history made for a bond, even if life together was often tense. (Abu-Lughod 1993: 90)

Emotions, evidently, are embedded in layered interactions, the inter-weaving of affect with perspective, history and character: they have a narrative construction. The effectiveness of the passage, its emotional conviction, depends in part on its placing among other scenes of domestic life, disputes over children, and tussles with husbands and sons; in part on the vividly presented personalities of the homely Gate-efa and her flashy outsider co-wife, the husband's favourite, who feature in many of the reminiscences. But it also has the strengths of good straightforward ethnography: exact description, apt quotation, deep

Persons and Particulars

familiarity with the protagonists, a feel for embodied sentiment and quiet significance, the authority of presence.

Another birth recalls an old woman to her younger self, her memories of how things were, the hardships of continuous pregnancies and lonely births in rough tents while the male world of work and hospitality goes on amid smoke and chatter, indifferent to the backstage drama. Prompted by the author, the grandmother ends her account with a lapidary judgment (1993: 53): 'Then I asked why it was said that the woman who has just delivered is close to God. She laughed at my piece of knowledge. "Yes, people say that. By God, it's difficult. Ask the woman who has given birth, ask her about death. She has seen it."' Only a personal narrative could justify that statement, and only verbatim reporting preserve its laconic beauty. It would be absurd for an ethnographer to assert, in the customary third-person fashion, that 'Bedouin women go through many hardships and see parturition as a kind of death'. The psychological and existential truth of the statement cannot be generalized or abstracted: it speaks from experience, not from factual expertise (like the author's 'piece of knowledge'). But neither is it subjective, mere opinion. It has the grainy truth of the particular yet refers to, and is part of, the larger scheme of things in which men's and women's lives are starkly contrasted but mutually entangled in life and death. Good ethnography is made up of such moments.

In her introduction, which serves as a manifesto, Abu-Lughod takes aim at ethnographic generalization, arguing instead for 'ethnographies of the particular'. Her stance, freighted with postcolonial anxieties, is broadly political or 'critical'. Generalization leads to the construction of the 'other' and the fetishising of cultural difference. Differences can only derive from and sustain greater inequalities. Other anthropologists of the time were arguing something similar – the *Writing Culture* volume (Clifford and Marcus 1986) served as a rallying point – and the concerted critique spurred several attempts at ethnography in a new key: less theory-driven, more personally engaged, with a strong narrative

Narrative

thread (Scheper-Hughes 1992; Wikan 1990). As the *Writing Culture* team had emphasised (*Writing Women's Worlds* echoing, in its title, their conceptual grammar, their belief that writing equals making), the anthropologist is complicit in the creation of 'cultures' as timeless, homogeneous, ripe for exploitation. Better, said Abu-Lughod, to 'write against culture'.

But what if otherness inflects all human relationships? What if cultural practices and human characters, perhaps even emotions, very different from our own – Javanese equanimity, Niha intensity, Bedouin resilience – are admirable, things of wonder? What if a recognition of difference, even of strangeness, is part of accepting another's humanity – and of recalibrating our own? We can set aside the worthy rationale yet accept the need for a change in writing practices.

As I argue throughout this book, a valuation of the particular – a refusal to abandon the actual – is vital to a proper appreciation of emotion. The truthfulness of Abu-Lughod's narratives depends on their emotional grittiness, their disdain for the abstract (at odds with the wordy manifesto). Which means that when a wife is 'sad' at her husband's neglect, or a mother 'angry' about her headstrong son's signing away the inheritance, we do not need an elaborate cultural exegesis of what Bedouin 'anger' might amount to; and we need not worry whether all Bedouin get angry in the same way. The meaning, the grounded content of the concept, is given in the narrative context; the story takes us there. *Trust the tale not the teller.* What Abu-Lughod's ethnography shows is that a story well told beats the inductive method of conventional ethnography on its own terms, surpassing it in realism, nuance, insight, and factual accuracy.

What goes without saying

The Bedouin are raconteurs, perfect sources for narrative ethnography. But what of those cultures where experience is not so readily verbalized

Persons and Particulars

or articulated? Do they undermine the case for the narrative *construction* of emotion, or merely suggest a difference in *expression*? Consider, briefly, some examples.

Pacific ethnographers frequently note a lack of speculation about motives and personalities. In Ifaluk, 'the emphasis is on explaining behavior rather than explaining individuals' (Lutz 1988: 111) – which makes sense in a small community where people have to get on with one another and personal history is common knowledge. Likewise, Levy (1973: 217–218) reports 'a caution about gossip', 'a general disinclination to explore and discuss private feelings and perceptions'. Mead's Samoan informants avoided psychological explanations of behaviour. 'The whole preoccupation is with the individual as an actor, and the motivations peculiar to his psychology are left an unplumbed mystery' (1972: 107). But there is no less interest in *events*. In fact, 'the [emotional] expressions of Samoans are classified as "caused" and "uncaused",' which suggests a cultural focus on circumstances, if not backstory (106). These examples – *prima facie* at odds with narrative – merely shift the focus away from psychology onto other aspects of emotional episodes.

A step further in resistance to psychologising, the scattered Pacific islanders gathered in Hollan & Throop's (2011) collection on empathy hold to a doctrine of the 'opacity of other minds'. In some cases, this amounts to a cautious focus on actions not motives; in others, a form of self-protection, a disclaimer of evil intent. What cannot be surmised cannot be blamed. The narrator, like the neighbourhood gossip, is surely checked; yet we can still dig for the story, building the socially convenient doctrine into our account. Hints of contradiction can be followed up. Among the suspicious folk of Yap, described by Throop, conversations held back-to-back, staring away from interlocutors, or conducted in evasive banter, might be presumed to suggest the *transparency* of other minds, the dangerous readability of word and gaze. (Is the ideology contradicted by practical knowledge, like the

Narrative

Trobrianders' dogma of 'virgin birth' (Leach 1966)?) Such examples might seem hopelessly unsuited to a narrative approach; at least they would frustrate enquiry. But they scarcely threaten the case I have argued, which is about the construction of emotion episodes, not their representation or official interpretation.

Working in the tradition of phenomenology, Robert Desjarlais presents a different challenge. Desjarlais lived among the Yolmo of Nepal many of whose 'experiences seem to be grasped and expressed through images' (1992: 30). 'Illiterate villagers like Meme and Nyima tend not to tell full-fledged stories much', he tells us, 'nor, I believe, do they see life through the same narrative lens that my American colleagues do' (ibid.). They recount dreams in 'snapshots' rather than stories, and 'in conveying suffering to others, villagers tend not to tell sequential accounts of how they hurt or heal, but rather to "tell images" that portray their plights: a witch's bloody assault, the "casting" of grief from the body' (31). Appropriately, in his sensitive account, Desjarlais emphasizes images, spatial configurations, and bodily presence in an attempt to capture tacit knowledge and embodied meanings, his intention being to 'retain a bit of this image-based reality' (ibid.).

Desjarlais' point is well made – and well taken. A narrative approach to emotion should not ventriloquize or verbalize what is tacit, embodied, or expressed in other ways. Nor should it convert vernacular genres into the linear narratives of the European tradition. If people like the Bedouin happily tell stories, all well and good; otherwise not. In fact, the Yolmo are rich in songs and litanies, and seem a lot more verbal than, say, the Utku. But Desjarlais is right in seeking a balance.

All these examples remind us that the apprehension of other emotional worlds requires a lot more than a transcription of native explanations; evidently, it is about grasping more than words. (Compare my recounting of the scene from *Tulpan*, in Chapter 4, where only the wind has voice.) The prominence of non-narrative interpretative genres, non-narrative frames (the Niha speaking heart), and impersonal perspectives

148

on agency (the stars, the humours) does not alter the fact that people everywhere link persons and events to comment, explain, predict, and blame. A sense of the evolving structure of persons-in-situations is built into social life, whether the apprehensions are worked up into stories, expressed as visual images, tactfully downplayed, or point-blank denied. In Chapter 6 I will show how our understanding of emotion episodes corresponds to that structure.

SIX

The Narrative Understanding of Emotion

I have set out a case for the narrative *construction* of emotion, an analysis that goes some way to explaining why, in real life, we tend to *understand* emotions narratively and that justifies a narrative approach to the *reporting* of emotion. Between these three perspectives on a theme the evidence must inevitably overlap, as the Utku and Bedouin examples showed. In the present chapter, the emphasis falls on understanding; in Chapter 7, writing. To facilitate what is, in any case, a rather arbitrary separation, and for other reasons that will become apparent, in this chapter I draw extensively on literature. Fictional examples have the distinct advantage of getting past the problem of 'privileged access', the inside view of other minds that is technically barred to the ethnographer. Fiction can also bring into luminous view the everyday, quasi-automatic process of how we read people and events, a process complicated in fieldwork by the cross-cultural encounter. This is not to say that literature furnishes transparent presentations of emotional understanding, even if the writer's art makes them seem so. Nor is it to suggest that anthropologists should set out to emulate Tolstoy or Conrad. Rather, through the exploration of fine-grained examples that have a quasi-ethnographic objectivity, I want to exemplify the narrative understanding of emotion and put my finger on where fiction and ethnography might agree or differ.

The Narrative Understanding of Emotion

How we understand emotions

Our understanding of an emotion episode, in life or fiction, depends on our ability to follow a narrative (which may lack words, as in the scene from *Tulpan*), to recognize and correctly interpret responses, to appreciate traits of character, to anticipate the array of possible outcomes, and to grasp point of view. It depends, in other words, on our real or imagined insertion in the scenario. Yet although the same processes of empathy, 'mind reading', and positional analysis are entailed, the nature of involvement in the fictional world is different from our immersion in the real world, however realistic the fiction, however constructed the real. Real-world engagement carries risks that fiction does not. To the extent that emotions misconstrue real problems and vainly attempt to remake the world, they become instances of Sartrean bad faith, blurring the line between fiction and fact. An Aristotelian measure of rationality, of what we should now call realism, is not *absence* of emotion but proportionate and apt emotion: anger justly directed at the offender, and with sufficient aggression.

Keith Oatley, one of the pioneers of the psychology of fiction, proposes that 'when we read, hear, or watch a story, we create and run a simulation of selves in the social world' (2012: 172). Fiction is a 'kind of play' (52), a safe space in which we can experience what it is like to storm the barricades, murder a king, or rebel against the Almighty. In the imagination, on page or screen, anything is possible and there are no real consequences or limits.

The question of how, or even whether, you can have real emotions about fictional characters – what's sometimes called the paradox of fiction – is one that has preoccupied philosophers and psychologists (Oatley 2012; Robinson 2007). One important difference is that in real situations we are not merely entering into the concerns of others and resonating with them but are assessing how *their* intentions affect *our* concerns. In every sense, we are interested parties. In many real

Narrative

situations, especially where we know the participants, we cannot help but take a position and become emotionally involved: the line between actor and spectator is crossed, even if we are not a central protagonist. (One who is merely told about the event, away from the action, is in a somewhat different position.) The ethnographer is highly anomalous in this respect: present in person, embedded in the action, but officially disinterested like a reader. She is that walking paradox, the 'participant-observer', neither one thing nor the other. In order to write her ethnography – and not get into trouble with the locals – she must correctly interpret the emotions of others; but *her* personal concerns are not relevant to theirs; and *theirs* are of no concern to her, except neutrally and therefore unemotionally as data. As the object of fierce critical scrutiny, almost everything that happens to the fieldworker rouses her emotion, but fieldwork emotions – at least in the early stages – are poor guides to the lives of others.

I consider the special case of the ethnographer's own emotions in Chapter 10. But let us stay briefly with the question of how we understand emotion in *familiar* surroundings. If we are part of the unfolding scene as, say, the object of anger rather than a bystander, we are implicated in complex and dynamic ways, though still dependent, moment by moment, on the narrative skills of empathy, causal linkage, and perspective-taking. In the passion play each of us is a moving target for the other. It is a truism, of course, that while emotions provide insights into our own and others' predicaments, they can also block understanding, as when we are blinded with rage or dizzy with joy. But in general an inability to take the other's point of view and grasp what is at stake for them entails a failure to recognize key elements of an emotion episode, and – if you are part of the story – respond appropriately. The tone deaf cannot pick up a tune, develop it, or modulate to a related key.

Moving from the familiar to the strange, the ethnographer *starts out* tone deaf. She must learn how to respond to relevant behavioural and

The Narrative Understanding of Emotion

narrative cues – a matter of cultivated attention and longterm immersion, the idle accumulation of life histories and gossipy detail. Briggs comments on a scene of rivalry between two young sisters:

> It became clear later that what seemed to me a 'mild' note of censure or of amusement was not necessarily so to Raigili. But at first, as unattuned to the highly modulated expression of friction as I was to the discreet expression of affection, I failed to note either the signs of tension or the context in which they most often occurred: Raigili's relationship with her sister Saarak. (Briggs 1970: 127)

Without acquiring a feel for narrative context and how it is channelled in emotion, much of what matters to the people we are living among passes unnoticed, slipping under the radar of formal research instruments. I say 'much of what matters', yet emotions are precisely about what matters. In nearly all definitions, emotions identify and respond to elements in the environment that impinge pleasantly or painfully on a person's interests and deepest concerns. And it is those concerns that cannot be read off from the immediate situation except in the simplest cases.

Non-narrative factors

Narrative isn't everything. The grasp of emotional meaning depends on other things too. What we casually call intuition is an ability to grasp situation, context, and significance in a flash, not a feat of cold Sherlockian observation or deduction. Something in ourselves answers to the scene; we feel it. But *what* is it? Neuroscientists, seeking bedrock, point to hard-wired dispositions, mirror neurons, and the architecture of the brain as factors in the biology of empathy: evolution has primed us to respond at a glance to the predicament of others, to feel at one remove what they feel, to shrink from what they fear. Such automatic responses

Narrative

are, of course, moments in an unfolding process rather than the complex assessments that narrative encodes.

Other scientists refer to the visual processing of facial expressions, which trigger a corresponding affect in the observer. Again, these have little or no narrative content, though they may communicate a judgment within an unfolding scenario. Psychologists have long recognized that postural mimicking facilitates emotional contagion and empathy (Heberlein & Atkinson 2009: 164). It is one of the tricks that psychotherapists use. The related phenomenon of bodily harmonizing helps explain crowd behaviour and conformity, joint activity stirring the sense of compulsion that overrides individual will. Recall the Niha penitents pulled into the Shaking and the Jumping. Think what it feels like to enter a dance. You can stay outside, but once within cannot resist or deviate. An early anthropological contribution to a theory of social bonding – Radcliffe-Brown's (1922) study of the Andaman Islanders – noted the emotional impulse that connected dancers. The coercive power of Andamanese society over the individual owed as much to the ritualized joining of bodies as to the fusing of wills. Such studies remind us that emotions are movements of the whole being, not simply agitations of the soul.

All these felt undercurrents are part of an explanation, clues to the recognition and understanding of emotion, an understanding both cognized and felt. But active engagement with others' emotions depends on more than biological priming and bodily feedback. Firstly, there is a developmental history to be reckoned with. However spontaneous in their mechanisms, 'fellow feelings' are not a creation of the moment; they are nurtured in the family, the group, and the culture. And they contribute to what social psychologists call emotional intelligence: 'the ability to monitor one's own and others' feelings and emotions, to discriminate among them, and to use this information to guide one's thinking' (Salovey, Hsee & May 2001: 185). I argue that emotional intelligence depends, additionally, upon an ability to read or intuit

The Narrative Understanding of Emotion

narrative: not just to follow a sequence but to make connections and derive implications. Whether or not we put our understanding into words (mostly not), this construal of meaning is essentially a narrative skill. Biology and personal development alone do not help with the more complex emotional episodes that unfold over the long run (remorse, guilt, hatred) or respond, however instantly, to enchained events. A more detailed microhistorical accounting that recognizes the interweaving of circumstance with point of view is necessary.

Time signatures

The narrative construal of emotion responds to its timebound construction, which has two dimensions, synchronic and diachronic (related but not equivalent to the egocentric and biographical perspectives discussed in Chapter 5). The synchronic dimension is explained by philosopher Aaron Ben-Ze'ev: 'An emotional change is always related to a certain personal frame of reference against which its significance is evaluated' (2010: 44). Ben-Ze'ev sees this framing as comparative: an evaluation of the change compared to what could be or what might have been. Personal frames of reference, I take it, vary with age, gender, class, culture, personality, temperament, and experience. My disappointment is proportional to my expectations, my stoicism or sunny disposition, my options and support networks, and the reactions of others. Ben-Ze'ev is not concerned with temporality, as such; but the 'personal frame of reference' appears to be a present-tense, immediate assessment of how one is affected. The conditionals and subjunctives of comparison (the *might haves* and *could bes*) refer backward and forward only to weigh the present. The diachronic dimension, in contrast, is the history of relations within which emotional episodes unwind – again, distinctive and particularized, if nested within culturally and socially shared frames.

Our sense of being short-changed in popular culture, whether airport novel or Hollywood blockbuster, is due to a neglect of one or other

155

Narrative

dimension. In formulaic acting we see emotion stereotyped, a simulacrum that references but does not express the real thing. Pop culture evokes shallow emotions from synthetic ones that lack the ripeness of real emotions. The effect of either alienness or banal predictability we get from reading thin ethnography is due to the same simplification. *Alienness* if we are denied sufficient backstory (the exotic effect); *banality* if general factors mask the determinate detail. Our understanding responds to the fact that emotions have a vintage as well as a structure.

Reading faces

The omission of context in work postulating basic emotions suffers from the same drawback. Researchers in this area tend to use very short time frames – the seconds that a smile or a surge of fear last (Ekman 2003). Appropriately, their materials are often photographic: mugshots that purportedly capture something essential. In Ekman's famous experiments (of which there are several variants), subjects from Papua New Guinea were asked to match photographs of faces to situations that implied sadness, joy, disgust, surprise, anger, and fear – Ekman's postulated six basic emotions. Americans, in turn, matched Papuan faces to similar scenarios. The consistency of results across cultures appeared to confirm the universality of facial expression of emotion: the smile for happiness, the frown and compressed lips for anger. But as critics noted, what they actually showed was that people in forced choice (i.e. limited option) tests correctly linked posed faces to simple scenarios. Who knows if or how emotions are involved, unless you define emotions *as* those grimaces and scenarios?

The methodology, the claims, and the ecological validity of Ekman's approach have all been seriously criticized (Crivelli et al. 2017; Russell 1994). Pictures of anonymous persons responding to generic stimuli (or posing the expressions) for interpretation by cultural strangers obviously lack real-life context and the results cannot plausibly be

The Narrative Understanding of Emotion

generalized to natural emotional episodes. Among the most damaging of criticisms is Fridlund's (1994) contention that facial expressions have evolved to communicate *intent* rather than convey felt emotion. In a social animal, expressions need to be distinctive, reliable, rapid indicators of intent, readable with minimal context. Emotions are more messy and complicated.

The face does not tell the whole story. The same expression can accompany different emotions, different expressions the same emotion. Fear of a mad dog looks different from fear of failure (prompting the question, in what respect are they both instances of 'fear'?). Joy at a birth looks nothing like the joy of revenge. Merely to state these alternative scenarios is to point out that in each case the emotion is a complex event, not an entity with a natural sign. The common ground between exultation over the enemy's corpse and exhilaration at the birth of one's child is very small. A big smile tells little.

In widely shared video clip, Robert De Niro gives the following advice to aspiring actors, who tend to overdo the mugging.

You don't have to do *anything*. Nothing. And you're better off, and it'll work the way people are in life. They don't do *anything*. I'm talking to you, and I'm looking at your expression. You could have been told that somebody in your family was this or that, some terrible thing. You're still gonna have the same look on your face; and that says more, allows the audience to read into it, as opposed to you telling them what they should feel . . . . You just have to do it, and it will take care of itself. https://cast44.com/famous-actors-give-their-best-advice-on-acting/

What allows the viewer to attribute emotion, of course, is the narrative context, not the expression. This is what the face experiments miss. Posed and natural expressions are quite different, by no means equally readable or as easily discriminated. Without knowing what has gone before or is likely to follow, we cannot be certain. The immobile face, Gombrich writes in a study of visual perception, is often ambiguous,

Narrative

'the node of several possible expressive movements' – in portraits, often deliberately so (1982: 117). In fact, the ambiguity of a living expression, its positioning within a time sequence, is what distinguishes it from a mask or caricature.

Naturalistic observation by emotion scientists contradicts the experimental results for posed pictures. 'The available evidence points to weak correlations between emotions and their predicted expressions in natural settings' (Fernández-Dols & Crivelli 2013: 125). It turns out that quite different emotions can be associated with similar facial expressions: 'an experience of intense sexual enjoyment consistently coincided with an expression strikingly similar to that of pain' (ibid. 117). How reliably, therefore, can we infer affect from image? And how are we to explain the connection between face and feeling – as sign, symptom, or communication? These questions have still not been satisfactorily answered. Others seem to answer themselves. What do we lose by omitting social and cultural context, character, and past history? Almost everything. Do we read the expressions of people we know more subtly and intelligently and in a different way from our reading of strangers? Obviously, yes.

In light of these sceptical findings, Fernandez-Dols and Crivelli suggest that *facial behaviour* would be a better term than *facial expression* (2013: 26). We do not necessarily know that a particular face expresses emotion; what we do know is that it is made to an audience in a certain dynamic context; it is part of an interaction; and beyond that, part of a story.

Beyond expression

People brought up under other skies and in other periods cannot be exactly like 'us' and we should be sceptical if they are made to appear so. Nor is there good reason to expect cultural others to be any less complex in their emotional and moral functioning than we take ourselves to be.

The Narrative Understanding of Emotion

(Utku emotional episodes may appear predictable and relatively simple, if inscrutable to the outsider, but their earnest moralizing of emotion greatly complicates things.) An emotionally engaged ethnography will fail to deliver if it ignores the particulars and assumes that the general frame is determinate or that everyone who fits a categorical profile will think, feel, and relate in the same way. With emotions, the devil is in the detail.

An approach to emotion through narrative recognizes the distinctiveness of emotional formation in other cultures and the possibility of sharply different kinds of experience. It offers a path to understanding specific episodes more empirically valid and more ethnographically interesting than a broad-brush static universalism. At the same time, it avoids the mystification of out-and-out cultural relativism, the assumption that people who have different concepts of emotion and inhabit different lifeworlds must remain opaque to us. For the narrativist, opacity lies not in alterity but in the observer's blinkered gaze, the shrinking of emotion to an instant.

Among philosophers, Peter Goldie is unusual in emphasizing time-depth and in recognising the amplitude of emotions like love and grief, whose expression may surface only in briefer moments and whose ebb and flow can mould character and shape a life. His characterization of emotion (which elides the difference with mood, the one lapsing in and out of the other) is close to the position I am developing here: 'An emotion, I have argued, is a relatively complex state, involving past and present episodes of thoughts, feelings, and bodily changes, dynamically related in a narrative of part of a person's life, together with dispositions to experience further emotional episodes, and to act out of the emotion and to express that emotion' (Goldie 2000: 144). Drawing on the Austrian writer Robert Musil, Goldie locates complex emotions in a person's sense of themselves and their place in the world, the manner of their engagement evolving through reflexive action and adjustment to the responsive world – what Musil calls 'shaping and

Narrative

consolidation'. This is good news for a narrative anthropology (though Musil himself was mistrustful of the orderly chronology of narrative [1995: 709–710]). And Musil is a star witness, a major emotion theorist in his own right. But in widening the evidence base I shall choose other models. I should say, other *examples*, for the aim is not to produce a weak imitation, a poor man's novel, but to learn something about how emotions operate, how they connect people and shape the world, how they feel. Where Musil was an analytical master of emotion, with an engineer's eye for intricate mechanism, Tolstoy was perhaps the supreme empathic observer and narrative exponent.

But before the examples, a question. What, in the case of literature, do we mean by evidence?

The evidence of literature: A cognitive approach

Theorists writing in a cognitivist tradition place the emphasis on different aspects of appraisal: judgment (Solomon, Nussbaum), evaluation and 'coping' (Lazarus), subject–object relations (Frijda), temporality (Goldie), and mental modelling (Oatley). They provide the anthropologist with diverse tools for prising open ethnographic nuggets, or, in combination, a frame-by-frame analysis of what may pass in a flash. Of these authors, Oatley (a cognitive psychologist) and the philosophers draw most frequently on literary examples. Oatley is of special interest in his concern with the structure of narrative, finding in literature much of what is lacking in experimental data. In *Best Laid Schemes* (1992), he defines emotions as mental states of readiness that arise when an event 'impinges on a person's concerns', in particular when the event bears on their goals and plans (1992: 21, 36). In everyday life our wishes are kindled, frustrated and fulfilled in unpredictable ways, and this conjunction of goals with happenstance is what produces emotion. Emotions enable us to respond to the contingent, to change plans and adapt to circumstances, which include the conflicting plans of others.

The Narrative Understanding of Emotion

Following Aristotle, Oatley argues that the very same clash of desire with facts is what drives narrative and what arouses emotion in the reader or viewer. It is narrative, with its goal-oriented plots, its purposive but ineffectual characters, that delivers the best insights into emotion, insights that experimental methods miss because they fail to take account of the improvisatory schemas that unfold in real encounters (1992: 24–25; 2012).

Oatley uses literary examples to illustrate the working out of emotion episodes as characters manage their responses to reversals of fortune, triumphs, and disappointments. His analysis of how emotions define and respond to predicaments is in a long tradition that runs through Aristotle and Spinoza, but in co-opting cognitive science to the task Oatley goes much further, proposing that our goal-directed behaviour obeys the computational logic of the modular mind (a conception of the mind as consisting of innate task- or domain-specific structures). In what he dubs a 'communicative theory', he further proposes that emotions have the function of alerting others, and ourselves, to our changed circumstances and to the urgency of managing a course of action (Oatley 1992: 44–54, 178–179; Oatley & Johnson-Laird 2014). Crucially, 'one of the effects of an emotion is to make the problem conscious', forcing a re-evaluation (Oatley 1992: 383–384). The 'communication' may take place between persons or within the organism, as one part of the system (e.g. for monitoring goals) is in dialogue with another (e.g. for communicating semantic messages).

Let me give an example from *Anna Karenina*, a favourite among emotion theorists, including Oatley himself. After an encounter on the train with her prospective lover, Vronsky, the heroine arrives at the station and greets her husband:

An unpleasant sensation gripped at her heart when she met his obstinate and weary glance, as though she had expected to see him different. She was especially struck by the feeling of dissatisfaction with herself that she

Narrative

experienced on meeting him. That feeling was an intimate, familiar feeling, like a consciousness of hypocrisy, which she experienced in her relations with her husband. But hitherto she had not taken note of the feeling, now she was clearly and painfully aware of it. (Tolstoy 1877/1901: 107)

In this example, the 'unpleasant sensation' enters Anna's consciousness as a moral feeling, forcing an adjustment, a taking stock. An internal 'communication' of sorts, it would seem to fit Oatley's theory. Various schemas are in play: of her husband as a spouse and as a man, of what she expects from her marriage, of herself as a moral being; while, in the background, the urgings of desire project Vronsky as masculine paragon and love object. In principle, some of these schemas refer to goals that come into conflict (though it is evident even in this brief extract that goals are only the half of it). The mix of feelings prompts a readjustment, or rather a dissatisfaction that suggests such a readjustment will prove difficult or impossible.

As with other expositions of modular theories, the non-specialist may puzzle over who or what is mediating between modules, who or what is conscious of their separate outputs, who joins the dots.[1] Raymond Tallis (2011: 186–208) makes the case that there can only be communication – the passing of information – via nerve impulses or between modules if there is someone or something *external* to them to read meaningful messages in dumb signals. It cannot be another module (e.g. a reading module), because the same conundrum would arise: Who or what is making sense of *that* output? In 'anthropomorphis[ing] the organs of perception' (202), he writes, the neuroscience model seems to call for a homunculus or ghost in the machine (cf. Scruton 2014: 60–61; Tallis 2011: 188).

---

[1] For a humanistic critique of neuroscience on person and self, see Scruton (2014: 57–66). For an exhaustive philosophical critique, Bennett and Hacker (2003). See also rejoinders in Bennett et al. (2009).

The Narrative Understanding of Emotion

This is not something anthropologists can help with, though they cannot safely ignore the arguments. Yet – the jury being out – our decision about what analytical course to follow must ultimately be based on the test of experience, or else we should be in the position of the economist who complained, 'That's all very well in practice, but will it work in theory?' Our course must also depend on what level of functioning we are trying to explain. If what we are trying to illuminate is action within meaningful contexts, an approach to emotion that deals in reasons, feelings and thoughts, rather than the neural processes that underlie feelings and thoughts, seems to work pretty well. (Bennett and Hacker [2003: 209] argue that events in the brain are not, in themselves, tantamount to thoughts and feelings; nor do brains have thoughts and feelings, only persons-in-the-world do.) For our purposes, the Computational Mind may turn out to be incomplete: self-sufficient yet lacking in what makes for selfhood. An ethnographer of almost any stripe – and certainly most authors of narrative fiction – would want to give more place to action, social relation, microhistory, personality, and cultural framing in the composition of an emotional episode. The meaning, tone, and tendencies of an emotion derive from those factors and are not separable from what the emotion is; they are not mere conditions for its generation. Perhaps this boils down (on my part) to a greater scepticism about the integrity of the emotion concept, or at least preference for a fuzzier definition. Oatley's confidence about basic emotions and their mental constitution is not something I would share. And yet, as literature abundantly confirms, the goal-contingency juncture he identifies and convincingly demonstrates is undeniably at the heart of the emotional process. An anthropologist would differ only in locating that juncture in social activity rather than the mind.

With his psychological penetration and command of detail, Tolstoy is a prize exhibit. Yet his superior claim on our attention surpasses his value as theory fodder. *Anna Karenina* serves as reminder of how far experience escapes formulation: a lesson to ethnographers who are best

Narrative

placed of all social scientists to capture it. What we learn about emotion from the Kareninas and Oblonskys overflows the hierarchical schemas of goals and plans. To be sure, plot is important, the scaffold of the story; and Oatley's notion of 'best laid schemes' usefully transfers to the goal-driven behaviour of colliding individuals. But other aspects of emotion – its transformation of perception, its recasting of past events, its personal resonances, its rhetorical uses, its shudders and sighs – need noting too.

The complexity of emotion within a natural sequence – its resistance to formula – becomes strikingly obvious if we consider an example of what is often taken to be its involuntary, unequivocal, natural symptom: the blush.

The blush as sign and symbol

My uncle Toby blushed as red as scarlet as Trim went on – but it was not a blush of guilt – of modesty – or of anger – it was a blush of joy; – he was fired with Corporal Trim's project and description.

Sterne, *Tristram Shandy*

In any narrative form, there are stylistic conventions that need to be considered, even in the mimetic art of realism where there is often an assumption of transparency. It is through artifice that the fictional universe is made to *seem* real. (In Ibsen's phrase, 'The illusion I wished to produce was that of reality.') The reader responds as if to the real world, but the reality-effect is contrived. We ignore the brush-strokes and see the face; yet without the brushstrokes there is no face. In using literature as evidence, we cannot always be sure when we are beguiled by the means (or convention), taking it for the fictional reality, the medium for the message. The blush is a good example: a natural sign that served, in nineteenth-century Russian literature, as 'a kind of code or banner that informs the reader of this or that character's feelings' (Nabokov 1981: 211–212).

164

The Narrative Understanding of Emotion

Despite there being no emotion-linked word in Russian for the blush (Wierzbicka 1999: 294), Tolstoy's characters frequently 'flush', 'redden', or 'colour', sometimes as memory impinges, sometimes out of embarrassment or suppressed anger, though Tolstoy typically avoids naming the emotion and lets the scene do the talking. When Levin (Kitty's husband) runs into Vronsky (her former suitor) at an election meeting, 'blushing crimson, he turned away immediately, and began talking to his brother' (1901: 635). His awkwardness towards an ex-rival comes over as rudeness, which he regrets and later tries to fix, causing more confusion. Later, when Kitty herself meets Vronsky for the first time since the ball at which he had jilted her for Anna, 'her breath failed her, the blood rushed to her heart, and a vivid blush – she felt it – overspread her face. But this lasted only a few seconds' (648). She regains possession of herself. The blush here betrays a painful memory and its mastering through a private struggle within an emerging moral context – that of her new, still fragile relation to Levin, his habitual jealousy, and her innocent tendency to flirt. A whole history is contained in that blush.

In his sea tale *Lord Jim*, Conrad gives us a painfully detailed account of blushing following a misunderstanding (2002/1900: 50–55). After leaving the courtroom where he is on trial for dereliction of duty, the hero Jim runs into the novel's narrator, Marlow. In the swirl of departing bodies Jim has overheard the words 'Look at that wretched cur' (people had been stumbling over a stray dog) and mistakenly takes offence. Primed for anger, he turns on Marlow who braces himself for an attack. On recognizing the error and putting Jim right, Marlow is struck by his adversary's florid and incapacitating blush. There is no doubt that the description is meant to be psychologically realistic – so far as psychology can be discerned in a novel obsessed with obscurity of motive – though its placing within the story is calculatedly pivotal and it packs a tremendous symbolic punch. Like the novel as a whole, and like most 'social' emotions, the blush is about judgment and misjudgment: the judgment of society, of a profession, of circumstances, and of

Narrative

oneself; and about the fatal consequences of misjudging an action, taking a false step. A banner raised above an army of causes, motives, and effects.

Without naming an emotion, Conrad-Marlow enumerates the symptoms, eventually labelling the *situation* 'humiliation'. We might have expected the emotion word 'shame' or 'embarrassment'. But 'humiliation' casts the net wider, referring to a predicament that could include various emotions. The blushing crisis points to many things, rippling outwards in significance:

- Jim's recognition of his inappropriate reaction to the imagined insult.
- The awkardness of a climb-down.
- His sense of injured pride.
- The circumstances of the trial, in which his reputation is on the line, making him alert to any subsequent insult.
- His habitual prickliness over a life-changing lapse of judgment when he abandoned a sinking ship, whether out of cowardice, folly, or negligence, we do not know.
- The blush recalls an earlier scene when he failed to rescue a drowning youth, a matter of acute regret and a spur to dreams of heroism. So the present 'humiliation' is doubly motivated, the blush deeper than the situation warrants.
- In plot terms, the encounter inaugurates the friendship with Marlow; the blush is the catalyst to make amends.

Conrad could have written, 'Jim blushed deeply in shame', but the description of developing symptoms conveys, as it were in real time, the dawning consciousness of moral implications without need to spell them out. The episode is obviously and intensely emotional; but Conrad would gain nothing by confining it to 'shame'. What matters here is not the identification of a certain emotion – the standard recourse of a lesser writer – but the total context in its dramatic and psychological dimensions; while the interplay of contexts and levels – the ripples – conveys

The Narrative Understanding of Emotion

the broader significance of the scene, giving it leverage in the novel as a whole. It is not a case study, of course, and from reading the episode we probably learn nothing new about shame. But we learn a good deal about masculine pride, colonial codes of honour and duty (how deeply they are embodied), and the formative power of an emotionalized judgment in the course of a person's life.

Ethnographers spend their days amid humdrum scenes, but they live for compacted yet explosive moments like this. And once or twice in every fieldwork they are sure to occur. How can we make more of them? A first step is in recognizing their dramatic density, the entanglement of emotional episodes in interlaced stories and lives. This is the point of the literary examples – not, as might be fancied, to set up impossible standards. Better prepared, we can now turn to the anthropological writing of emotion, identifying weaknesses and omissions, and asking what, given our workaday skills and resources, can be done about them.

SEVEN

Writing Emotion

Anthropologists, as writers, should take their models where they find them. Consider *Salvatore Giuliano* an Italian documentary-style film made in 1962. The eponymous hero was a Robin Hood figure – Eric Hobsbawm called him a social bandit – who joined the cause for Sicilian independence after World War II and held out in the mountains for years, supported by the people of Montelepre. Officialdom pinned on him the massacre of a communist rally. In 1950 he was lured to town and killed in an execution made to look like a shoot-out.

The film is a meticulous recreation of events through re-enactment, flashback, and court testimony. The director, Francesco Rosi, used only one professional actor, who plays the judge. The rest were local people who had lived through the events. The court scenes are concerned with establishing causes, and with the difficulty of finding the truth due to police misinformation and the bandits' *omertà*. Like Rosi's other work, it is a film about the quest for the truth – the forensically established facts and motives, and the larger contextual truths, the politics. In such a case, narrative cannot be linear, seamlessly consistent, or univocal.

Despite the exciting action *Salvatore Giuliano* is not a histrionic film. There are very few close-ups of faces. Many scenes are depicted from afar or from above. Apart from the keening of Giuliano's mother in the morgue – Rosi cast a woman who had lost a son – and a couple of angry outbursts in court, it is not a film of emotional display. Which

Writing Emotion

makes the director's comments in an interview made years later all the more interesting:

All this, this method, this system, is to try and elicit the same emotions [*emozione*] that were felt at the time... *This* is the great affirmation of realism. Realism is a feeling [*emozione*] that depends upon the way in which you manage to bring back to life on the screen the feelings of a population, the feelings of a whole country, the feelings of the people who had lived through the events and who now are living them again. I think *this* is the result that every director wants to achieve in reliving certain events connected to the relation between citizens and the state, citizens and the events that made history and are still making history. *This* is realism.

(Rosi 2014)

The 'relationship' between the inhabitants of Montelepre and the events 'was so genuine that it made it look like a documentary. But it wasn't a documentary.' To achieve realism was to discover how events were lived out and above all how they felt – no need for melodrama or 'acting'.

Rosi's comments on the mise-en-scène are particularly striking:

[Through] my friendship with the cinematographer we were able to create a platform of emozione, a way of feeling [*modo de sentire*] and of succeeding in making the audience feel the emozione that I wanted them to experience through the creation of the ... [he gropes for the word and uses French] *mensonge* [lie] of the cinematographer. I say 'the *lie* of the cinematographer' to indicate that he recreates reality. But that reconstruction – which is the same as a lie – once again becomes a great act of emotional [*emotiva*] participation for the people who have lived through those events; and for me who brought them back to life.

The truth is in the emotion. But the aim is not psychological. As he explains in a separate interview about *Hands over the City,* a film about crooked property developers and corrupt councillors in Naples, what interests Rosi is the 'social mechanisms' and the unpredictable clashes

169

Narrative

that issue in the emotions. To get the emotions right is to illuminate these processes.

Emotion and realism are not usually paired, least of all in political film-making. If the master of neo-realism sees emotion as central to the making of events, to their artful depiction ('the lie'), and to the audience's understanding, we do well to listen.

As my ethnographic examples have, I hope, shown, taking emotion seriously does not signal a retreat into psychology or away from social realities. Still less is the 'emotional stuff' an optional extra, the feelgood human interest that lazy reviewers look for in narrative ethnography. An emotionally alive anthropology is not a soft alternative to the real thing: sentiment for structure. It promises, instead, greater realism through a steadier attention to the flow of social life and a Rosi-like determination to render that complexity with fidelity and probe its truths. Which requires a different kind of writing – and, in turn, a different kind of reading.

In this chapter I identify the flaws in standard ethnographic approaches to writing about emotion, finding a persistent set of constraints than runs through a century of anthropology. I might have begun this book with a brisk historical survey; but it is only now, having disentangled the elements of emotional episodes and presented some exemplars, literary, cinematic, and anthropological, that the holes in the ethnographic hand-me-downs show up. A retrospective on how anthropologists have handled emotion gives us an alternative history of the craft. It also points the way back to emotional realism.

The problem

In understanding how emotion got written out of ethnography we can identify two separate but related problems: on the one hand, a patchy *recognition* of emotion, often amounting to neglect; on the other, a failure in *reporting*, a critical lack of detail. You can underrate emotion by ignoring it, or you can underrate it by putting it in the wrong words, letting it slip through the gaps. If the problems are related, so are the solutions. To give emotion its due we have to think harder about what goes on in the field *and* how best to put experience into words.

Many anthropological readers will doubt there is a case to answer – unsurprising given that for most of our discipline's history emotion has not been a focus. Its integrity as a concept has been assumed, its cross-cultural identity taken for granted, its empirical role in social processes either scorned or obscurely acknowledged as fundamental. 'The aspects of things that are most important for us', writes Wittgenstein, 'are hidden because of their simplicity and familiarity. (One is unable to notice something – because it is always before one's eyes.)' (1953: 50).

The centrality of emotion in human life explains its ethnographic invisibility. Ubiquitous but intangible, neither out there nor in here, emotions are all-important or totally irrelevant, nebulous, ungraspable. The difficulties are conceptual and methodological, and – like many of the most taxing issues in anthropology – they are perennial. So the selective history of emotion-writing that follows is of more than antiquarian interest: it identifies problems and positions that remain starting points for any discussion. I shall be sketching a history of neglect that runs counter to the progress achieved in other anthropological fields – a story of missed opportunities and roads not taken; all retraced with the comfort of hindsight.

Off the verandah

As every anthropology student knows, the modern tradition of fieldwork-ethnography was more or less founded by Malinowski. In the manifesto-like introduction to *Argonauts of the Western Pacific* (1922), he made a distinction between the collection of data about social organization and the 'imponderabilia of actual life' – the moment-by-moment flow of behaviour which the anthropologist was uniquely able

Narrative

to record. To grasp the imponderabilia and, through them, the 'native point of view', you had to come down off the verandah, the creaking stage of old-style fieldwork interviews, to observe speech in its living context. It was the newly-discovered, or at least newly-theorized, method of participant-observation that revealed to Malinowski the critical contrast between what people do and what they say or think they do. The method emphasized what Roger Sanjek, in a review of fieldwork practices, calls 'situated listening' and 'speech-in-action participant-observation' (1990: 233), as opposed to 'formal interviews with seated informants' (246). We must bear this crucial contrast in mind in assessing recent studies of emotion. All too often we have forgotten the lesson of the master.

The extraordinarily rich descriptions that Malinowski produced from his fieldwork in the Trobriand Islands would not have been possible without his clearly articulated discovery of 'subject, method, and scope', as his first chapter is entitled. However, what worked for ceremonial exchange and garden magic did not work quite so well for emotion. Consider a well-known example, cited by his biographer as a prototype of the extended-case method (Young 2004: 402; cf. Chapter 4). This was the story of the expulsion of the chief's son, Namwana Guya'u, from Omarakana, Malinowski's village in Kiriwina. Namwana had accused his rival, the chief's sister's son, of seducing his wife and had reported him to the colonial Resident. The outrage that followed the seducer's imprisonment led to Namwana's formal denunciation and exile. For village and ethnographer the consequences were momentous: the loss of an influential man and key informant, the chief's semi-withdrawal from active life, the grief-stricken death of his wife, and a 'deep rift in the whole social life of Kiriwina' (Malinowski 1926: 105).

Malinowski presents the case in structural terms as a struggle between matrilineal authority and paternal interest (1929: 13). The personal elements that would thicken the meaning are edited out. You cannot blame him for seizing the opportunity to clinch a decisive sociological point. But the emotions – the imponderabilia – have been filtered. The backstory is summary; the description sparse. Malinowski's hero and literary model, Joseph Conrad, would not have approved. But what of specifically *anthropological* interest is missing? How about what the participants felt: felt in the fullest sense – how they judged the events; how public humiliation affected the imprisoned philanderer and the well-born cuckold; how the longstanding feud between them stoked anger and retribution; how the linking but invisible women – the chief's sister and the unfaithful wife – judged the unfolding situation and were reconciled with the warring men; and how, emotionally and linguistically, the whole thing was framed by differently positioned parties. All these aspects are central to an account of the social life of emotion, in fact, to the social life *tout court*. The sociological case is nailed, trophy-like, for future admiration; but we learn little from Namwana's story about the way Trobriand emotions are constituted or experienced. We can see they matter a good deal; but the method of reporting does not let us see how or why they matter. By and large, emotions were just too imponderable for functionalist methodology; they escaped the subject, method, and scope.

One might sum up the problem as a reversal of background and foreground. The functional framework (of positions and motives) gets in the way of what is immediately important – manifest in the emotions – *and* what is carried forward from the past: the emotional hinterland. Both past and present are eclipsed.

After Malinowski: Structure and sentiment

Nor do we learn much about emotion from Malinowski's students. Raymond Firth restricted his coverage of emotion because of a preconception about what might count as psychology. In documenting family sentiments, Firth warns with a shudder: 'But the use of the term "sentiment" in this book [*We, the Tikopia*] implies not a psychological

Narrative

reality but a cultural reality; it describes a type of behaviour which can be observed, not a state of mind which must be inferred' (1936: 160).

To be fair, a late essay delivered on Malinowski's centenary *does* directly address an emotional episode, another case of a chief's distraught son (Firth 1985). But Firth's analysis concerns intelligibility; it says little about emotion, or indeed Tikopia emotion. And I say this in spite of Michael Carrithers' otherwise persuasive appreciation of the case, which he incorporates into a powerful argument for the narrative understanding of behaviour (Carrithers 1992: 159–160).

I shall dwell a moment on this example, both to highlight what is missing in Firth's account and to show where I diverge from Carrithers' more positive assessment. It concerns an incident during Firth's fieldwork in 1929 when his friend, Rangifuri, the chief's son, was seen leaving his father's house in turmoil (Firth 1985: 35–41). As it turned out, Rangifuri was upset that the chief had refused him an axe to cut bark needed for a mortuary ritual to mark the loss of his (Rangifuri's) son at sea, presumed drowned a year before. Worse still, the chief had complied with the wishes of Rangifuri's brothers to stage a dance festival, 'so making their drain on family resources take priority' over the death rite. Rangifuri's outburst appears to be compounded of grief and anger at his brothers' manipulations and his father's refusal of the axe. Working backwards from the outburst to its origins, Firth identifies 'areas of similar basic experience of the external world' (35) as a key to the general intelligibility of the situation. (We recall Lazarus's 'core relational themes'.) Carrithers (1992: 159–161), in turn, refers to our grasp of a 'universal pattern' in 'the basic idea' that Rangifuri was 'upset' and in 'distress' (166). We recognize distress because we have all 'been there'.

But have we? We need to ask what *kind* of distress. How was Rangifuri's acting *teke* ('angry', 'objecting') conceived, felt, shared, resisted, or ignored? Beyond a rough orientation, how much do basic patterns help? Only a fuller narrative could tell us why Rangifuri's father appeared not to share his grief; how, given the depth of feeling

Writing Emotion

surrounding the outburst (which insulted the chief's dignity and caused a village rumpus), Rangifuri and his father could be so swiftly reconciled; and what were the chief's own sentiments towards the dead youth, his ultimate heir. To these ethnographic questions basic patterns offer no clues. Firth's account is too laconic and schematic to dispel the mysteries or illuminate the nature of *teke*.

So it is all the more surprising – and revealing of how narrative trumps summary reporting – when we turn to a version of the same incident first published in 1951 (Firth 1971: 61–72). In this much richer account the background is presented *before* the outburst is related rather than filled in retrospectively to demonstrate a theoretical point. The hierarchical but loving relation between the chief and his son is much clearer, and the emotional stances of all concerned emerge with life-like detail and credibility. Crucially, we learn that Rangifuri had been 'in mourning, with food taboos and abstention from public affairs, for about a year, and wanted to be free' (65). We learn that the night before the incident he had dreamed of a quarrel with his father and that, in the dream, his son had appeared to him for the first time since he was lost, urging Rangifuri to make the barkcloth for his funeral. Firth gives us all this and describes the tears and gestures in which the dream was conveyed to him: 'It can be understood, then, that when Pa Rangifuri went to see his father the morning after his dream he was in a highly emotional state, ready to react violently to any opposition to impulsion to proceed with the funeral rites. He said of his acts then, "My belly was like as if fire had entered into it"' (1971: 72). The cumulative detail tells much about the dramatism of Tikopian emotional episodes, and much about their collective mediation. With sympathetic words and gestures, Rangifuri's fellows patiently humour his distress ('one of them lay with his nose pressed to Rangifuri's thigh . . . a conventional token of sympathy, expressing also a rather flattering respect'); they acknowledge his grievance but steer him from violent or rash acts. In a scene straight out of Conrad, the reconciliation is mediated by Firth when he deputizes as facesaving mediator and ceremonially leads the faux-reluctant penitent 'by the wrist' back to his enthroned father. Once the chief's outraged dignity is soothed (more rubbing of noses), and misunderstandings righted, the funeral can be arranged.

Vivid and convincing, without false familiarity, it could not be done better. Considered as an emotion episode, the timing, the motivation, the stagecraft, the distinctive feelings (burning belly), the settlement and aftermath are all carefully reckoned. Background and foreground are in proper focus. Yet reframed thirty years later (1985) to explore a problem about intelligibility, the emotions are obscured, and so, therefore, are the configuring details.

What does all this prove? That emotions really could be given their due when 'subject, method, and scope' were relaxed a little and the writer, fully alive to human possibility, was allowed free rein. Early Firth, starchy and hypercorrect, excluded them by disciplinary prejudice; late Firth, inclining to theoretical gravitas, tailored emotions to argument. But in the middle of the journey Firth got it just about right. And the lesson? Whatever the virtues of narrative as an ethnographic tool and recipe for a humane anthropology – virtues nicely elucidated by Carrithers – when it comes to emotion, the narrative must be considerably fuller and must go beyond basic pattern recognition. In particular, the temporal dimension – the past in the present – is crucial.

Malinowskian descriptive functionalism, forged in the Jazz Age, lasted well into the 1980s; and it remains the default method of reporting in anthropology, if trimmed of circumstantial fat. On functionalism's other wing, one foot on the verandah, Radcliffe-Brown and his followers also shied away from an exploration of naturally-occurring emotions, preferring standardized 'social sentiments' unmixed with idiosyncrasy, temperament, or curriculum vitae. The structural functionalists followed Durkheim in their ruthless purging of individual psychology and history. 'Psychological facts' had no bearing on 'social facts', which were the sole concern of sociology and anthropology.

French structuralism took up a different strand of the legacy but kept the taboo. Like Evans-Pritchard, who dismissed Durkheim's theory of religion as derived from crowd psychology, Lévi-Strauss faults the master for breaching his own principles and deriving social phenonema from 'affectivity'. 'His theory of totemism starts with an urge, and ends with recourse to a sentiment' (1962: 70). Lévi-Strauss went further in rejecting *any* explanatory role for emotions. 'Actually, impulses and emotions explain nothing', he wrote; 'they are always results, either of the power of the body or of the impotence of the mind' (1962: 71). A strict Cartesian dualism prevented him from seeing emotions as having any cognitive content, or, to put it slightly differently, intellect as embodied (1981: 667–668); which meant omitting the motivations, judgments, tactics, and expressions that comprise emotions and animate social life. For Lévi-Strauss, emotions are mere effects. Yet, as we know, in the flow of events effects are causes of further effects. Emotions have a history, hence motivational value. We seek pleasure and avoid pain; hope springs eternal.

Even granted a narrow view of emotions as sentiments, Lévi-Strauss cut out much of what the fieldworker observes. And relying mainly on published texts, his examples are doubly depleted. It was only a small step from the functionalist schemas he drew upon to an algebraic notation of dispositions, with + and − signs denoting sentiments. Call it abstract expressionism. This was kinship drained of human significance. In a generation, anthropology had passed from Malinowski's exuberant realism, in which people and their emotions were at least visible if not a focus in themselves, to a plane of abstraction which left them far behind.

After Boas: Emotion and ethos

As the home of what became psychological anthropology, America was more hospitable to emotion. Built on the edifice of Boasian descriptive

Narrative

ethnography, American anthropology made culture its cornerstone. Boas himself was keen to distinguish culture as a historical product from individual thought and feeling. Above an assumed 'psychic unity of mankind', what varied across cultures was the content of cognitions, not the faculties or forms of experience (Shore 1996: 22). Although his students – the Culture and Personality pioneers – saw emotion as a key variable in a design for living, they took for granted the conception of emotion and its objective status as a natural kind. Their concern was not with what emotions *were* but what they *did*; how they were shaped by everyday routines, how they moulded the ethos. This was the focus of their writing.

The attempt to pin feelings to forms was most explicit in Bateson's *Naven* (1958/1936), an ambitious synthesis of British structural and American cultural approaches conceived in the Sepik River region of New Guinea. Bateson's reporting strategy is instructive. He fixes on stereotyped sequences in Iatmul encounters, coining the term *schismogenesis* for the competitive escalation and breakdown between partners. Schismogenesis, he proposed, was a widespread form of interaction evident in marital squabbles, class war, even the arms race. Curiously, in Bali where he later worked, it was lacking. Instead, a tendency to excite then dissipate emotion – an 'absence of climax' – led to what he and Mead (1942) called a schizoid personality. On almost every measure Bali was different; but no less than in the Sepik, Balinese emotions, daily routines, and cultural values were tightly interlinked in a functional circuit.

This crystalline clarity came at a cost – people with a past, a biographical present, whatever it is that generates emotion. A focus on patterns discounted the specificity of emotion episodes, winnowing out the passionate individual, turning the love and anger of real people into the synthetic passions of generic Balinese, Papuans, and Samoans: culture-specific, not person-specific emotions. Despite its lively tone and one's memory of it as rich in emotions, Mead's Samoa book

Writing Emotion

contains not a single description of an emotional sequence witnessed by the author. The technique is one of ethnographic generalization – 'Cases of passionate jealousy do occur, but they are matters for extended comment and amazement' (1972/1928: 131); or summary – 'The rage of Lola was unbounded and she took an immediate revenge, publicly accusing her rival of being a thief and setting the whole village by the ears' (145). The discursive manner sacrifices verisimilitude for presentational coherence.

Naven, one of anthropology's Great Books, illustrates the gains and losses of pigeonholing emotions. I cite it here because the balance sheet is still relevant and because Bateson was unusually – obsessively – reflexive in his approach and knew very well what he had to leave out. In his introduction, Bateson asks how the ethnographer can capture scientifically what literature conveys by 'impressionistic' techniques. 'The emotional background,' he writes, 'is causally active within a culture, and no functional study can ever be reasonably complete unless it links up the structure and pragmatic working of the culture with its emotional tone or ethos' (1958: 2). But his focus is on formalized behaviour and sentiments; and his argument, frustrating and dazzling by turns, succeeds only to the extent that he can persuade us such sentiments do indeed dominate Iatmul life. From the evidence, we cannot know. *Naven* is famously theory-driven, with Bateson a kind of anti-Malinowski, herding the facts like docile sheep from one hypothetical fold to another. Here and there among the confining frames are glimpses of stray facts, unformulated emotions – the feelings *behind* the 'emotional background', one might say. Bateson witnesses a funeral and puzzles over the half-hearted sobbing of the men and their relieved lapse into competitive boasting. 'They escaped entirely from a situation which was embarrassing, because it seemed to demand a sincere expression of personal loss, an expression which their pride could scarcely brook' (154). Ethos triumphs over inchoate feeling. But the psychic cost, like the ambivalence Bateson found in Iatmul sexual antagonism, remains

Narrative

unexplored. How are unauthorized emotions experienced? What subterranean life do they lead? How does the personal trauma of initiation get transformed into the 'pride of the male ethos'? Legitimate anthropological questions, but they could not be asked when the object of enquiry was 'culturally standardized behavior'.

Triumph of the cultural

I have been tracing the lacunae to show what needs to be restored – the unwritten shadowing the written, the gaps in history that are gaps in the present. But we are not quite finished.

Functionalism and structuralism had reduced emotions to dispositions, shadows of structure. In Talcott Parsons' mid-century rethinking of the social sciences, emotion was even more elusive. Parsons' maxim was the irreducibility of psychological, sociological, and cultural phenomena, each 'level' having its own characteristics (Kuper 1999: chapter 2). In the division of labour, anthropologists were assigned 'culture', sociologists 'society', and psychologists 'personality'. But where did emotion belong? Each scholarly tribe could claim emotion as its own only by losing two of the dimensions. For the anthropologists, it had to be cultural or nothing. But what was emotion torn from its psychological moorings?

The answer came with a different conception of emotion, one that better fitted the cultural mould. If human beings were cultural beings, as Parsons' chief anthropological exponent argued, so must their emotions be cultural. 'Not only ideas, but emotions too, are cultural artifacts', wrote Clifford Geertz in 1962 (1973b: 81). This was a radical claim, far from the dilute Freudianism that set limits to the relativism of the Culture and Personality school. But in its strong sense it was not picked up for many years, not even by Geertz himself. In this early essay, Geertz was moving towards the idea of culture as a tissue of symbols, a kind of text. He later gave philosophical ballast to the conception by appeal to Wittgenstein's

Writing Emotion

strenuously public concept of meaning, for which the axiom 'an "inner process" stands in need of outward criteria' (1953: 153) might serve as banner. In the Bali essays of the 1960s and 1970s, however, emotions appear as manipulable *entities*, psychological ready-mades rather than cultural artifacts. Here's an example: 'What the cockfight says it says in a vocabulary of sentiment – the thrill of risk, the despair of loss, the pleasure of triumph ... Attending cockfights and participating in them is, for the Balinese, a kind of sentimental education' (Geertz 1973c: 449). This is not very different from Bateson and Mead on Bali. Thrills, despair, pleasure: culture shapes what nature provides. What's new is the idea that the *parade* of emotions serves as a social commentary, part of a cultural 'text'. In a later essay on Bali, Geertz goes a step further in the depersonalizing of emotion: 'It is dramatis personae, not actors, that endure: indeed it is dramatis personae, not actors, that in the proper sense really exist' (1983: 62). Where would emotions figure in a play without actors? Geertz's Platonic formula reverses ethnographic perception, ideas coming before people. Whether Balinese worldview totally subsumes Balinese experience is not, for Geertz, an interesting question. They are a 'dramaturgical people with a self to match'. Ethnographic reality fits theory hand in glove. We are a long way from the thrusting individuals of Malinowski's *Argonauts* or Firth's Tikopian idyll, far removed from real imponderable emotions.

Geertz's bracketing of the biographical, his focus on cultural framing rather than subjective experience, set the course for a generation. Anything outside this programme amounted to mind-reading. Interpretivism inspired many fine-grained accounts of the person that enriched the literature but left out actual persons. It was as if the symbols and models had the experiences on the actor's behalf. What was left over when texts had been interpreted and symbols logged was private sensation, amenable to neither observation nor analysis. In this perspective, individuality was equated with privacy (in the philosophical sense), an anthropological no-man's-land.

Narrative

Such was the orthodoxy as constructionism took hold from the 1980s. Contrary voices arguing for transcultural factors lingered here and there. Rosaldo (1989) and Wikan (1992) argued from common experience; phenomenological anthropologists continued to assert the primacy of the body, the experiencing self, or other avatars of consciousness; but the dominant modes remained the summary report, the case study fitted to a thesis, the colourful vignette, and the generalizing comparative statement.

Emotions in focus

But what about those full-length studies that prioritize emotion, such as 'person-centred ethnographies' (Hollan 2001; Levy 1994)? With the scope to depict and describe, to mine biographical formation, surely they keep a steadier eye on the actuality, on the people inhabiting the emotional landscapes? Well, yes and no. I do not want to take away from what are, in other respects, outstanding contributions to anthropology, but in two flagship specimens of the genre, long sections devoted to emotion contain no examples of actual occurrences witnessed by the authors (Hollan & Wellenkamp 1994: 107–123; Parish 1994: 190–230). The ethnographic material consists of responses to questions like: 'What is the relationship of hopelessness with desire?' (Parish 1994: 229); 'What happens inside you when you have *pastae*?' (Parish 1994: 224); or 'Can you remember a time when you were really angry?' (Hollan & Wellenkamp 1994: 116). In both books context-free, present-tense generalizations hark back to the summary statements of an earlier era: 'Toraja believe that if one avoids getting angry . . .', 'In the Toraja view of emotions . . .' (Hollan & Wellenkamp 1994: 119, 110); 'What Newars know, as moral beings, is mediated by this pain and fear' (Parish 1994: 215). As a reporting practice it's hard to avoid; I've done it myself. This is the plaint of a repentant sinner.

Writing Emotion

Though person-centred ethnography can, with some justice, claim to give us the 'native point of view' – or at least the *elicited* native point of view – it violates the other Malinowskian axiom of testing word against practice. Parish is aware of the objection and stresses that 'we should not ignore the ways emotion is embedded in action and practice in ways that go beyond what cultural theories of emotion say' (1994: 215). In his conclusion (1994: 278), he affirms that 'culture is lived – it is embodied in experience, action, and life. It emerges in lives.' But a reliance on interviews is not well suited to such a conception. The original person-centred ethnography, *Tahitians* (Levy 1973), is, happily, packed with people; yet Levy's influential essay on emotion contains not a single account of an emotion episode, offering only a brief hypothetical case (1984: 219).

What these diverse approaches – functionalist, structuralist, constructionist, interpretive, person-centred – have in common is a limited temporal context, an optic that moves swiftly outwards to factors of ideology, cultural framing, and generic experience rather than deeper into individual stories: wide-angle rather than long focus. In most cases, the context is immediate and reducible to generalities, the approach synchronic – as if the actors, like the ethnographer, were fresh to the scene. How can the writing not be emotionally depleted?

This is not a repetition of the old complaint that ethnographies fail to tell the story of the field: many now do. It is a more radical criticism that (with exceptions) ethnographic writing, *by design*, gets emotion wrong, filtering out what for actors is of principal significance: history, character, implication, strategy, and plot – all those elements that the filmmaker Rosi painstakingly recreates in pursuit of the real.

A theatrical analogy. To respond to a Hamlet soliloquy, you need a knowledge of sixteenth-century English, a familiarity with the conventions of Elizabethan theatre, with the world of castles and courts, hawks and handsaws. (That, or good footnotes.) But the meaning of the speech lies not in its exemplary nature – as an instance of stagecraft, courtly

Narrative

intrigue, or the Oedipus complex – but in the revelation of character in action, the motivations and ruminations of Hamlet at that moment in the plot. The rest is mere background. In considering emotion, we have got background and foreground reversed – trained, as we are, to read significance in general forms, in the paradigmatic instead of in particulars. But the remedy, the cure for abstraction or functionalist thinness cannot be ever-thicker description, which merely takes us deeper into social structure and cultural frames, as Rosaldo (1989) rightly discerned. Nor, however, can it be Rosaldo's appeal to the ethnographer's own sentimental education, which misses the personal-historical complexity of emotions, their grounding in interwoven stories and characters.

Towards emotional realism

What Briggs, Abu-Lughod, and Firth (of 1951 vintage) show is that a certain narrative density is needed before the humane significances that define the emotional life can emerge. The reality effect, as Rosi argued, depends on achieving an emotional integrity. For the ethnographic writer, working on a smaller scale than the film-maker, an awareness of emotion in narrative context brings to light the contradictions and conflicts that people experience as social beings, their *not* fitting, their resistance or unwilling capitulation to social pressures (or their happy conformity), their abrasions with reality, their struggles for meaning. For the same reason, narrative works against a relativism that would encompass emotion within culture – depersonalizing it – as if nothing escapes the cultural embrace. A narrative approach leaves opaque what resists social analysis; it acknowledges the irreducible; it does not force an answer.

Here we come to an important difference between the narrating of emotions in fiction and non-fiction. Fictional emotions are accountable within self-contained plots, whereas non-fictional narrative implies the open-endedness of real life. (Bayley [1966] maintains that *War and Peace*, which Tolstoy refused to see as a novel, shares this life-like character.) But plot is only one dimension. In classical theory, plot is the revelation of characters in interaction. What befalls the tragic hero is a function of his flawed make-up. For Henry James (1972: 37) this equation is the engine of fiction. 'What is character but the determination of incident? What is incident but the illustration of character?' Emotions transpire within the tight organic whole.

In the looser weave of ordinary life extraneous factors intervene. Stuff happens. The procession of events does not run on the rails of character but expresses the vast complexity of the world, of which we know only our own little corner. Most realist fiction – James notwithstanding – is a compromise between the poetic compression of stage or page and the ungraspable complexity of offstage reality. Narrative plausibility depends entirely on the plot–character mechanism, so that what people say and do follows from the past without being entirely predictable. But plausibility is not verisimilitude. (A melodrama may be plausible within generic conventions but lack verisimilitude.) What makes a fiction seem *true*, rather than merely plausible, is its representativeness, our sense of its fidelity to experience of the external world. It is in this sense that the reader of *Anna Karenina* feels 'that what he is reading is being effortlessly reported rather than laboriously made up', as Janet Malcolm (2015) writes of Tolstoy's 'preternatural realism'.

The truth conditions of standard ethnography are different. Lacking a narrative perspective on a self-contained world, you don't ask yourself, 'Would this person do that, given what we know about her?' but 'Would she do that given the cultural premises?' Ethnographic plausibility is about logical consistency. Verisimilitude is harder to specify. When Levy (1973: 304) tells us that a Tahitian man, abandoned by his wife, felt not *sad* but sluggish and ill, the account is plausible, given the premises (no explicit concept of sadness, a resistance to negative emotions), but without narrative background it remains mysterious. We have to take the

Narrative

point on faith. Levy, whose background is psychoanalytical and who staged psychodynamic interviews in the field, sees such cases as culturally shaped misrecognition, so that a loss that *we* should associate with sadness is experienced as fatigue (Levy 1984). Even granted the cultural premises, can it be true? Misrecognizing emotion is a common enough event. But the fatigue following loss of a spouse is surely unlike the fatigue following a day digging taro. Levy's account requires the Tahitian to misconstrue not only his sadness but also his tiredness.

To be sad or to grieve is to recognize the source of pain, to acknowledge and struggle through certain feelings, and thereby to elicit sympathy and mobilize help. But to collapse in lethargy is to renounce action or remedy. It can be a failure of coping as well as a failure to confront one's feelings. More (or less) than a misattribution, it is an interruption of normal emotional service. Briggs describes how the Utku, deprived of their canoes by Canadian sportsfishermen, and – thanks to the taboo on anger – unable to confront the *kaplunas*, spurned their peace offerings of salmon, leaving the gifts to rot. Immobilized, they 'were afflicted with a most unusual lethargy. They yawned, complaining of sleepiness in midday, something I had never seen at any other season. Innuttiaq and Allaq once fell sound asleep at noon' (1970: 281). Puzzled by this passive refusal, Briggs recalls other instances of emotional lockdown: 'I remembered that lethargy one autumn day after the kaplunas had gone, when Amaaqtuq was describing to me how one could recognize that a person was upset (huqu). "He will sleep long hours during the summertime when people usually stay up late," she said, "and he'll sit idle instead of working"' (ibid.). A reaction of this kind, without cultural charter and seemingly instinctive, can *in extremis* overtake a whole community stricken by calamity. In her great memoir of the Stalinist Terror, *Hope Against Hope* – a study in modes of fear and coping besides much else – Nadezhda Mandelstam describes the enervating effects of rearrest on the victim's family, which are quite unlike the fearful hope and frantic activity that follow a first arrest. Beyond hope and despair, beyond emotion, a

Writing Emotion

bodily inertia sets in that seems to enact the death sentence to which many Russians felt themselves doomed.

We had rushed around to see her [their friend, a singer] on learning that her husband, recently released after five years in a camp and allowed to come to Voronezh, had again been arrested. This was the first time we had heard of someone being immediately re-arrested like this, and we wondered what it could portend. The singer was lying in bed. People are always literally prostrated by this kind of misfortune. My mother, who as a doctor was mobilized after the Revolution to help with famine relief in the Volga region, told me that the peasants just lay quite still in their houses, even in parts where there was already something to eat and people were not totally exhausted by hunger. Emma [a lecturer] once told me how she had gone out to work on a kolkhoz [collective farm] with some of her students, and that all the kolkhozniks were lying down. It is the same with students in their hostels, and with office workers when they get home in the evening. We all do this. I have spent my whole life lying down. (Mandelstam 1970: 185)

We are a far cry from the listless Tahitian. But those hibernating Utku and petrified Soviet workers – candidate versions of the same phenomenon – strengthen the case that reporting cannot stop with anomaly. There is always a story to be excavated, whether personal, collective, or even national. The extreme cases conform neither to cultural logic nor to biographical origin; but they are not recalcitrant to narrative. As Mandelstam shows, the new is urgently made sense of against the old; the latest phase of the Terror throws up novel questions ('we wondered what it could portend'), but the response – so shocking and alien, so terrifying in itself – calls to mind, and perhaps depends upon, longer established patterns.

If plausibility depends on internal consistency, one of the ways in which verisimilitude – especially in the reporting of emotions – is enhanced is through *inconsistency*, the out-of-character lapse, the capacity to do things that surprise. When 'best laid schemes' fail, emotions generate new plans (Oatley 1992), and the individual is forced to improvise, drawing on diverse resources, sometimes making an existential

Narrative

choice. But there is more to it than that. Real human beings surprise us because we are fallible observers and because we lack access to all the facts: the secret histories and stutterings of motive that occasionally break cover. It is the pressure of the past – the traces of previous encounters in memory, dispositions, expectations, and emotions – that make for what E. M. Forster called round characters: individuals with depth, agency, and the capacity to surprise. This hidden aspect – emphasized by Epstein in his Tolai cases; epitomized in Lord Jim's blush – is especially significant in emotion because of its reflexivity and partial privacy; and the point holds even in societies where the individual soul is not a matter of much interest. I think back to a curious incident during my fieldwork in Nias. Though not much in itself, it gives a glimpse of an obscure emotional history – and, as emotions sometimes do, points the way into a much bigger story (related in *After the Ancestors*).

The tell-tale heart *redux*

After a thirty-year reign the chief of Orahua had died – a prolonged, public passing both welcomed and regretted as the end of an era. In the hall of the great house that was the hub of village life he lay in state, hair combed, a plug of betel in his mouth, dressed for eternity. Around his open coffin (hewn from a rice bin) clustered family members, some pressing handkerchiefs to their noses in the fetid heat. All day, clansmen and villagers had streamed in to pay their respects, and by mid-afternoon the air was thick with betel breath and the clamour of a hundred people. From below decks, through the floor, came the grunts and shrieks of pigs gathered for slaughter.

A funeral, like any occasion in Nias, means speeches. Form required a mix of flattery and criticism: the spirit's path to the otherworld would be blocked by unvoiced resentment ('painful heart'), and there was plenty of that in the air. The chief had many faults and not a few enemies. Nobody paid much attention to the worthy sentiments and complaints that fell

Writing Emotion

from the mouths of the elders as they rose one by one to say their piece. ('You are a bird in the treetops, soon to depart. We won't dwell on your offences.') But when the chief's great rival, his deputy, got up to speak, there was a perceptible change of rhythm, a collective shuffle. People put aside betel bags or replenished their chews, ready to watch his face and hang on his voice. He was the best orator, the master of staged emotion. He would find words for their feelings, 'tell their hearts'.

Ama Darius had waited half a life for this moment. But how to strike the right note: magnanimous but not triumphant, sympathetic but gently critical? And how would he conceal a lifetime of rancour beneath the formulaic praise? Everyone *knew*, but it was necessary to make a show: the prize of leadership was within his grasp. As often before a speech, I noticed him grimacing and making faces at the floor, trying on masks. But when he stood up and hailed the crowd – a little feebly, I thought – he fumbled for tone. The speech was unmemorable, the words mechanical. He seemed agitated as if itching to be elsewhere and fell into an uncharacteristic mumble. It was as if he had been thrust onstage unprepared and was desperate to get off. The chief's older brother, who lived on family reputation, glared disapproval. Among the crowd, attention drifted, betel bags rustled, and then – midway through his eulogy – the deputy's voice cracked. As his chin dropped the words choked in his throat; in place of the usual passionate flow, a strangled cry. He was suddenly wiping his eyes. Those who had resumed chattering or relaxed their concentration looked up, startled. The words, the tone, had not prepared us. The tears did not belong in the speech but came from somewhere else – an eruption of feeling that concerned the chief but was not, in its sudden violence and equally sudden suppression, one of grief. Stranger still was the effect of his appearance. Something about him was different, but what? Only when I turned again to the chief's usually silver-maned brother, did I realize. Using diluted boot polish, both men, overnight, had dyed their hair jet black; both rejuvenated by the chief's death. I cannot separate the uncanny

Narrative

effect of this transformation from its symbolism and the situation that evoked it. The occasion demanded sorrow, and half found it in the deputy's stifled sob; but the checked words and the youthful appearance suggested liberation, perhaps even elation in his rival's passing. The black hair was a personal symbol; one that the audience registered but whose meaning could not be spelled out.

The disturbing transformation – and the same collective double-take – was repeated a year later when, hours after a murderous clash between his lineage mates (both rivals for his land), Ama Darius passed – some say *ran* – through the shuttered, terrified village in tennis shorts. It would be trivializing to call it a fashion statement; but the deputy's white shorts and pale unsunned legs had a startling effect on the villagers who had only ever seen him in sombre sarong or trousers. Everyone knew he had been the intended victim of the killer, his nephew; everyone could see he had profited from the murder of their kinsman. But why the parade? With one rival killed and another led away to justice, what was he playing at? Was it a gesture of defiance, a triumph not only over his enemy but over death? For his enemy – like the grim reaper   had been stalking him, dagger in hand, for days.

A narrative of the fieldwork would have to make something of these oddities – the black hair and the white shorts – precisely because they fall outside ethnographic stereotype. Closer to parapraxis than praxis, they tell us nothing general; but therein lies their significance. They remind us that the occasion, expression, and meaning of emotion are personal and particular; and that emotions focus a range of concerns, which is why they are anthropologically interesting. In fact, no synthetic example or capsule summary could tell us half so much about power and status in Nias as emotion-laden incidents of this kind. To make proper sense of them I'd have to unravel a history of reversals and humiliations. I'd spool back twenty years to the deputy's wedding day, when the chief had barred the door of the great house to him, turning him away with a foul oath. I'd recover the tale, scarcely mentionable, of how his grandmother had been abducted on a headhunting raid and had married into the chief's lineage, a slave become a bride. I'd retrace the stories of how he had subsidized the bridewealth of his nephew, the future murderer; and of the resentment that had grown between them until the day fate had placed the wrong victim in the way. I might not come away with a hypothesis, but I would have a better understanding of the play of emotion, the twisting together of envy, resentment, humiliation, and revenge; and of how the little, half-intended details mean everything. This would not be a psychoanalytic history; instead it would return to the broad context, which has a powerful transpersonal reality: perspectival, but not purely egocentric, historical but not stratigraphic in the Freudian manner; a story embedded in other stories. Once again, as Rosi showed, the truth is in the emotion; but we come at it through narrative history, big and small.

Frame and focus

If we are interested in giving emotions their due, we have to work into our ethnography the confrontation between the teeming complexity of the world and the first-person perspective that reorders it: the capacity of emotions, as Solomon puts it, to constitute a world (1995: 41). Call it frame and focus or panoply and perspective: emotions seize what pertains to us; they respond to what external reality casts up in the way of frustration, loss, and opportunity; and they do so according to our dispositions, training, and history. Yet I want to insist that neither a phenomenological account nor a psychoanalytic one tells the whole story. For if, as Solomon has argued, an emotion is a judgment, an assessment of the circumstances affecting *me*, it is also an action in a world made by others: a response of pleasure, fear, or anger to what lies beyond our control, to what disturbs our equilibrium, our goals, and desires. And this tension between inner and outer imperatives – to overstate an opposition – must be at the heart of a fully anthropological

Narrative

account and can only be captured in narrative. The dialectic of provocation, judgment, response, and re-evaluation, however swift, is not the work of a moment. Life is a movie, not a snapshot.

In her book, *Upheavals of Thought*, the philosopher Martha Nussbaum has argued the case for a cognitive view of emotions, as opposed to Jamesian theories which make cognition secondary to visceral response. She differs from certain other cognitivists in rejecting a synchronic explanation that would 'sever emotions from their past and depict them as fully and reliably determined by present input about one's current situation' (2001: 177).[1] But her point is equally applicable to constructionist accounts that ignore or compress the temporal dimension, which Nussbaum takes to be essential. 'In a deep sense', she writes, 'all human emotions are in part about the past, and bear traces of a history that is at once commonly human, socially constructed, and idiosyncratic' (ibid.). Those three time-bound properties have been taken up in different kinds of inquiry: the commonly human in developmental psychology, the socially constructed in anthropology, and the idiosyncratic in fiction. All three belong in ethnography. Recall Ama Darius and his dynastic struggles. What history issued in that stifled speech of tribute and that puzzling rejuvenation? The *common human factors* are thwarted ambition, sibling (or, rather, cousin) rivalry, personal offence, loss, and survival; factors that no doubt echo deeper childhood experiences. We recall Lazarus's 'core relational themes': the abstract scenarios that frame appraisals of situations and motivate emotions. Each of them in itself is a capsule story, a story basic to the human condition.

The *socially constructed elements* would include the record of feasting and ceremonial exchange that organize status competition among big men; but also ongoing tensions in the lineage cycle, such that cousins

---

[1] Among her targets is Solomon, though his position *does* take past occurrences into account: 'Every emotion is a judgment that presupposes the entire body of previous emotional judgments to supply its context and its history as well as "paradigm cases" for it to consider if not follow' (Solomon 1993: 137).

Writing Emotion

farming different tracts of shared land begin to assert individual control at the expense of rivals: a ready motive for murderous conflict.

The *idiosyncratic history* would be the dark memories of raiding and abduction, the repressed past out of which the dynastic struggle is spun. This history casts the deputy as Edmund to the chief's Edgar, the natural talent against the legitimate heir, the man of words against the figure of authority. As a personal history, not a bare record of fact, it would include the hallmarks of character that shaped their rivalry for a generation: the chief's wooden correctness, his booming certitude and simple piety; the deputy's subtlety and resentment, his restless scepticism, and his capacity to surprise: the black hair and the white shorts.

Pan-human, culturally specific, idiosyncratic: I can tease apart the factors, but no account of the emotions at the funeral scene could justly privilege one set over another. Take away one dimension and the whole thing collapses.

*

History, big or small, is not the whole story; and the case for narrative I have been developing in the last chapters will not apply in every situation. Brief reactive emotions and simple responses of the kind enacted in Ekman's posed photos require no narration: a caption for snapshot. More unsettling is the charge that the persistent self is a Western construct, in which case, the feeling subject needs no history: emotions, like persons, are prisoners of culture (Geertz 1983; M. Rosaldo 1984). (The counter-charge is that cultural ideas are distillations as much as determinations. Life overflows and undermines them.) But there are other challenges that strike deeper at a narrative approach to emotion. One of these, the subject of Chapter 8, throws out both emotions and persons, making narrative totally redundant; this is the so-called turn to affect.

Part III

Perspectives

EIGHT

Affect
A Wrong Turn?

Affect Theory, as its advocates call it, has emerged as a new research programme in a range of disciplines – cultural studies, human geography, feminist theory, sociology, and, latterly, anthropology. The meaning of the word 'affect' in this new endeavour diverges markedly from both ordinary and scientific usages. Drawing on the philosophy of Gilles Deleuze, and before him Spinoza, Affect Theory returns to the etymological roots of 'affect' in reconnecting the meaning of the word as a *verb* (to affect, have an effect on) and as a *noun* (from the Latin *affectus*, 'affection', bodily affect). As geographer Steve Pile puts it in a useful overview, in the new paradigm, 'affect describ[es] both a capacity to be affected, and to affect, and also specific flows of affect that lie beyond cognition' (2010: 12). Writers in this vein evidently intend something quite different from the concept of affect as understood in mainstream emotion theory. What they mean – and what they mean for anthropology – we shall come to. But first, what of the standard, semi-technical usages in psychology and Anglo-American philosophy?

Affect in psychology and philosophy

It is encouraging, and unusual in our overspecialized world, that emotion researchers in psychology, analytic philosophy, psycholinguistics, history, and cognitive science talk to each other and debate one

Perspectives

another's theories and findings. A community of interest has blossomed in international conferences, learned societies, and thriving interdisciplinary journals. What has emerged from decades of debate is a broad field of emotion studies in which participants from the humanities and the 'affective sciences' speak a common theoretical language. Naturally, several of the key terms are hotly contested – including 'emotion' itself. Others have a rather ad hoc designation. In particular, the usage of 'affect' has been quite loose and variable, as some examples will illustrate. A psychology textbook gives the following gloss: 'general, slightly old-fashioned term used to include emotions, moods, and preferences' (Oatley, Keltner & Jenkins 2006: 412). A recent special issue of *Emotion Review* on 'affect dynamics' uses 'affect' and 'emotion' interchangeably (Kuppens 2015). A reader in social psychology assigns *affect* or *affective states* to the broadest category of 'emotional feelings': '"Affect" refers to any psychological state that is felt and in some way is evaluative or valenced (positive or negative). Indeed, the range of phenomena encompassed by the term "affect" includes not only moods, emotions, and emotional episodes, but also pleasures, pains, likes, and dislikes' (Parrott 2001: 4). In contrast, the cognitive psychologist Frijda (1994: 61) uses the term more narrowly to refer to 'pleasant or unpleasant feeling', a sense also signalled in the term 'experienced affect' (Niedenthal 2008). Likewise, in discussions of components or dimensions (two rival approaches to emotional phenomena), 'affect' usually has this narrower denotation. Although the sense is usually stipulated in context, the designation varies in scope. Inconsistency has made general discussion more difficult, leading Solomon to question 'the vague, general (and technical) notion of "affect" and its cognates ("affective tone")', and to wonder whether it merely substitutes for 'feeling' (2008: 10).

Anthropological usage is similarly wayward. Blurring important differences, the older studies of socialization employ 'affect' as a synonym of 'feeling', 'emotion', and 'attitude' (H. Geertz 1959; Harkness & Kilbride 1983). As in psychology, when a narrower sense is intended,

Affect

'affect' tends to mean the feeling-tone or valenced subjective response, the 'feeling good' or 'bad' about something; as such, an element in a larger process of evaluation and action. Once again, designation is usually clear from context; ambiguity arises only when generalizations are proposed. When Michelle Rosaldo claims that 'affects, whatever their similarities, are no more similar than the societies in which we live' (1984: 145), it is not clear whether she is referring to feelings, emotion episodes, or vague mental states. The intention is to defend cultural relativism; but to what does it apply?

In a bibliographic review of 'language and affect' in anthropology, Niko Besnier applied 'affect' inclusively to feelings, emotions, and '*affect*, the subjective states that observers ascribe to a person on the basis of the person's conduct' (1990: 421). Besnier eschews definitional concerns in order to widen the scope of enquiry, a sound anthropological principle. But as Louis Charland notes: 'an important feature of domain names of this sort is that their precise theoretical meaning depends on research in the very fields they are supposed to delimit. In the case of 'affect' this has led to an intriguing situation where both the term and the domain have been called into question' (Charland 2009: 9). If you want to have your cake and eat it, it helps to know what counts as cake.

A central debate about affect in emotion theory has hinged on how it relates to cognition – how it is triggered, how modified in conscious experience (Clore & Ortony 2008; Scherer 2005). A celebrated mid-century experiment by Schachter and Singer seemed to show that both affect and cognition were necessarily involved in fully-fledged emotion – the 'two-factor' theory. To simplify, a feeling of nervous agitation caused by an injection of adrenaline was experienced as 'emotion' only when a motivating context was supplied to the injectee. Then the disturbance was felt as *anger* (offensive scenario) or *joy* (humorous scenario) (see Cornelius 1996 for a review). Since then, and notwithstanding the continued catch-all usage, the accumulation of evidence has driven a

Perspectives

trend towards a sharper distinction between *affect* as an undifferentiated process of arousal and *emotion* as, variously, a syndrome of components (including affect), an Anglo folk category unrecognized in other traditions, or an emergent state that arises from a combination of biological, social, and cultural inputs – to name only some of the options (Clore & Ortony 2008).

Recent work on affect in neuroscience and cognitive psychology is difficult for non-scientists to assess, although plenty have weighed in with opinions, backing favoured theorists like prizefighters in the ring. Unlike the bitter culture wars of the humanities, however, debate is increasingly collaborative across party lines, as shown by new interdisciplinary journals like *Emotion Review* (I declare an interest here). *ER*'s founding editor, James Russell, himself sceptical of the scientific utility of the emotion concept, puts the case for a big tent approach to theoretical discussion as follows:

> In much the same way that the concept of thought is treated by cognitive psychologists, emotion is treated here as a constitutional monarch: The word *emotion* remains as a name for the general topic of discussion but is denied any real power, such as the power to determine borders. Thus the scope of the proposed framework [discussed below] is broader than emotion (including states such as comfort, serenity, drowsiness, and lethargy). Gone is the assumption that all events called *emotion* or *fear* or *anger* can be accounted for in the same way. These concepts are not abandoned but are put in their proper place as folk rather than as scientific concepts, and their role limited to whatever role folk concepts actually play in emotion (and in the perception of emotion in others).
>
> (Russell 2003: 146)

Boundary anxieties are a perennial problem in anthropological discussions of emotion. How does emotion relate to context? Where does affect belong? Is emotion different from thought? What is essential, what peripheral? So Russell's strategic ecumenism ought to work for us too. It casts the net wide and opens up enquiry to the unexpected, a precondition of good fieldwork.

Perhaps surprisingly, and in contrast to older theories, recent work in cognitive psychology leaves the anthropologist considerable freedom in an enlarged field, gates thrown open. Basic emotions theories like that of Ekman had limited cultural variation to 'display rules' – cultural rules modifying facial expression and what to feel. In cognitive approaches, the workings of the nervous system are seen to be in dynamic relation to situation, categorization, action, and felt experience – all of which cry out for ethnographic attention (Barrett & Russell 2015; Parkinson, Fischer & Manstead 2005; Scherer 2004). A focus on components and their contingent interrelations therefore leaves everything to play for. You might, for example, place the emphasis on *situation* rather than affect or category. Ortony and Clore (2008: 631–632) argue that 'the distinctiveness of an emotion may lie in the nature of the situation it represents, not in a stored pattern of latent emotional potential'. To which the anthropologist would add: show me a situation and I will show you *many* emotions, situation itself being a construct depending on point of view, biography and 'narrative'.

James Russell: Core affect and psychological constructionism

Russell's inclusive approach to the data, trailed above, is compatible with several characterizations of emotion, but it differs from some in dealing *not* in notional wholes like 'emotion' or 'emotional episode' but in more primitive building blocks. On his account (but in my non-scientific words), 'core affect' is the fluctuating current of feeling prior to cognition and action, the hum of interior life, the purring of the engine: 'Core affect is a pre-conceptual primitive process, a neurophysiological state, accessible to consciousness as a simple non-reflective feeling: feeling good or bad, feeling lethargic or energised' (Russell 2009: 1264). It has two dimensions, each a continuum: activation/deactivation

Perspectives

(i.e. level of arousal) and pleasure/displeasure (i.e. valence), corresponding to two independent neurophysiological systems. What English speakers call 'rage' corresponds to a state of core affect high in both arousal and displeasure; 'depressed' corresponds to low arousal/high displeasure; 'joy' to high arousal/high pleasure; 'contented' to moderate pleasure/low arousal. As challenges and opportunities arise and fade, core affect swims in and out of consciousness, making itself felt with greater or lesser urgency. Fear and disgust might be similar in intensity and unpleasantness, but their subjective experience *as* fear or disgust is the result of a process that unfolds *after* the alerting change in core affect. In this respect, Russell follows William James. Relevant changes in the internal or external environment (a sudden memory, a strong coffee, an insult, a charging bull) activate a change in core affect which prompts an automatic search for an object congruent with the feeling, a process of 'attribution'. One can feel pleasurably energized and attribute the feeling to an achieved goal (hence 'satisfaction', 'pride'), a lover ('love', 'lust'), or an event ('excitement'). One can feel bad and attribute the feeling to a foe ('hate') or misattribute it to an innocent target ('Now look what you've made me do!'). The cause need not be the formal object.

The object hit upon has an 'affective quality', a propensity to affect the subject that depends on a range of factors, cultural, social, and biographical. A pig possesses different affective qualities for a Niha feastgiver, a Muslim, and a child hearing bedtime stories. These affective qualities are not intrinsic, but derive from cultural values, social position, and experience. Without discussing them – his framework is strictly psychological – Russell fully acknowledges the importance of social, cultural, and idiosyncratic factors in emotional experience. They are our entry point, the ethnographer's meat and drink.

In Russell's theory, which refers to 'psychological construction', words like 'anger' and 'fear' denote concepts with associated scripts that are culturally specific. In the process of appraisal of the 'object'

Affect

(the thing to which affect is attributed), the subject categorizes the experience with a relevant concept, 'anger' or whatever. This in turn shapes the experience. Feeling 'angry', I am motivated to behave in a certain way – with aggression, say. If I categorize my agitation differently (thanks to upbringing) as 'indignation', I will respond differently. We have seen how Utku and Javanese, having different emotion concepts, respond in ways sometimes puzzling to us. Even the dictionary equivalents of 'anger' in Javanese and Niasan possess slightly different scripts, different models of context, feeling and behaviour. Russell calls these *categorized* experiences 'meta-emotions' – psychological constructions that correspond to what emotion realists (e.g. basic emotions theorists) call 'emotions'. Tomkins (1984), for example, defines affects as 'innate mechanisms', but uses English words like 'terror' and 'contempt', which have distinctive cultural profiles. In Russell's terms, once Tomkins applies such labels to biological processes, he is talking of meta-emotions. Meta-emotions serve to organize subjective experience according to cultural scripts; they are not natural kinds.

The theory has much more to it, and the elaboration of the detail – building on half a century of work by an army of researchers – is fascinating, though in essence the framework is beautifully simple (see Barrett & Russell 2015 for the current state of debate). The bald summary above is directed by my concerns and limited by a layman's understanding. But it shows where anthropology retains an interest and a foothold in cross-disciplinary emotion research. It also serves as a baseline from which to assess the new paradigm of Affect Theory, which seems to deal with some of the same elements.

Readers who have followed the examples – literary and ethnographic – in this book will see how closely they match Russell's theory. (And they were not pre-cooked or retrofitted: I have had them in mind for years.) Such examples also underline the necessity, at least for the anthropologist, of going well beyond immediate situation (minimally conceived in Russell, both in timespan and complexity). So, let me end

Perspectives

this section with a final example from Tolstoy – who else? – that descends from the abstract to glorious particulars.

The following scene from *Anna Karenina* offers a striking instance of the interplay of core affect, unfolding context, feeling, and meaning – all within a narrative rich in character and plot. The lovestruck Levin – presented with the gentlest irony as a thinker pitched into life, a Hamlet who says Yes – is on his way to find Kitty and propose to her. The passage begins in a manner Tolstoy's contemporary, William James, would approve: 'At four o'clock, conscious of his throbbing heart, Levin stepped out of a hired sledge.' (The Maudes' translation has the hyper-Jamesian 'feeling his heart beating'.) Levin's agitation is increased by the fact that his proposal will come as a surprise – more, in fact, than he realizes – and may be rejected: 'He walked along the path toward the skating-ground, and kept saying to himself: "You mustn't be excited, you must be calm. What's the matter with you? What do you want? Be quiet, stupid," he conjured his heart. And the more he tried to compose himself, the more breathless he found himself' (2001/1877: 34). We might call this love compounded by hope and fear, but would gain nothing by naming the emotions other than pointing out that within a single sequence, itself within a larger emotional frame ('in love'), different, even contrary, emotions (Russell's meta-emotions) are intermixed. And then, in a remarkable passage that captures point of view, affective transformation of perception, affective quality of object, attribution, and bodily feedback: 'He walked on a few steps and the skating-ground lay open before his eyes, and at once, amidst all the skaters, he knew her. He knew she was there by the rapture and the terror that seized on his heart' (ibid.). What Tolstoy lays out is a unitary experience that comprehends perception, all-over disturbance (not to limit it to the body), feeling, and thinking. To feel the rapture of love is not merely to judge someone as loveable and feel accordingly, as Solomon (1993) would have it, but to see, feel, and know in a certain way: 'for Levin she was as easy to find in that crowd as a rose among nettles. Everything was made bright.'

The ingredients of the narrative are instantly recognizable: it is a portrait taken from life. But as always with Tolstoy, the greater narrative context brings to the episode other dimensions – the contrast with the unhappy Anna–Vronsky–Karenin triangle, a sense of the springs of life, the pivotal moment of self-discovery, the beauty of the ordinary – which is what gives a simple human story, fodder for many a soap opera, its emotional reach. The scene is affecting because affect is given its proper narrative place.

Affect theory

How different from all this is the brave new world of 'affect theory'! So different that the two bodies of thought hardly touch, their leading lights inhabiting different intellectual spheres. Which of these spheres, we might wonder, pertains to *our* world? To ask that question is to assume a shared or – at least in principle – shareable world that includes the broad field of scholarly enquiry and science. But that cannot be taken for granted. We come abruptly to a paradox. Affect theory draws freely, if haphazardly, on biology and neuroscience, but its practitioners are not scientists, they are mostly unaware of – or show no interest in – the range of what I have loosely called emotion theory, and their line of argument is often hostile, or at least orthogonal, to scientific methods and reasoning.[1]

Still, there are points of contact. The favoured emotion scientists – among the few cited – are in the Tomkins–Ekman–Izard tradition of biologically-based explanation, of which Antonio Damasio is the

---

[1] Good discussions can be found in Hemmings (2005), Leys (2011), Pile (2010), and Wetherell (2012). Leys' critique – which gives more importance than I would to 'basic emotions' theory as the 'dominant paradigm' in emotion theory generally (2011: 437) – includes a painstaking demolition of Massumi's influential speculative reading of neuroscience. Gregg & Seigworth (2010) offers a representative sample of writing.

Perspectives

current distinguished standard-bearer. But affect theorists diverge in which biological systems they prefer. Some go for the central nervous system (Massumi 2002); others look for affect in the recesses of the brain, the endocrine glands, or even in the vapours of emotional contagion (Brennan 2004). The irony of mixing outré *post*-poststructuralist rhetoric with wide-eyed scientism is inescapable. It is as if the New Atheists – Dawkins, Hitchens, and Grayling – had adopted Mother Teresa as their mascot.

Why this should be the case is an interesting byway of intellectual history. In their parallel reviews, Papoulis and Callard (2010) and Leys (2011) argue that the movement's proponents found the separation of affect from cognition espoused by basic emotions theorists convenient to their larger project, which is to recognize and celebrate the bodily energies that escape intention, meaning, consciousness, and therefore ideology. The mind imprisons; the body liberates.

So how should we grasp this other mode of being moved? Here's how the historian Ruth Leys characterizes the field: 'For the theorists in question, affects are "inhuman," "pre-subjective," "visceral" forces and intensities that influence our thinking and judgments but are separate from these ... affects must be noncognitive, corporeal processes or states' (2011: 437). *Pre-*, *in-*, *non-*: easier to say what affects are not than what they are, or *where* they are. But the general aim is clear enough: to get away from individuating, conscious, interior, verbally articulated, and culturally formulated emotions to something *prior*. Affect is an inchoate energy that emerges from the body, or is generated between bodies by contagion or collision. Hence the link – never satisfactorily explained, but implied by the double meaning – between affect as sensation or energy and affect as 'capacity to affect or be affected'. Out of mind, affect eludes representation and manipulation. Once verbalised, tamed or domesticated, it runs out of steam and becomes something else. As Leys points out, this characterization of affect is not altogether different from what certain emotion theorists have argued and demonstrated experimentally; though it is much closer to Russell's 'core affect' than to Tomkins or Ekman, whose fixation is on the face.

What chiefly distinguishes new-style affect theory from old-style affective sciences, however, is the grander agenda, which is to reshape cultural and social theory rather than merely understand human functioning. Like 'embodiment' before it, affect theory aspires to paradigm status, a new broom that will sweep away the cobwebs. And behind the urgent 'theorizing' burns a hunger for something new: a millenial vision that will overthrow the tyranny of language and banish the old warhorses of positive science, social constructionism (the very words sound tired), deconstructionism, and humanism.

As commentators note, affect theory frequently gets drafted into an emancipatory agenda, as in the work of the literary/queer theorist Eve Kosofsky Sedgwick for whom the determinism of social constructionism is a strait-jacket to be cast off. Without evidence of follow-through, however, one is hard pressed to know what an affect-powered reformist project would entail. 'The goal is a kind of "emotional liberty" ... a politics of hope', wrote Nigel Thrift (2004: 68) – not yet the powerful university vice-chancellor he was to become. In a more playful mood, affect theory brings an air of celebration, a delirious flouting of grammar and logic akin to the surrealists' automatic writing. There is fun to be had, but also nuggets of insight.

On the whole, though, the preferred manner is oracular and declamatory. The editor of a volume called *The Affective Turn* introduces the central concept as follows: 'Affect constitutes a nonlinear complexity out of which the narration of conscious states such as emotion are subtracted, but always with "a never-to-be-conscious autonomic remainder"' (Clough 2007: 2).What are we to make of this? Does affect *constitute* anything? Who is the narrator? Does the arithmetic of subtraction and remainders add up? When a film theorist (quoted in Leys 2011: 442) declares that affect is a 'non-conscious experience of intensity; a moment of unstructured potential', it sounds

Perspectives

vaguely like Russell's core affect; but where Russell stipulates meaning, here the terms remain undefined.

One persistent side-effect of the evasive manner is to distract attention away from concepts, arguments, and evidence onto the words themselves. Definitional logorrhea is symptomatic, as if the need to communicate overflows the ability to formulate. Content is smothered in style:

Affect arises in the midst of *in-between-ness*: in the capacity to act and be acted upon. Affect is an impingement or extrusion of a momentary or sometimes more sustained state of relation *as well as* the passage (and the duration of passage) of forces or intensities. That is, affect is found in the intensities that pass body to body (human, non-human, part-body, and otherwise), in those resonances that circulate about, between and sometimes stick to bodies and worlds, *and* in the very passages or variations between those resonances themselves ... Affect is persistent proof of a body's never less than ongoing immersion in and among the world's obstinacies and rhythms, its refusals as much as its invitations. Affect is in many ways synonymous with *force* or *forces of encounter* ... affect need not be especially forceful (although sometimes, as in the psychoanalytic study of trauma, it is.) In fact, it is quite likely that affect more often transpires within and across the the subtlest shuttling intensities: all the miniscule or molecular events of the unnoticed. The ordinary and its extra-. Affect is born in *in-between-ness* and resides as accumulative *beside-ness*. Affect can be understood as... (Seigworth and Gregg 2010: 1–2; not my italics)

What comes to mind is Louis Armstrong's witty, if unfair, putdown of bebop – 'one long search for the right note'. (As a Monk fan, I protest.) But the quoted passage, in its dizzy effervescence, seems closer to glossolalia than to Dizzy Gillespie: a speaking in tongues, a vivid instance of the phenomenon it seeks in vain to define. In the Great Repentence, Niha penitents broke into streams of affect-laden God-speech when they could not say what they meant. No one could doubt their sincerity, but no one could understand.

Sympathetic critics, anxious not to be wallflowers or intimidated by the intellectual heavies standing in the wings, strain to understand and incorporate. Mostly they back off, letting quotations speak for themselves. 'When quoting Massumi', writes Margaret Wetherell of a key figure, 'it is almost impossible to stop. His words are so evocative and dizzying. What he is suggesting is so vague, breathless and escaping' (2012: 56). As long as you stay inside the terminology, the incantatory repetitions have a self-confirming, hypnotic effect. And there are many tangled tendrils and backstories that complicate interpretation and provide cover. Easier to dig up a root than a rhizome.

Rather than get sucked into the infinite regress of who-meant-what-about-whom, in this chapter I am concerned with what affect theory can offer anthropology, whether it overlaps with or supersedes big tent emotion theory, and whether it is adaptable to ethnography in both senses of the word, the fieldwork and the writing.

How best to approach the task? The fizzing diversity of the affect enterprise is part of its appeal; but its disparateness makes it hard to engage. In earlier chapters I developed a narrative approach to emotion through a discussion of what academic managers (irritatingly) call 'best practice', with some negative examples thrown in. Without a cohesive 'affect theory' to unpack, it makes even more sense to structure a critique around discussion of a few exemplars, which I shall now do. My points could be applied to affect theorists more widely; but a general discussion would quickly get lost. The strongest critique will be one that deals in depth with the best representatives.

I begin with an example that conveys the breathless plethoric style and thesauric overkill of the new school before moving on to a more straightforward work of anthropology, one that draws on affect theory but that departs from the house style while offering challenges to conventional thinking on emotion, ethnography, and much else.

Perspectives

Ordinary Affects

Reviews and commentaries encourage us to read Kathleen Stewart's book as a pioneering work, flagbearer for a new paradigm (Blackman & Venn 2010; Martin 2013; White 2017). 'The appearance of *Ordinary Affects* augurs well for new and productive forms of ethnographic enquiry and cultural study', wrote one reviewer in *American Ethnologist* (Staples 2008). 'It pushes ethnography to the brink and beyond, scoring high in poetics and resonant voice', says another (Krause 2010). 'Affect theory is emerging as a, if not the, dominant mode of critical discourse in the humanities and social sciences ... Stewart's *Ordinary Affects* serves as a paradigmatic example of this re-emergent field': thus, a contributor to *Feminist Theory* (Warner 2009). Evidently, affect theory is an important, boundary-bursting venture, and – for the anthropologist – *Ordinary Affects* is as good a place as any to see what it is all about.

So what *is* it about? To misquote an old song:

What is this thing called affect?
Just who can solve its mys-ter-ee?
Why should it make a fool of me?

Sometimes affect is very like emotion, or feelings available to emotion: 'Free-floating affects lodge in the surface tensions of low-level stress, loneliness, dread, yearning, a sense of innocence, backed up anger, the ins and outs of love' (Stewart 2007: 94). The imprecision of the sentence – can something lodge in a tension? does loneliness have a *surface* tension? – signals the oblique approach, an effort to capture the inchoate. You could paraphrase: 'vague feelings and background moods find expression, or objects, in yearning, dread, etc.'. But that would presuppose an affect/feeling equivalence, and 'feel' – something quite concrete, a conceptual and linguistic universal (Wierzbicka 1999) – would commit to a different kind of argument. Stewart is not sure what she means by affect, so she circles round it, evoking it in short scenes. A keyword in this evocation is 'something'. Affect is something, perhaps something happening. 'For some, the everyday is a process of going on until something happens, and then back to the going on' (10). 'Everyday life is a life on the level of surging affects, impacts suffered or barely avoided. It takes everything we have. But it also spawns a series of little somethings dreamed up in the course of things' (9). As a sympathetic critic notes, '"Or something" does a lot of critical work in Stewart's project' (Vogel 2009: 257).

'Somethings' are different from 'things'. Things just are, whereas somethings happen or surge, just like affects. 'Something surges into view like a snapped live wire' (9). (Do wires snap? Do they surge into view?) Everyday life contains the potential of something happening, hence 'the ongoing vibrancy of the ordinary' (21). However, 'the ongoing' is different from 'the going on', which is not vibrant until something happens. Daily life is quivery, and you never know what may happen next. 'Matter can shimmer with undetermined potential and the weight of received meaning' (23). We have to be alert to this potential: 'Things happen! Here's something that might be for you! It's the paying attention that matters – a kind of attention immersed in the forms of the ordinary but noticing things too' (27). Here *things* seem very like *somethings*. But this paying attention permits insights, such as when the author comes upon people floating in a hotel pool: 'A fantasy tentacle floating in the stormy placidity of the nowhere of dully compelling force peppered by dreams of getting out or *something*' (24, original emphasis).

As the image reveals, we are at several removes from standard academese, and not too close to the world described: the reader struggles to see past the words to the reality conjured. To be sure, the language is intended to be performative, evocative, not analytic or discursive. But if the action is happening on the page, not in the field, the proper response – at least the initial response – must be aesthetic.

What, then, are the hallmarks of the house style? Like the fantasy tentacle, the tone hovers between the vaguely powerful and the

Perspectives

powerfully vague. As is standard among affect theorists, nouns are mercilessly pluralized ('banalities', 'knowledges', 'somethings') – probably justifiable with reference to Deleuze's multiplicities and connections. Lists of plurals proliferate: 'Little undulations are felt as pleasures and warning signs, as intoxications and repetitions in daily routine' (28). Social science abstractions alternate with concrete observations and vignettes of the kind endorsed by creative writing tutors.

> Sentences are short.
> Often one to a line.
> A kind of pseudo-
> Poetry

Verbs are imprecise: 'Ideologies happen. Power snaps into place . . . Identities take place. Ways of knowing become habitual at the drop of a hat. But it's ordinary affects that give things the quality of a *some*thing to inhabit and animate' (15).

The pathetic fallacy rules, partly a matter of projection (shimmering reality, bubbling with potential), partly of metaphor, usually mixed metaphor. 'The animate surface of ordinary affects rests its laurels in the banality of built environments and corporate clichés' (29). Do affects have surfaces? Do surfaces have laurels? Do they *rest* their laurels (a non-corporate cliché that)? The prose is less a window onto a world than a verbal vision, a hallucination of disturbed objects and prepositions that recalls the effect of magic mushrooms: 'Weirdly collective sensibilities seem to pulse in plain sight' (28). But the idioms – wires sparking, charges, circuits, forces, 'vibratory motion, or resonance' – are from *Popular Electronics* magazine, not The Doors psychedelia: 'The potential stored in ordinary things is a network of transfers and relays' (21). If Stewart could specify what these networks, forces, and relays were, that really might be *something*.

Sometimes it all comes together – the ordinary, the energy flows, the plurals, the potential, the random lists, the pathetic fallacy, the choppy sentences and cod-verse:

Affect

The ordinary throws itself together out of forms, flows, powers, pleasures, encounters, distractions, drudgery, denials, practical solutions, shape-shifting forms of violence, daydreams, and opportunities lost or found.

Or it falters, fails.

But either way we feel its pull. (Stewart 2007: 29)

A quotation from Alphonso Lingis comes from the same manual: 'Trust is a break, a cut in the extending map of certainties and prob-abilities. The force that breaks with the cohesions of doubts and deliberations is an upsurge, a birth, a commencement' (Lingis, quoted Stewart 2007: 119).

What of the vignettes, the scraps of jargon-tormented life served up as ethnography? The scenes of lower class small-town America, of pallid epiphanies in postindustrial suburbs, seem familiar even if you have never been there. The theme of something (mostly not) happening, or trying to make something happen, was that of the great short-story writer Raymond Carver in his sparse depictions of drab simmering suburbia – done to death by legions of imitators. 'Everything left unframed by the stories of what makes a life pulses at the edges of things', writes Stewart, in a kind of echo (44). But Carver famously had a ruthless editor, deft with the scissors.

Something very strange has happened on the way to the mall.

Like a live wire, the subject channels what's going on around it in the process of its own self-composition. Formed by the coagulation of inten-sities, surfaces, sensations, perceptions, and expressions, it's a thing com-posed of encounters and the spaces and events it traverses or inhabits.

Things happen. The self moves to react, often pulling itself someplace it didn't exactly intend to go. (Stewart 2007: 79)

Even from these short extracts it is plain that the prose offers something new; it incarnates what the other affect theorists merely promise. You have to admire the author's pluck.

Perspectives

Can we run with it? There are various ways of evaluating a new concept. Does it illuminate an episode? Or suggest new and interesting questions? How does it link up with other explanatory concepts? In a brief sketch Stewart tells of a remembered scene in a doctor's waiting room in Virginia. The men awaiting the doc are striking miners. They exude defeat. But one man spins a fantasy of their storming the governor's mansion and looting it, briefly drawing in the others. What's going on? '[A] live event – a fleeting conduit between the lived and the potential hidden in it (or hidden from it). Potentiality resonates in the scene. It's an experiment compelled by the drag of affect in the room, and when it's over the men just sit calmly together, as if something has happened' (98). We note the skimpy unobserved context, the omission of dialogue (though it was a verbal fantasy), the lack of evidence for the men's interest or for the 'drag of affect' that 'compelled' the event. 'Event' is meant here in the Deleuzian sense of 'the potential immanent within a particular confluence of forces', a kind of vital happening (Parr 2005, sv. *event*). But what practically, ethnographically, is conveyed by this formula? How would it be different, you wonder, if someone had merely cracked a joke at the company's expense? That too would have dispelled the gloom.

And yet something strikes a faint chord in ethnographic memory:

Ordinary affect is a surging, a rubbing, a connection of some kind that has an impact. It's transpersonal or prepersonal – not about one person's feelings becoming another's but about bodies literally affecting one another and generating intensities: human bodies, discursive bodies, bodies of thought, bodies of water. (128)

It could be a description of the Great Repentance in colonial Nias when converts crowded into huts to jump, shiver or shake, surrendering to trance (Beatty 2012). The affects were not ordinary – far from it – but *affect* in Stewart's and Deleuze's protean sense does seem to apply.

Affect

I think, too, of Massumi's (2002) characterization of affect as the bodily autonomous, the non-discursive, the out-of-mind. The Niha penitents were out of time, out of their minds. In Chapter 2, I situated the Repentance among key emotions ('resentment', 'spite', *weltschmerz*) and cultural forms (the speaking heart). But the sacred symptoms – glossolalia, contagion, compulsion – were not limited to 'emotional' episodes. The rebounding energy of the movement burst its channels and could not be expressed, much less captured, by formulaic emotions or articulated forms. *Something else* was happening (there, it's catching!): a breaching of barriers between past and present, self and other, conscious and unconscious, word and feeling.

Can a single word do for all this? 'Affect', a label for too many processes, mystifies as much as it explains. If the energy transmitted between Niha penitents was 'transpersonal' (so, too, is much emotion), that is because the event, the choreography – the method in the divine madness – made it so. More things were in play than agitated bodies: traditions trashed and recomposed, cultural models reinvented, pop-up evangelists, oracles for outcomes. More was surrendered than individual autonomy and selfhood. The timing, periodicity, and strength of the movement – its ebb and flow – were geared to acts of colonial conquest and cultural repression. The historical context *overwhelmed*. Robbed of power, desperate for release and absolution, the penitents were broken people, morally annihilated. Behind the spontaneous happening was a modern history, a dark past, a veritable clash of civilisations. And behind its recurrences, a failure to find the right words, to match affect to object. One long search for the right note.

Ordinary Affects resists evaluation as anthropology. Too slippery to grasp in any critical frame (those tentacles!), it can only be appreciated as performance, an enactment of what it purports to describe. Among anthropologists it figures as an exemplar of 'the turn to affect', a model for the new paradigm; but other, more conventional works have a better claim. Consider, for example, Yael Navaro-Yashin's *The Make-Believe*

Perspectives

Space (2012), a study with a solid foundation in fieldwork and something interesting to say. In assessing what the 'turn to affect' can offer anthropologists, especially those with an interest in emotion, Navaro-Yashin merits close attention.[2]

Affect and ethnography

The Make-Believe Space has many merits. It makes original contributions to our understanding of the modern state. It says important things about war, historicity, and nationalism. It shows us what binds people to ideology. My interest, however, is in the book's concern with what the author calls 'affective geography'; in particular, the 'affective geography' of the Turkish Republic of Northern Cyprus (TRNC), a statelet created in 1974 by the ethnic cleansing of Greek-Cypriots from the north of the island (with a symmetrical expulsion of Turkish-Cypriots from the south). The resulting division, secured by Turkish military occupation, is unrecognized by the UN and scarcely legitimate in the eyes of its citizens who guiltily conserve, trade, or use the homes and personal effects of their former neighbours and counterparts as 'loot'. The author's central question, stated in an earlier publication, is 'What affect does such an exchanged and appropriated environment discharge?' (Navaro-Yashin 2009: 4).

The wish to enjoy the fruits of violence while recognizing them as illegitimate, the mix of bad feeling and bad faith, we might characterize as 'guilt'. But that concept does not explicitly figure in the testimonies the author collected. Decades of propaganda and legislation affirming rights to the spoils of war have created an uneasy acceptance of the status quo. Redrawn maps paper over memory and sentiment. On the

---

[2] A recent collection in the same vein, *Affective States* (Laszczkowski & Reeves 2017), takes Navaro-Yashin, Stewart, and other affect theorists mentioned above as its inspiration.

Affect

TRNC side of the partition, a derelict zone strewn with rusted vehicles and abandoned household paraphernalia leaves the border a permanent scar of war, obsessively fingered yet thrust out of mind. The ruined landscape makes people 'melancholic'. It reminds them of bad things done to them and done by them. And it makes them reflect on their altered identity: formerly Cypriots with a complex heritage; now simplified Turkish-Cypriots categorically opposed to Greek-Cypriots. The old city walls, pockmarked with bullets, remind them they live in a prison, a frozen construct of the past. The better off have moved to new suburbs, leaving the old town to poorer settlers. But they are a haunted people: haunted by the past, by the people they have displaced, by their buried selves. As Navaro-Yashin tells it, the landscape itself is haunted, as are the looted objects, a mute testimony of their former owners.

All this is fertile terrain for an exploration of emotion, taken in the broadest possible sense. But the author eschews that path, seeing emotion in the narrow terms defined by biology or social constructionism or the inner quest of psychoanalysis, none of which will do. And if emotions were confined to discourse, the psyche, or visceral feedback to the brain she would be right. But as we have seen they are much more. They connect, respond, communicate, apprehend, appraise, model, and project. At any rate, the range of activities that we group by the term 'emotion' includes those functions. All of which can be captured through such writing strategies as narrative, dialogue, and what in fictional terms would be called dramatization – the depiction of people in their everyday exchanges, their dilemmas and predicaments. Adequately presented, an ethnographic account grounded in experience and responsive to life yields what the old conceptual alleys shut out.

So what does the author propose instead? First, a focus on objects – the ruins of old buildings, the debris of war, the materiality of things that resist interpretation. Navaro-Yashin picks over the ruins and asks denizens what it is like to live among them. She pores over maps and

Perspectives

charts, palimpsests on which geography and history are rewritten. She tours private collections of war loot – garage-museums of dusty finds that leave visitors perplexed, unsure what to feel.

Second, a focus on space: enclosure, occupation, partition, *Lebensraum* for people who don't belong among other people's belongings. The friction interlopers encounter, their sense of not fitting, she calls 'irritability', and makes this stand for 'a dis-resonating [*sic*] feeling produced by environments that harbor phantoms'. Irritability is 'representative of the affects invoked by the environment' (20).

Third, an interest in the tools of domination – maps, plans, offices, title deeds – whatever imposes the order of things and generates affect. Documents 'transmit specific kinds of energy among their users'; they are 'affectively charged phenomena' (125); 'they produce and effect affect' (126). What kinds of affect? What count as examples? 'Irony, cynicism, familiar contempt, and wit' (126), but also fear, apathy, and dissatisfaction. These are recognizable human responses, suggesting an overlap between the concepts of affect and emotion. But Navaro-Yashin takes a further step. 'We can conceive of institutions as having nerves or tempers or, alternatively, as having calming and quieting effects … Here I study administration as animated, as having its own charge' (33).

As can be seen from these examples, affect is given varied denotations. Sometimes undefined and undifferentiated, as in 'This book is about the affect that is discharged by a postwar environment' (17), affect is also equated with a 'force' or 'energy' given off by objects, spaces, and institutions, something that 'exceeds' human signification but is nevertheless felt. 'It is this excess, explored through the terms of affect, that I study ethnographically in this book' (18). The terminology echoes Stewart (who is quoted), as well as Deleuze and Massumi. But affect is also differentiated and pluralized, and (in my terms) equivalent to emotion, mood, impulse, feeling, sentiment, even disposition or expressive act – as in the awkward formula: 'an affect of thanksgiving to Turkey, as well as one of independence' (93). Sometimes the equivalence

218

is explicit, undermining claims to originality. 'Administration, I argue, evokes a complex spectrum of affect. In northern Cyprus, this is experienced through seemingly opposed emotions: Turkish-Cypriots feel desire for and apathy toward their state administration at the same time ... This is a study of affective civil service or of bureaucracy as an emotive domain' (82). A different kind of ethnographic approach might usefully distinguish between a reigning office ethos, personal dispositions, background moods, and fleeting emotional episodes. But no interactional episodes are presented through which such distinctions could be explored. We are stuck with the single word 'affect' as, variously, the precursor, elicitor, vehicle, or equivalent of emotion; or else as something undefined and altogether different.

What, then, are the 'terms of affect'? Affect becomes 'qualified' through human interaction with the environment; which is presumably why affects (plural) can be labelled and distinguished with familiar emotion words like 'anxiety' and 'sadness' that respond to varying context, as well as with words for dispositions or attitudes such as 'irony' and 'cynicism', or affective tendencies like 'irritability' – to use a more conventional terminology. Navaro-Yashin only develops the notion of 'qualification' (via a discussion of Tarde) at the end the book, and links it obscurely to metaphor; but it serves to recover areas of emotion and subjectivity that her favoured theorists exclude. What the left hand takes away, the right hand gives back.

Nonetheless, we are very far from what an anthropology of emotion – or an emotionally-alive anthropology – would require. We do not see people interacting with one another, quarrelling, at play, in anger or in love; nor do we know what they are like or how they act. Despite mention of an 'emotive domain' – whatever that may be – there are no accounts of emotional scenes among people. It remains unclear whether this is because (1) the author's interest was limited to environment–person interactions or (2) affect is supposed mainly to occur in impersonal transactions (though, following the cultural theorist

Perspectives

Teresa Brennan, she also speaks of 'transmission of affect' between persons). At any rate, the effect of the presentational focus is to animate objects and de-animate persons, who – except when they speak – become objects in the field like any other. Among believers, this would not necessarily be counted as a criticism, though from my point of view it highlights a limitation. Recourse to Actor Network Theory, one of the author's inspirations, justifies the exclusion of a vast range of experience and observations that might have cast a different light on the genuinely interesting problem she uncovers, namely, a deep ambivalence about identity, biography, place, history, and personal relations in the wake of partition.

A glance back at my summary of Russell's 'psychological construc-tionist' discussion of affect reveals some superficial similarities, which both authors would probably find surprising, coming at the problem, as they do, from opposite directions. In Russell's theory, undifferentiated 'core affect' (analogous to Navaro-Yashin's 'energy') becomes qualified through a process of attribution in response to the 'affective quality' of things, thoughts, and events. Core affect is distinguished from full-blown emotions (or 'meta-emotions') of the kind we call 'anger', and it may influence behaviour out of consciousness. Like many emotion theorists these days, Russell gives an interactional (or 'relational', in Navaro-Yashin's term) account of affective states in which the environ-ment, including other people, forms a necessary part of the account. The major differences from the alternative approach discussed here are in the psychological emphasis, the greater analytical precision, and the experimental methodology. As I say, the similarities are superficial, even coincidental; but since we are dealing with a shared term – a term trending among social scientists and cultural theorists – it is good to know what's what, and what isn't.

My chief concern, however, is to road test the affect concept. How does it work in the field? Does it open up new ground? Does it overlap with 'emotion' or have nothing to do with it? Does it require a different

Affect

approach to fieldwork? Is the 'turn to affect' a wrong turn, a chimera? Given an expertise and patience I lack, it would be possible to construct a genealogy of the concept – something that Leys (2011) has attempted with some success. The patient reader would be taken on the trail of Chinese whispers through Spinoza, Deleuze, Massumi (a Deleuze exponent), and Massumi's followers. Other branches of the genealogy would lead back through cultural critics like Sedgwick to the scientist Tomkins, whose psycho-biological account of emotion figured as a minor influence in an earlier period of anthropology (Chapter 4).

But the test of a tool is not whether it looks good on the drawing board or comes with the right credentials but whether it works. If a new concept turns out to be ineffective in the field, better discard it and get new tools, or do better with the old ones. Navaro-Yashin's book is extremely useful in this respect. It sets out its terms and conditions with admirable clarity, in contrast to some of the cited theorists, and it provides us with enough context to form a judgment.

Navaro-Yashin's approach to what she calls 'her material' is emphatically theory-driven and, in a way common with much recent ethnography, only loosely grounded. Her interpretations are suggested as much by her reading as by what her 'informants' say and do. (Use of the old distancing term 'informant' is revealing: there is little intimacy between ethnographer and subjects; many of the informants are anonymous and generic: an old woman, a Turkish settler, a government official, a Turkish-Cypriot.)

Theory-driven, how? 'Bataille's work might assist us in studying the energy discharged by ruins and rubbish' (150). Or: 'Through Kristeva, I am able to consider what the ruins, the rubbish, and the war remains in northern Cyprus stand for in the Turkish-Cypriots' subjective and internal psychical mechanisms' (150). Each static scene is viewed through a different theoretical lens – now Kristeva, now Benjamin, now Derrida, Deleuze, Guattari, Agamben, Brennan, Bataille, Latour, Butler, Freud, Thrift, Tarde. And with the same objective: Does

Perspectives

'my ethnographic material' fit the theory (or vice versa)? Would another theory work better? Can one have both, some, all? Shifted this way and that, the 'ethnographic material' only comes into focus through a specified optic. It does not live, but is inertly subjected to varied 'readings'; and where the material challenges, through not fitting, it is only to provoke some new compromise 'reading' or triangulation. Ethnography made subordinate to theoretical positioning.

Balancing Deleuze/Guattari with Benjamin requires nimble footwork: 'Yet I prefer to describe my ethnographic material – these prickly plants and wastelands – in terms of ruins, shards, rubble, and debris (à la Walter Benjamin's imagination) rather than the [Deleuzian] rhizome ... How would affect be theorized were we to work with the metaphor of the ruin rather than the rhizome?' (170–171) How indeed? How to pick your way among ruins both topographical and metaphorical? 'Thinking through my material from northern Cyprus', the author writes, now on a different tack, 'I agree with Latour that there is a need to attend to the centrality of objects in the making of politics' (162). I agree, too, up to a point. Walls, frontiers, and official forms have tangible effects that reinforce, sometimes exceed, their purpose. In another old formula – anathema in this context – the medium is the message. Who (of a certain age) has not shuddered at the telegram, unopened in its blue envelope? Or winced at the dentist's buzzer? Yet the effects of material things depend greatly on their non-material aspects – what the documents *say*, how the place-names signify, how the frontier separates, what the relics recall – and would seem logically to require human agency, a human context of invention and use. Emotions are not conceivable without people to experience them; and affect (new style), if it has any connection to affective states (old style) needs people too. In an oft-quoted declaration, the high priest of affect theory rejects any such link: 'emotion and affect – if affect is intensity – follow different logics and pertain to different orders' (Massumi 2002: 27). Yet even Spinoza, whose word is God in these matters, lists among 'affects' such recognizable emotions as joy, hatred, love, envy, and fear – and goes on to explore their logical structures, explaining how the 'passive affects' that lower our spirits may be mastered through reason. Which is why he is sometimes claimed as successor to the Stoics and precursor to cognitive theorists of emotion – at the opposite pole from contemporary affect theory (Calhoun & Solomon 1984; Nussbaum 2001).[3]

Let us accept that there are other takes on 'affect', alternative uses of the word in quite different systems of thought that include such acceptations as 'capacity to affect or be affected', 'potential', and 'becoming' (though it is not clear whether 'affect' is *defined* as these concepts or just related to them). Let us suppose, however, that despite the disavowals of hardliners, this other kind of affect, as it concerns us ethnographically, *is* connected with emotional phenomena. Navaro-Yashin, citing geographer Nigel Thrift, thinks so, even if she wants to have it both ways: 'Affect does refer, broadly, to an emotive domain, but its scope goes far beyond that of human subjectivity or the self' (167). Following Latour, Navaro-Yashin wishes to 'redistrib[ute] subjective quality *outside*' (167, original emphasis). Objects, on this view, can be said to 'discharge affect'; likewise, affect 'can be studied in sites and spaces beyond the scope of the human subject, her subjectivity, or her psyche' (168).

In my world – the place where you and I meet – things need us to be able to generate affect. They can't do it on their own. At least, no one is

---

[3] It is possible that the difference senses of 'affect', and a source of confusion, derive from contrasting senses of Spinoza's Latin equivalents, as mediated through later interpreters. In Spinoza's ontology *affectio* ('affection') refers to 'modes of substance' or the 'modifications of bodies'. *Affectus* ('affect'), a term he uses much more frequently, refers to 'affections [i.e. modifications] of the body which diminish or increase the power of the body (affects of the body) and the ideas of such affections (affects of the mind)' (van Bunge et al. 2011, s.v. *affectio, affectus*). This is close to Frijda's notion of 'action readiness'. Or compare Calhoun & Solomon's (1984: 71) cognitive interpretation: 'Like the Stoics, [Spinoza] viewed emotions as a species of thoughts, albeit misguided thoughts.'

Perspectives

explicitly arguing that objects discharge affects among themselves, green walls making red walls sad, rusting cars feeling sorry for themselves. Yet to distribute affect (as it concerns the 'emotive domain') among material objects one would need to make such a claim, or at least attribute it to others. In fact, Navaro-Yashin's informants resist such projections. They are quite clear in talking about their feelings of unease as interior, using the term *maraz* for 'a state of mental depression, deep and inescapable sadness and unease', an 'inner lack of calm' (161), in contrast to the author who sees 'this melancholy not only as an expression of the inner worlds of my informants, but also as the mark of the energy (or affect, as I am calling it) discharged on them by the dwellings and environments they have now lived in for decades' (161).

We need not take people at their word, of course. It is hard to put feelings into words, hard sometimes to know what you are feeling, or why. And when you try, there is not much difference semantically between saying 'I feel bad inside prison walls' and 'prison makes me feel bad', unless you attribute malice to the brickwork. But the analytical leap to an animate geography – whether or not Cypriots think in such terms – is not warranted by the evidence. There *is* a malice in electrified fences and bristling walls, but only imaginatively.

The anthropological question – do Cypriots experience the landscape in the way the ethnographer does, fresh to the scene? – requires a fuller answer than Navaro-Yashin is able to give. She does pretty well in conveying the desolation, but can we tell *their* experiences from hers? 'The space through which we walked exuded a melancholy that I could feel intensely . . . the atmosphere discharged a feeling of the uncanny, a strange feeling derived, in this instance, out of a sense of impropriety, haunting, or an act of violation' (166–167). When informants' testimonies *are* quoted, they do not always support the 'reading' placed on them. An old Turkish-Cypriot woman, asked how she felt about living among ruins, says: 'No, I don't feel bad seeing them. I don't notice. We got used to these ruins' (155). The author comments: 'perhaps due to

224

this involvement [of her family in the making of the ruins], the affect generated by these ruins, which appeared like a shocking war zone to my eyes and senses, had been repressed and abjected over the years' (155). The woman's tale of initial unease, gradual familiarization, and eventual indifference hardly warrants the conclusion. An interpretive leap is required to fit the findings to Kristeva's theory of abjection.

I have pursued the argument of *The Make-Believe Space* to try to put my finger on where exactly in the economy of affect the non-emotional and non-human part company with the emotional and human (the 'emotive domain'). The strong claim is that objects 'exude' or 'discharge' affect, independently of human agency (or presence?) and 'beyond the scope of the human subject'. This seems difficult to substantiate. The weak claim, to which Navaro-Yashin retreats, is that 'neither the ruin in my ethnography nor the people who live around it are affective on their own or in their own right; rather they produce and transmit affect *relationally*' (172; author's italics). It is possible that, by 'relationally', the author means something like the bare 'associations' that arise between 'actants' in Actor Network Theory (Latour 2005), i.e. connection without presumption of a *social* relation. But more is explicitly entailed, including 'language and subjectivity'. In which case, the 'relational' claim is not very different from what emotion theorists have long argued. See, for example, Frijda (1986) on appraisal, Russell (2006) on 'affective quality', Burkitt (2014) on relational contexts, or Parkinson, Fischer and Manstead, who write: 'emotions are ways of aligning and realigning interpersonal and intergroup relations' (2005: 235). When Navaro-Yashin concludes: 'my material calls for a conceptual merging of affect and subjectivity' (172), you have to wonder why they needed to be pulled apart.

An object-oriented ethnography certainly offers a novel, if tightly cropped, perspective; but 'affect', in the revamped sense, casts a dim light. The affect paradigm excludes the shared life that is the strength of fieldwork, the possibility of human connection, and the source of so

Perspectives

many anthropological insights. Is it perhaps the latest instance of that turning away from ethnographic reality that facilitates theory but which, in the case of emotion, destroys its object? When I read Thrift's assertion that affect theory 'cleaves to an "inhuman" or "transhuman" framework in which individuals are generally understood as effects of the events to which their body parts (broadly understood) respond and in which they participate' (2004: 60), I concede that – marionette shows aside – this might well describe certain Melanesian thought-worlds (in an essay on urban affects, very much *not* his point), but it offers little to the man or woman in the field; in fact, it makes the deep engagement of fieldwork inconceivable. Clifford Geertz once contrasted exact scientific accounts with immersive interpretive ones as 'experience-distant' versus 'experience-near'. Without being scientific, much less exact, it is clear where on the scale affect theory lies.

Conclusion

'When I use a word,' Humpty Dumpty said, in rather a scornful tone, 'it means just what I choose it to mean – neither more nor less.'

'The question is,' said Alice, 'whether you can make words mean so many different things.'

'The question is,' said Humpty Dumpty, 'which is to be master – that's all.'

Lewis Carroll. Through the Looking Glass.

For affect theorists, emotions are putative properties of individual subjects, interior states that are expressible and available to consciousness. In an obsolete, cosily human world, emotions are experienced and shared by people. Affect theory, in contrast, belongs to that chilly poststructuralist world from which the human subject has been banished.

The affect/emotion divide, already wide enough in some disciplines to suggest a paradigm shift (though scarcely registered in analytic philosophy or the affective sciences), does not, however, map neatly onto established and emerging ways of doing anthropology. Why? Because nowhere has the conventional conception of emotion been more criticized. Over a period of twenty or thirty years, anthropologists have chipped away at the model, questioning the boundedness and fixity of 'the person', showing how emotions are mediated through discourse, at once framing encounters and pervading politics. In deconstructing Western concepts of emotion and exploring modes of relation in other cultures, anthropologists have already encroached on the territory annexed by 'affect' in other disciplines. We have, in several senses, *been there*. And this deep ethnographic engagement with other modes of being gives us a practical and comparative perspective on other lifeworlds that affect theory cannot match. Can we therefore do without 'affect'?

If the Alice-like disagreement over what 'affect' designates and how it might be made useful to anthropology is intriguing, its applications have so far not been encouraging. They mostly signal a retreat from ethnographic precision and a loss of analytic power. Unresolved problems with constructionist, evolutionist, and phenomenological approaches to emotion have created a hunger for a theoretical messiah. But as the new paradigm stubbornly refuses to take shape a definitional fog has settled over the ethnographic terrain, blurring outlines, reducing vision, turning everything grey. In the new climate, the people we struggle to understand across cultural divides seem remoter than ever. At risk is anthropology's greatest asset: news from the frontline, the field in all its unsettling strangeness, its spikiness and vigour.

NINE

Concepts, Words, Feelings

Doesn't the terminology affect the emotion in any case? Shouldn't I have just said *je t'aime* (and who's to say I wouldn't have been telling the truth)? Naming can lead to making.

Metroland, Julian Barnes

Like the other human sciences, anthropology moves with – or a beat behind – the times. Questions that obsess one generation fade with the next; not because they have been answered but because the questions themselves change and key terms accrue new meanings – witness 'affect'. Some problems, perhaps the hardest, remain unsolved and anyone coming fresh on the scene is forced to go back to them, from the other side of the hill, as it were. Anthropologists are forever 'rethinking' kinship, morality, religion . . .

One particular problem, a real mountain, has to do with meaning: in our case emotional meaning; that is, the meaning (in various senses) of the events we call emotions and the meaning of the words we use to denote them. In approaching this many-sided problem, it would seem sensible to start with the current wisdom – at least, as anthropologists see it – sketching the state of the art, and then work back omnisciently to past errors. But if you want to do more than rearrange ethnographic snippets in a comparative anthropology of emotion, and especially if you want to understand why there isn't a state of the art anyway, much better retrace your steps and go back to square one. My task in this chapter is not the genealogical one of showing how we got to where we are now, wherever that is, but to examine critically – and rather unhistorically, as if they were our contemporaries – some foundational texts and theories about emotional meaning in the hope of better tackling those unsolved and presumed-solved problems. At least we can then aim for some clarity in our present uncertainty – or are better placed to undermine present certainties.

The following checklist serves as a reminder of aspects of emotional meaning covered in this book, leading into a discussion of what emotion words refer to, what they mean semantically, how they are used pragmatically, how they can be translated, and what to make of the 'gaps' and 'inconsistencies' in a given emotional lexicon. A persistent concern is the psychological reality of the emotions identified. What do linguistic and social science methods actually reveal?

The meaning of 'meaning'

Emotions can be said to possess, or involve, meanings in several respects, none of which can be ignored by the ethnographer.

(1) **As intentional mental states**. The meaning of emotions, in the sense of their intelligibility, derives in the first instance from their intentionality, their being *about* something (de Sousa 2014). This property is integral to the concept of anger, shame, etc., part of their semantic structure as well as part of an emotion's phenomenology – how it is experienced, what it feels like.

(2) **As comparisons**. 'Emotional meaning is mainly comparative', writes Ben Ze'ev (2010: 44). An emotional evaluation of a situation (in hope, defeat) corresponds to how things might be or might have been.

(3) **As appraisals**. Emotions respond to appraisals of situations relevant to personal well-being (Lazarus 1991). Their meaningfulness derives

Perspectives

from cognizance of 'core relational themes', sadness being a response to the appraisal of loss. Frijda's take on this idea is that 'each emotion corresponds to a different appraisal – a different *situational meaning structure* – and is characterized by it' (1986: 195; my italics). A property of situational meaning structures is that the experience of emotion appears 'objective' in that 'the subject experiences himself as being affected and passive in this regard: he does not confer meaning . . . In emotion, events carry their significance as inherent features' (Frijda 1986: 204). This point is important in gauging local understandings of emotional episodes, how people explain behaviour, motivation, and person–world relations.

(4) **As judgments** that shape our reality (Solomon 1993). Emotions are not merely interruptions in our experience of the world: they 'set it up' (Ratcliffe 2010). They are 'constitutive of our world' in the sense that things appear to us as *inviting, disgusting,* or *scary*; emotions determine in what respects and how much things matter to us. With his notion of judgment, Solomon introduces an element of agency and choice, whereas Frijda emphasizes the quasi-objectivity of emotions as passions, things that affect us, urges that move us to action.

(5) **As constituted in actions embedded in social relations**. In a larger sense that goes beyond semantics, 'the significance, meaning or social value of emotions is constituted in the pragmatic relations of social transaction', as Myers (1988) writes of the Australian Pintupi. Among tribal Pathans in Northwest Pakistan, the meanings of honour and shame are constituted in acts of hospitality and revenge, as well as in the organization of gender (Grima 2004).

(6) **As conceptual structures**. For each emotion word there is a conceptual structure, *a script*, which it is the ethnographer's task to discover. 'To know the meaning of a term like happiness, fear, or jealousy is to know a script for that emotion' (Russell 1991: 442).

(7) **As scenarios**. An emotion word evokes a prototypical scenario – the sick child that excites an Ifaluk's *fago*, 'compassion'; the offence to

an elder that epitomizes *song*, 'justified anger' (Lutz 1988). Emotion words are meaningful in terms of how people think about contexts, which is tied up with their ethnopsychology and 'worldview' (Lutz 1988: 157; White & Kirkpatrick 1985).

(8) **As discursive practices**. Emotion words are commentaries on social life that reflect and channel power plays (Lutz & Abu-Lughod 1990: 11).

(9) **As indices of inequality**. The significance of *emotionality* varies across time, cultures, and social categories, so that subalterns, women, children, the mentally ill, and colonized peoples have been regarded as more susceptible, less controlled, than men, grown-ups, and dominant groups (Dixon 2015; Matt & Stearns 2014).

(10) **As words standing for things**. In an older positivist psychology, anger and fear were discrete psychobiological events, facts of nature that the English vocabulary conveniently names. As most now recognize, what 'anger' refers to is far from obvious. As Jenefer Robinson puts it: 'explaining behavior by reference to ordinary language concepts for emotions – jealousy, envy, *amae, fago* – is making an after-the-fact cognitive evaluation in the terms of folk psychology, summarizing a particular emotion process, a particular sequence of events' (2004: 39).

(11) **As a product of categorization**. Conceptual Act Theory, a new variant of psychological constructionism, prioritizes the role of language in differentiating emotions – not just descriptively but constitutively, in interaction with bodily processes. Language constrains, *in the flow of events*, both the meaning and the phenomenology of emotion (Barrett 2017). Meaning arises in the act of categorization, which happens automatically, as a product of cumulated 'emotional' experiences and the predictive activity of the brain. The expansion of vocabulary enables nuances of discrimination and emotional *granularity*, the ability to experience, and to recognize in others, distinct instances of anger, irritation,

Perspectives

frustration, etc. (Barrett 2017: 106–107). Controversially, 'you need an emotion concept in order to experience or perceive the associated emotion ... Without a concept for "Fear", you cannot experience fear' (141).

The problem of reference

A distinction between what a word refers to and its larger significance or purport in an utterance has long figured in linguistic and philosophical discussions of meaning (Lyons 1977: chapter 7). The distinction, variously formulated, helps us think about what is entailed in emotion language. The meaning of 'disappointed' in 'I'm disappointed our team lost' is captured adequately in its dictionary definition: 'sad or displeased because someone or something has failed to fulfil one's hopes or expectations' (*Oxford Dictionary of English*). Its *reference* is unambiguous. Contextual or situated meaning, on the other hand, is more complicated and unpredictable. The *sense* of 'I'm disappointed in you' is quite different when said by a boss to an employee – implying a threat – and when spoken with irony or mild reproach among friends. To grasp situated meaning, and therefore practical implication – getting fired, the need for restitution or riposte – you need a grasp of context and intention, tone, mutual status, personal history, and conversational etiquette.

As James Wilce (2009) has emphasized, most linguistic and psychological accounts of emotion language are fixated on reference; but emotion words are less often used referentially, to identify or describe an emotion, than pragmatically, to strike an attitude or effect a change. Anthropology's signal contribution to emotion research has been to demonstrate that the passionate speaker has an agenda: to persuade, manipulate, or complain – as does the commentator on others' emotions (Lutz & Abu-Lughod 1990). Emotion talk, as a moral idiom (White 1990), is more often concerned with characterizing morally fraught situations than with describing mental states.

Concepts, Words, Feelings

Geoffrey White provides examples from the Pacific Islands where emotion words figure in a practice called 'disentangling', a talking-it-out form of conflict resolution in which events are rehearsed and relations readjusted 'through performative production of (new) emotional meanings' (2005: 250). Disentangling is unlike the heart-to-heart or *tête-à-tête* of Euro-American confessional – always a private matter – though it might serve a similar end. As is common in face-to-face societies, the aim is not straight talking or soul-baring (*face* being more important than *heart* or *tête*), but mutual accommodation, the necessity of going on and getting on.

As White argues, on Santa Isabel in the Solomon Islands, emotion talk is effective in repairing relations *because* it is indirect and ambiguous, enabling the reframing of events in terms acceptable to all parties (which is why, in Chapter 2, I compared it to Niha heart-speech). The 'sadness' and 'shame' 'rhetorically produced' in disentangling are not necessarily *felt* – that is not the concern; nor is feeling the key criterion of named emotions in many Pacific cultures. What is important is that the revised emotions, however rhetorical, insulate antagonists from the threatening implications of 'anger' – the starting point, the knot to be untangled. It would be a mistake to insist on a literal reference to felt emotion, or indeed to subjectivity, when the context is expressly public and performative, though presumably the performance depends on a shared understanding of what being 'sad' or 'angry' usually entails for the individual.

Despite the enormous differences between a stand-off in the Solomon Islands and a dose of office politics in the West, the framing of emotion talk as moral idiom is perhaps not that different. Other than in dictionaries, emotion words are not, for the most part, labels for entities but elements in a complex communication, a mini-drama played out in the mixed media of words, intonation, gesture, and expression. In speech and action, emotions are conveyed – and do their work – with or without naming: most are anonymous. Fishing for an abstract definition

233

Perspectives

in the field – asking what X or Y means – is too simple. Who's asking? Who's telling?

Nonetheless, emotion words must in some way refer, or they would not be much good for doing the other things. If they do *not* refer – or refer obscurely, as in the Niha hairy-heart expressions – there is still a presumption that they *do*, the 'reality' of the named emotion being part of the language game.

Semantic meaning: Indonesian examples

Semantic analyses aim to reveal knowledge and mapping of the putative domain of emotion language in a speech community, highlighting word-clusterings, agreement among speakers, and prototypicality (i.e. discovering which words count as the best examples of 'emotion'; 'anger' rating above 'curiosity' in English). In an ingenious variant of procedures, Karl Heider (1991, 2011) constructed constellation-like maps of Indonesian emotion words based on closeness of association. Words grouped by informants as near-synonyms are bunched closer together, while weaker equivalents lie further apart. Dense thickets of related words indicate areas of cultural interest.

Heider's contention is that the meaning of a term derives from its penumbra of synonyms. Contrasts in mapping reveal 'an important difference in the cultures of emotion: American English "love" is closer to "happiness," whereas the Indonesian equivalents are closer to "sadness"' (1991: 70). Heider draws on popular culture to illustrate these patterns, which he links functionally to social structural features, reflecting what Geertz called 'ethos' and the historian Stearns (2008) calls 'emotionology': the affective styles, norms and codes of a particular group in a given period. For example, in the cluster of terms for loss, words meaning 'missing' and 'yearning' are linked to the Minangkabau custom of *rantau*, spells of exile that young men take to seek their fortunes, away from the confining matrilineal household.

234

Concepts, Words, Feelings

Semantic studies of Indonesian emotion language have usually required speakers to sort words in relation to *perasaan hati* ('feelings of the heart/liver') (Fontaine et al. 2002; Heider 1991), as in 'Tell me instances of *perasaan hati*'. But this phrase – a presumed equivalent to 'emotion' – lacks the currency of the English word and is not widely accepted as a generic term for the emotions. According to Goddard (2001: 170), in Malay (the basis of Indonesian), *perasaan hati* 'designates feelings that are relatively longstanding, involve evaluation, and are directed toward another person (as opposed to transient or impersonal feelings such as *terkejut* "being startled" and *takut* "fear")'. Evidently, a category that excludes 'fear', one of the most prototypical English emotions, must be a very different creature. Put plainly, a domain of *perasaan hati* language is not a domain of emotion language.

The polyglot context adds a further complication. Outside the metropolitan centres, Indonesian is mostly spoken as a second language. Though fairly able in Indonesian, my Javanese companions were not confident about the usage of *perasaan hati*. Our cook thought it meant being considerate to others, 'like when you put out cakes when the cook arrives'. (Was this a prompt?) The chief's mother, who had been looking after her ailing son following his defeat in the mosque, said: 'It's when you show someone you care about them' – a sentiment of kith or kin. But as Javanese speakers they would not naturally use this term. Nor is there an equivalent to the generic 'emotion' in Javanese, though the language is rich in meta-emotional terms deriving from *rasa*, 'feeling'.

Variable usage adds yet another twist. As everywhere, some people use a narrower range of terms than others. When I presented a neighbour – a peanut trader who was 'aunt' to our children – with contrasting scenarios that would indicate 'annoyed', 'hate', 'dejected', 'jealous', 'envious', 'resentful' and 'disappointed', and which Javanese is well equipped to discriminate, she applied to most of them the same word: *bangkel*. As we went through the scenarios and I asked her how in each case one would feel, she found it odd, and oddly discomfiting, that her reply should be always the same, pausing longer with each example as if the differences in feeling, engagement, and circumstances eluded language. 'Ah, it's like having the same name for different children, Andrew!' she shrugged. Perhaps, in her restricted usage, there *is* a family resemblance between these different emotions that justifies a single label. But it was not one that others recognized.

Something of Aunt Jiah's consternation might be felt by an English speaker put on the spot over 'love'. A man might be said to love his children, peanut butter, and arguing, but nobody equates these sentiments; equally, it matters only to lexicographers that we use the same word for what are distinct affective dispositions: in my example it would hardly change things if they were differently named. Nor, when we speak of loving peanut butter or loving our children do we imagine these dispositions to be subtypes of 'love'. Word, concept, and affect are only loosely related.

Such inconsistencies in reference should give us pause when faced with neat, experimentally-derived semantic clusters – let alone the more florid pragmatic usages found in the wild. Does it matter that statistical groupings and cluster hierarchies miss the tactics of practical understanding and the flexibility, irony, indirection, and invention of actual usage? Only a detailed ethnographic example – such as follows in the next section – can really answer that question. The technical wizardry employed in semantic analyses distracts from the problem of ecological validity. The suspicion must be that the systematic form of enquiry confines and misrepresents the object. The tasks of pile sorting, rating for prototypicality, free listing, grouping by synonyms, and so forth, are remote from the improvisation of emotional discourse. Emotions are moving targets, not fixed entities. Words, meanings, actions, and emotions interact in ways quite different from reference to inert objects in the world. To capture this dynamism we need to turn from what people mean by words to what they do with them.

From semantics to pragmatics

Three decades on, the most influential linguistic study of emotion by an anthropologist remains Catherine Lutz's *Unnatural Emotions: Everyday Sentiments on a Micronesian Atoll and Their Challenge to Western Theory* (1988). Lutz's findings have become part of the received wisdom of cross-cultural research; her people, the Ifaluk, and their open-air emotions famous beyond the Pacific; her book a benchmark in cultural constructionism – a position nailed in its title. In thinking about how anthropologists might tackle emotion language, it remains the point of departure. In Chapter 5, I contrasted Lutz's interest in discourse and ideology with the narrative approach to emotion pursued in this book. Here my focus is linguistic meaning.

Lutz's publications from 1982 to 1990 (when she moved on to other pastures) traced the paradigm shift away from a concern with semantics and mental models that grew out of an older cognitive anthropology to pragmatics and the politics of everyday life. It is in the early (1982) semantic study of Ifaluk emotion words, however, that we find exemplified those stubborn methodological problems that persist in the later work, so there we must pause for a moment.

As a rule, ethnographers don't work with samples: they live with them. In social science jargon, participant-observation makes for low reliability (i.e. consistency) but high validity. In settings where total immersion is required, and blending in a priority, the introduction of formal instruments can be fraught with misunderstanding. The very idea of a formal sample – an unnatural section through the social body, like a biopsy – becomes problematic. It is never a 'slice of life'. Though ample for a population of 430 on an island covering half a square mile, Lutz's sample of thirteen was too small to rule out adventitious errors and inconsistencies of the Aunt Jiah kind. Other doubts emerge in the interpretation of results. After getting her informants to sort by similarity thirty-one emotion words written on index cards, Lutz asked them to explain why particular words

Perspectives

went together. She found that they grouped them according to situations of danger (e.g. *metagu* 'fear/anxiety'), connection and loss (e.g. *liyemam* 'longing', *fago* 'compassion/love/sadness'), good fortune, human error, and inability. This sorting into unnamed categories was not altogether surprising, for although Lutz's emphasis is on the cultural evaluations of situations and her argument emphasizes cultural relativity, the situations resemble the 'core relational themes' commonly identified as underlying all emotions. In fact, Ifaluk sort emotion words in ways similar to the semantic groupings of American English (Shaver et al. 1987). Oceans apart, but the cross-cultural differences seem smaller than the similarities.

What do semantic groupings of emotion words indicate?

The novelty of Lutz's analysis consists less in the groupings she derives than in the claim that Ifaluk define and organize a domain of emotion words by *situation*, whereas, for North Americans, 'the focus of perception in emotional situations is presumed to be primarily *internal*' (1982: 124). Put a bit differently: 'while Americans define emotions primarily as internal feeling states, the Ifaluk see the emotions as evoked in, and inseparable from, social activity' (124). We should not forget that *seeing* things a certain way, *defining* them, and giving *reasons* why they might belong together are distinct cognitive activities demanding varying degrees of reflection. The two perspectives – inward- and outward-looking – though sharply opposed in Lutz's account, could be seen as complementary. Indeed, it seems to be the case that Ifaluk emotion words *refer* to feeling states but are *defined* by situations. Or is that what the methodology requires? For Lutz arbitrarily delimits a 'domain of emotion words' in advance as a set of thirty-one terms that Ifaluk say are 'about our insides' – a formula mirroring the American folk concept of emotion, the very thing to be contrasted. The significant cross-cultural difference would then be restricted to the mode of definition.

Cited as an established fact in countless publications ever since, how much weight can this finding bear? It is worth reflecting for a moment on

238

Concepts, Words, Feelings

the oddity of the test for an Ifaluk, and reminding ourselves that in real life one *never* defines or sorts emotion words, though one might explain *why* one is angry. Reasons, of course, are not definitions; but pressed into this bizarre routine by a (literally) card-carrying cultural outsider, how else would you differentiate the words? In Lutz's case, as well as signalling cultural alienness, the artifice of the procedure highlights the outsider's inevitably limited knowledge of her companions, their personal histories, their language, and their speech practices. Her approach, in these circumstances, would tend to favour a situational answer because it invites a hypothetical explanation, a this-is-how-we-do-things-here response less likely to occur to an informant who is a fellow American.

Similarly, definitional abstraction invites formulations in which the impersonal *we* is the subject of the sentence. As Niha were apt to say with finality when I remarked on some practice: 'That's how *we* do it!' (which may be very different from how *you* do it). *Contra* Lutz (1988: 87–89), *we*- and *our*-forms do not require that emotions are shared, that the locus of emotion is collective, in contrast to Western psychology in which 'thought and emotion are taken to be the property of individuals' (56) (cf. Markus & Kitayama 1991). This is to mistake ideology for experience. An individual need not be an Individual.

Supposing, nevertheless, that Ifaluk *do* pay more attention to situations than introspective, ego-centred Americans do, as well they might. What does that demonstrate, apart from the sociability that consorts with a way of life premised on sharing? What are the implications for the conception and phenomenology of emotion? Once again, it is hard to know, since the process of opening something to inspection can change its nature. Self-report, the basis of much emotion research, can be problematic.

The practical diversity of usage

If the practical import of emotion categories and clusterings cannot be predicted from tests and definitions in the Ifaluk case, can we broaden

Perspectives

the sceptical critique to apply more generally? It may be instructive to compare Ifaluk with Javanese – two distantly related languages. Ifaluk group *metagu* 'fear/anxiety' with *lugumet* 'guilt/discomfort' and *ma* 'shame/embarrassment' because these words are used 'when one must go someplace where respectful behavior is required' (Lutz 1982: 116). Hildred Geertz (1959) identified a similar set of Javanese words linked to situations demanding respect (see Chapter 3). At least, that is how she frames them. But it is not obvious that Javanese themselves group *isin* 'shame/embarrassment', *wedi* 'fear', and *sungkan* 'reluctance' in this way, for there are other circumstances unrelated to respect in which those words are used. They are not like a spatula, whisk and rolling pin, grouped as 'kitchen tools' because that is all that they are. Like most emotion terms – indeed, like most emotions – they fit a variety of situations. People are *wedi* towards snakes as well as social superiors, *isin* among friends after a bad haircut as well as *isin* about their rustic dialect before a townsman, *sungkan* about joining a neighbour's work group as well as *sungkan* visiting VIPs after Ramadan.

Nor do such semantic groupings reflect the diverse phenomenology of emotion, the fact that embarrassment, reluctance, and fear (or their analogues) feel different and are differently embodied, even in similar situations; the *isin* felt after a social blunder being a sensation of surfaces, of burning face and tingling ears (so I was told); the *isin* that motivates avoidance when faced with a superior much more like *sungkan* – an awareness of posture, a shrinking or hanging back. Emotion words code not only culturally evaluated situations but diverse forms of engagement.

Consider – further afield – the Japanese word *haji*, which goes with a distinctive embodiment of shame-like emotion, in which the individual is painfully aware of 'self-exposure', an unwelcome display of the normally hidden self (Lebra 1983). To cope with the stressful experience of *haji*, or of the situation to which *haji* responds, Japanese manage their social lives so as to alternate between controlled, formal situations that soothingly minimize exposure of self (the tea ceremony) and informal events that liberatingly require it (after-hours drinking bouts with colleagues, communal bathing). A wedding gratifyingly combines the two, beginning with the tight formality of scripted toasts and ending with raucous singing and lewd jokes.

As these examples suggest, practical emotion merges with etiquette as a mode of managing encounters – configurations of persons and intentions from which meanings cannot simply be abstracted. Emotion language – if that is how we want to style it – is a key element in interpersonal adjustment depending on a flexibility of reference belied by semantic tests. As we saw in Chapter 3, in the close-packed, humming villages of Banyuwangi (Java), where boundaries and distinctions are scant, emotion serves as a compass, enabling villagers to feel their way without presuming on others or commiting *faux pas*. Emotion *language* figures in the plotting of moves and evasions, justifying entry or excusing withdrawal. It may also help conceptualize the gambit, especially if, as Lutz argues, an emotion word summons up a scenario, a script for the emotion. In the Javanese village, ambiguity of reference is tactically essential. Language ostensibly refers to a feeling while coding relation to a situation and justifying an action, allowing everyone to feel good, or at least neutral, about an encounter. Pragmatics and semantics cannot be sharply separated.

A generic category of emotion

All attempts to classify emotion terms face the issue of what larger categories such terms might belong to in a given language. The lack of a superordinate category of 'emotion' frustrates efforts at cross-cultural theorizing and threatens to derail the whole project of comparison, if not the very possibility of a theory of 'emotion'. In a landmark study of emotion categorization, the psychologist James Russell remarked: 'The possibility that [the concept of] emotion is not a recognized domain in

Perspectives

all cultures is perhaps the most important issue about emotion raised by the ethnographic record' (1991: 430).

It is an issue about which there is plenty of evidence. Tahitian, Utku, Javanese, Balinese, Niasan, and other Indonesian languages lack a translation equivalent of 'emotion'. In the Ifaluk case, it is unclear whether words that are 'about our insides' (*niferash*) are of a kind – a genuine folk category – and tantamount to a domain of emotion words, or whether the form of enquiry brings them into association. This empirical question masks trickier theoretical questions such as (1) whether emotion words form a coherent category in *any* language; (2) whether emotions themselves are a natural kind; and (3) whether there is a relation between (1) and (2).

Let's stick with the empirical question. We are told that Ifaluk see *song, metagu* etc. as 'coming from inside', consistent with their view that thoughts and desires originate in the gut, even if they explain *song* and *metagu* as having an external context and use these words pragmatically as a way of talking about situations (Lutz 1988: 95, 102). Grief is expressed in the phrase 'my gut is ripping' (99) – no ambiguity there. 'My insides are bad' means I am experiencing bad thoughts or feelings (92). 'Anger', in turn, is something to be suppressed (97), which would not be the case if it were purely a construal of situations or a mode of discourse. As in Java, unexpressed emotion is harmful: 'Both illness and unpleasant thoughts/emotions must "come out" in order to alleviate the trouble they can cause. In addition, emotion not expressed may cause illness' (100).

So an *internal reference* of emotion language has pragmatic, not merely psychological, implications. The force of the moral idiom – the voicing and effect of 'justified anger' – depends on the psychological reality, or at least the presumption of its reality. The words matter because of the feelings they trail; and the feelings matter because of the self-involvement implied. In this respect, the Ifaluk case fits rather than flouts Western psychological theory.

Concepts, Words, Feelings

Yet Lutz elects to 'treat emotion as an ideological practice rather than a thing to be discovered or an essence to be distilled' (4). Which seems to overstate the case. Does it have to be either/or, all or nothing? In emphasizing contextual meaning Lutz 'may be conflating sense with reference', suggests Russell. 'The sense of *song* [justified anger] can involve anger-inducing events and external relationships, although the reference of *song* is still an internal state' (1991: 445). If not, there is nothing about *song* that qualifies it as an emotion word. As Russell puts it, 'If *song* were a member of a class of words that, like *marriage* or *kinship*, referred to a relationship, then the reason for calling *song* an emotion word is unclear' (ibid.).

*

An audit of 'meaning' in the study of emotion has taken us through problems of reference, semantics, and pragmatics to the difficulties of formal testing in the field and extrapolation to real life, where meanings are more complex and inconsistent. In that shift from test results or conceptual analysis to actuality we feel most keenly the discrepancy between our own experience and the emotional world presented by the ethnographer, which is often forbidding or slippery in its sheer alienness. Well, you might say, *Vive la différence!* But the discrepancy raises the problem of credibility. Claims to radical alterity or incommensurability obviously undermine comparison and generalization, or else raise them to a level that once again loses the object in abstraction. What to make of those cases where 'sadness' or 'love' is 'lacking', or where the emotional spectrum is segmented in ways we cannot quite see? How can we approach emotional phenomena for which we have no words, or grasp words for which we have no common reference? One author more than any other has tackled this problem head on, the linguist Anna Wierzbicka. In the following sections I consider her comparative project in some detail, showing how it might apply to ethnography and how it might help in understanding the most intractable ethnographic cases. As

Perspectives

with the discussion of Lutz, my aim in analyzing Wierzbicka's work is not only to assess a key theoretical contribution, but to use it to explore general issues of meaning, practice, and reporting.

Anna Wierzbicka: Defining particulars by universals

Wierzbicka's vast and commodious project takes on, and arguably resolves, the relativists' paradox of comparing the incomparable. Like Lutz, she argues that 'emotion' belongs to a certain cultural tradition and cannot stand as a neutral scientific concept (1999, 2009). Linguistic relativity shakes the grounds for comparison: as a yardstick, we would do as well or as badly with Ifaluk *niferash* or Javanese *rasa*. But in order to compare emotion-like concepts found in other languages Wierzbicka has to assume that emotions, as 'cognitively-based feelings', are the common human lot.

Wierzbicka gets round this contradiction, at least to her own satisfaction, by an orderly yet catch-all approach that recognizes the polythetic nature of emotion classification and seeks the commonalities at a lower level. Wants, desires, feelings, and situations cohere in motley combinations named by emotion-like words that it is the job of linguists and social scientists to describe and explain:

The semantic question 'what does the English word *emotion* mean' is valid but is probably of limited interest to psychologists. From a more general (rather than purely semantic) point of view, the central question is not 'what emotions really are,' but how feelings are related in human lives with thinking and wanting, and also, with what happens in human bodies (brains, faces, and much else). (Wierzbicka 2009:10)

What characterizes emotion words and enables their comparison is not the kinds of situations they engage (the relational themes of Lazarus), or the predicaments they help constitute (the judgments of Solomon), or

244

Concepts, Words, Feelings

their position on a dimensional model, but their implicit conceptual structures. In a series of studies, Wierzbicka and her colleague Cliff Goddard worked out script-like definitions for an array of emotion words using 'linguistic primes', a set of sixty-three irreducible concepts (e.g. FEEL, THINK, GOOD, BAD, SOMEONE, DO, LIKE) represented in all languages that can be drawn upon to explicate the meaning of a given emotion word. This system of universal primes, printed in small capitals to distinguish them from vernacular terms, they call Natural Semantic Metalanguage (NSM). In principle, any word can be paraphrased using NSM, whether or not translation equivalents exist in the languages compared.

Why does this matter? For the first time, it gives us an explicit method to deconstruct, compare, and match language words and concepts across cultures – a Swiss Army knife to deal with any situation. Unfortunately, unlike that essential gadget, NSM does not make for easy handling. I will give just one example, not to stretch the reader's patience. As an aid, read the following script as a series of connected thoughts that convey the semantic shape of the emotion concept.

The NSM explication of English 'happy' goes as follows:

Happy (X was happy)

(a) X felt something (because X thought something)
(b) sometimes a person thinks:
(c) "some good things happened to me
(d) I wanted things like this to happen
(e) I don't want anything else now"
(f) when this person thinks this, this person feels something good
(g) X felt something like this

(Wierzbicka 1999: 52)

In contrast, *joy*, a stronger emotion, refers more emphatically to a current happening – 'something *very* good *is happening*'; it lacks the

Perspectives

self-referral 'to me'; and it lacks the component expressed in (e). In such manner, the method facilitates discriminations between near-synonyms while avoiding the circularity of dictionary definitions. 'Facilitates' is perhaps not quite the right word: set out in their curious stanzas, NSM scripts are hard to parse, though occasionally Wierzbicka puts them in handier form. Thus *'afraid* means, roughly, "feeling like a person does who thinks: something bad can happen to me, I don't want it to happen"' (305).

How does the method help us with the larger problem of making sense of emotional episodes abroad? We need to be clear about its limitations. Wierzbicka's theory is about the referential meaning of words; it is not about psychological processes – a theory of emotions – as her critics tend to forget (Izard 2010); nor is it about pragmatic implication or connotation (Quinn 2015). Her concern is not with what actually goes on in the organism (i.e. occurrent emotions), but with how people *conceive* of those disturbances that English speakers call 'emotions'. Her indictment of mainstream research is precisely that many psychologists, especially those wedded to basic emotions, have mistaken English-language concepts like *anger* and *fear* for psychological realities labelled by words that 'carve nature at its joints' (Wierzbicka 2010: 379).

Nevertheless, given the involvement of language in perception and subjective experience, some larger claims seem to be suggested.

(1) Set out as culture-independent definitions enabling translation of vernacular terms – etic models of emic concepts – the models are *also* held to represent prototypical scenarios embedded in cultural patterns or ways of life (1999: 15, 46, 284). There is plenty of evidence that supports this claim (e.g. Niha 'painful heart', Javanese 'shame', Utku 'anger', Ifaluk 'fear').

(2) With their premises and inferences, the definitions imply a series of logical steps, a mental sequence rather than a Gestalt. Explicitly, the scripts represent thoughts ('thinks like ...') in response to

Concepts, Words, Feelings

situations, the situation being part of the definition. In this they resemble some appraisal theories. Nevertheless, the avowed cognitive claim – untested, if profusely illustrated – is about concept-formation, not about the constitution of emotions (Niedenthal 2008: 591–592).

Feeling: What's in the black box

As we have seen, the NSM emotion-word scripts are formulaic, precise, and explicit – a brilliant aid, machine-tooled for translation. But wrapped inside each script is an enigma. The feeling element is left opaque ('feels like *this*'). There is no effort to capture the *qualia*, the subjective stirrings often taken to be the essence of emotion. You can no more imagine the feeling from the script than the taste of a dish from the recipe. According to circumstances, one either 'feels bad' or 'feels good'. Wierzbicka's contention is that – for communicative purposes – you cannot get inside the feeling; you can only point the way with a scenario and a thumbs up or down, or with a figurative comparison like 'I felt like I was walking on air.' Some psychologists likewise see 'phenomenological tone' as an 'unanalyzable primitive' (Oatley 1992: 86). Yet the bad feeling of guilt is, surely, different in more than situation and intensity from the bad feeling of annoyance. The jangled nerves of annoyance, the gnawing of guilt, the surge of love, the hot flush of shame, and the ache of regret are what characterize these feelings, peculiarities that dominate the experience and influence how we think of them and respond to their causes. (This is also a weakness of dimensional models of emotion with their gradients of pleasure and intensity.) Emotion metaphors – 'bursting with anger', 'heavy hearted' – are evidence that, as Lakoff and others have argued, 'metaphors show linguistic correlates of embodiment' (Lakoff 2016: 270). The 'warmth' of love and the 'simmering' of anger are rooted in the physiology of those emotions, even if there is no precise mapping of emotions onto bodily

Perspectives

states, and even if *love* and *anger* are Anglophone concepts, not universals. The skeletal NSM definitions are not enough to specify the feeling of what is felt. Which is one reason why you cannot back-translate from NSM scripts to vernacular emotion words. For *elation* (my example), 'feels good' + scenario will not do it; nor, for a non-English speaker, would 'walking on air'.

Wierzbicka's general claim is that while FEEL is a semantic primitive – a universal – 'emotion' is a complex, culture-specific concept, a term from ordinary English borrowed by psychology and roughly meaning 'feelings based on thoughts'. Lacking in many other linguistic traditions and poorly matched across European languages, emotion is unsuitable as a scientific concept; it cannot be used to explain other things when it requires explanation itself. *Feel* is more basic than *emotion* and cannot be explained by it, whereas a definition of *emotion* requires a feeling component (Wierzbicka 1999: 4–16). Yet, paradoxically, in order to identify feelings – the bedrock of comparison, the 'stepping stones' out of the hermeneutic circle (8) – we need the cumbersome apparatus of an emotion definition. If feeling is a black box, we need the scripts to suggest what's inside.

From script to narrative

I end this review of a major research programme with a brief look at how it complements the narrative approach espoused in this book, followed by some reflections on persisting puzzles that may account for the fact that its significance has not yet been fully realized in emotion studies generally.

Whether or not Wierzbicka would accept the designation 'narrative-like' for her models, I am not sure. It would not add anything to her theory, though it adds something to the narrative perspective on emotion I am trying to advance. The NSM method enables fine discrimination among analogous emotion words within and across languages. But

Concepts, Words, Feelings

what it does in addition is supply a skeleton key to emotional worlds, something that the fuller recitals of narrative proper can specify with greater precision. If NSM opens the door, narrative takes us inside. Naturally occurring emotions will have a more complex genesis and realization, a denser narrative weave than the script playlets through which we conceive them (supposing we do) in concepts like 'fear' and 'anger'. This bigger-scale complexity, however, is not amenable to experimental investigation, which controls for the very elements that comprise the experience and determine both subjective feel and social impact. For that very reason, triangulation – verification by alternative means – is ruled out. I cannot agree with Russell that 'the claims from the ethnographic method can be accepted only tentatively, until verified by other methods' (1991: 434). As anthropologists see it, the boot is on other foot.

Except for a few hostile critiques from within linguistics (Riemer 2006; Wawrzyniak 2010), commentaries on the NSM programme have tended to be vaguely appreciative or vaguely dismissive. Everyone struggles with the stanzas. Non-specialist readers – like this one – are awed by the scope of the project, quality of argumentation, and copious illustration, but puzzled by its cognitive implications and extra-curricular uses. Nonetheless, some of the criticisms seem off-target. I do not see the project as a simplistic attempt to 'reduce emotion definitions to different types of primitive feelings' (Mulligan and Scherer 2012: 345), but rather as a reduction to the common denominators capable of expressing a myriad scenarios – feelings themselves being ineffable. Which is fine so far as it goes. From standard bricks ornate baroque palaces can be built. What continues to perplex, however, is the question of psychological reality – or indeed *social* reality. Are the NSM scripts merely definitions, context-free tools for translation, or cultural models shared within a population? Are they presumed to run through the minds of natives experiencing or observing the emotion? If the 'lexicon suggests particular cognitive structures' (Wierzbicka 1994:

Perspectives

136), whose structures are they? Are the models operational (how to *fago*) as well as descriptive? In Geertz's formula, are they 'models *of*' or 'models *for*'? And if they are models *of* folk concepts, how come they all resemble in structure the generic English *emotion*, as if the blueprint as well as the bricks were universal?

*

As will be all too evident by now, we cannot make a clean distinction between emotions and emotion words and opt to talk about one to the exclusion of the other because language interacts with experience rather than simply labelling it. Attempts to handle aspects of emotion language separately or serially are quickly frustrated, try as we might. Frustrations aside, in the first part of this chapter we looked at conceptual issues, in what I hope is a logical order; in the latter part we considered two powerful and distinctive approaches to emotion language, those of Lutz and Wierzbicka. We are now in a stronger position to take up a challenge, one that occurs to anyone interested in what anthropology can tell us about emotion. The challenge is simple enough to state: Are emotions that are not named or otherwise formulated in a given culture nonetheless experienced? *Do the X have a word for it?* And if not, what then? This is more than a problem of translation. Such apparently trivial questions take us into the heart of the ethnographic encounter, testing the limits of cross-cultural understanding and empathy.

Categorization and hypocognition

We can learn a lot about emotional worlds from classifications and usages. But much escapes linguistic formulation. You don't need to be German to like *bratwurst,* nor to feel *Schadenfreude.* Pleasure in others' misfortune is a staple of gossip, an undercurrent of humour almost everywhere, not only in the wicked West. Categories delineate areas of

Concepts, Words, Feelings

cultural interest, but lack of a word does not mean lack of the emotion or the concept. Nor does having few words for a concept imply disinterest. Although the Indonesian word *malu* ('shame') refers to a culturally prominent emotion, it lacks the rich range of synonyms that cluster around *marah*, 'anger'. In Heider's emotion-word constellations *malu* is an outlier, a lone star (Heider 1991).

In some cases, however, a concept that would seem positively required by context is bizarrely lacking. A brief example – which is not centrally about emotion but quickly leads there – may illustrate. Until missionization, the Waorani of the Ecuadorian rainforest used to engage in long cycles of revenge killings (60 per cent of adult deaths were due to violence), but they have no explicit concept or verbal formulation for revenge, and it is difficult even to talk about revenge in the abstract (Boster, Yost, and Peeke 2003). When the Bible translators came to *Vengeance is Mine, I will repay, saith the Lord,* they were obliged to put an extraordinary circumlocution into the Lord's mouth: *Upon seeing people do bad things, I myself, who should be the one that judges and punishes on account of their bad deeds, shall, in turn, do enough to them that they will suffer* (ibid. 475). You might say that the unwieldy periphrasis needed to capture the pithy biblical phrase shows that vengeance cannot really be *thought* in Waorani: that nobody reading such a sentence could possibly get God's message, let alone apply His concept or do His will. Vengeance might be '*Mine*' but it cannot be *theirs*.

In fact, 'the Waorani did not need an abstract labeled category of "revenge" to either practice or explain vendetta, as all concerned shared a good understanding of the motives of allies and enemies alike' (ibid. 476). Only an external perspective on Waorani morality – that of Christianity – could necessitate an explicit concept in order to frame what had always been taken for granted. Instead of categorizing an act of *revenge* – the complex idea conveyed by the Bible translators – Waorani express retaliation by simple juxtaposition: 'Wëwä bewitched Äwä, he died. We killed Wëwä, he died' (472). Killings are explained narrowly, not

Perspectives

by a narrative of causes and consequences, but by an attribution of emotion ('anger'), which refers to a simple unvarying schema of offence. 'Because each emotion term indexes a shared understanding of what causes one to feel that way, further elaboration may be unnecessary.' In the small-scale, face-to-face Waorani world where everyone is known, personality descriptors are 'largely absent' and emotion terms few.

The authors draw a provocative conclusion: 'The observation, following the Gricean maxim of quantity ... that one need not make explicit that which everyone understands implicitly, helps explain the 'hypo-cognition' of personality and emotion among the Waorani' (Boster et al. 2003: 476). We name only what we need to distinguish. On this view, which links language and cognition tightly to function, breadth of psychological vocabulary is related to the *scale* of the society: a big society of varied human types in varied settings requires a richer set of distinctions to facilitate communication – a point relevant to my discussion below of another laconic forest people, the Chewong of Malaysia. As we shall see, this peaceful people – the mirror image of the Waorani – get by with hardly any psychological vocabulary at all.

Explaining the gaps: The Chewong

Lexicalization offers useful pointers to the researcher (Ogarkova 2013), but the 'gaps' need careful interpretation. It is perfectly possible to have a concept without having a word for it, as Wierzbicka's theory explains. Her thesis extends even to the shortlist of semantic primes. A word for FEEL, a component of all her emotion-word scripts, is reported absent by some ethnographers. Levy writes 'there is no Tahitian term for either "feelings" or "emotion"' (1973: 271). The task of constructing a typology of Tahitian emotions depends on other indications, such as reference to the 'intestines' or (post-missionization) the biblical 'heart' as the seat of the emotions.

Similarly, the Chewong – who lack both 'think' and 'feel' – do not say 'I feel fine', but 'my liver is good' (Howell 1981: 139). A Chewong version of the Beatles lyric, *She's in love with me and I feel fine* would go: *She likes me and my liver is good.* For Wierzbicka, such body-part phrases are not metaphorical (1999: 277–279). 'My liver is good' *means* 'I'm feeling good.'

Levy, who took emotions to be natural phenomena in cultural dress, introduced the notion of hyper-/hypocognition, where *hypercognition* refers to a cultural focus or cultivation of an emotion, and *hypocognition* its denial or de-emphasis (Levy 1984). Anger is the typical candidate for either treatment. Modern Europeans and North Americans, with their road rage and anger-management classes, hypercognize anger, deploring it for its harmful effects while valuing it for its air-clearing honesty. Anger is harnessed in protest and confrontation, finding voice in the political march, the Day of Rage, the Indignados. The tradition goes deep. As Aristotle first noted, sometimes when you suffer an offence it is right to be angry.

In striking contrast, among the Chewong: 'while it is recognized that anyone might experience anger at some time, and engage in a quarrel, most would not admit to having done so. I never witnessed a serious quarrel or observed anyone I would describe as angry' (Howell 1989: 54). In Levy's terms, they hypocognize anger.

Levy was concerned with the cognition of *specific* emotions. His general point is about the power of culture to shape nature. Cultural training overrides the natural impulse; a secondary appraisal eclipses the primary appraisal, the presumed universal reaction. Specific emotions, say anger or shame, can be cultivated, suppressed, or misrecognized. Levy espouses a moderate relativism that recognizes the distinctive profile of emotions in different places but leaves room for residues of the culturally unformulated in dreams, fantasies and unexpressed desires. But the Chewong example suggests a more radical difference, allowing us to take Levy's insight a step further.

Signe Howell, who lived with the Chewong, tells us that they withdraw from anger or aggression. People who are wronged, for example by marital infidelity, get depressed or ill rather than angry. They take 'an

Perspectives

extremely passive line', their 'livers are not good'. This is not just a matter of self-control but of avoiding emotions *generally*, whether positive or negative. Shunning strong emotions as 'potentially destructive', Chewong possess only seven words that might count as emotion terms.

This finding is arresting enough in itself without contemplating its broader significance (which we shall come to). By way of contrast, think of nineteenth-century German with its 573 heart-terms (Ots 1994), or Nias with its eighty-eight+ states of the heart. Recall the moralism of Ifaluk emotives, the verbal ballet of Java, or the Utku with their unspoken, deeply considered anger. So much is entailed by the breadth – and creative use – of an emotion lexicon: it is about much more than cognitive mapping and a naming of hearts.

Compared with these cases, what Howell limns in that leafy emotional desert is not just a different *emotional* world but a quite different way of being in the world. With apt understatement, she writes: 'The Chewong language is poor when it comes to expressing emotional or inner states' (1984: 35). But neither do Chewong attend to, or moralize about, 'outer' conditions, as the Ifaluk do in their discourse. In fact, emotional behaviour of any kind is scarcely to be observed. Interactions are undemonstrative, conflict and competition avoided. People do not greet, acknowledge, or help one another; they have an 'ideology of non-interference' or 'non-involvement' (1984: 38) – a crucial point, given that emotions, classically, require a sense of involvement.

Except for 'fear' and 'shyness', which are encouraged in children, 'most emotions commonly acknowledged in the West are suppressed' (209). (We note the absence while reserving judgment on the mechanism.) A battery of taboos prohibiting the anticipation of pleasure, 'the nursing of ungratified desires' (184), and the display of pain, might be held to imply that Chewong *do* register what we would call emotions, if minimally. But an effect of the 'rules' is to 'discourage emotionality' (1988: 148).

Even in the placid forest – we assume – situations of loss, frustration, disagreement, and attainment of goals must arise; but their

Concepts, Words, Feelings

contextualization in the chilled-out cosmos governed by supernatural sanctions means they are not defined in a way that would entail *emotional* appraisals. Which does rather call into question Wierzbicka's nettle-grasping conclusion that 'my liver is bad' = 'I feel bad'; or, granted her equation, that 'I feel bad' in Chewong means something resembling what *we* call an emotion, namely, the self-involved apprehension of a situation that entails a change in circumstances and a motivation to action. In this case, a minimal psychological vocabulary is not compensated in other ways. The gaps really are gaps.

What the Chewong – or their far-seeing ancestors, or cultural evolution – seem to have achieved is an ability to side-step the emotional entailments of everyday life, a feat that Javanese villagers can sometimes, exceptionally, pull off – though as an individual achievement informed by a philosophical psychology and long practice in self-discipline. *Not being involved*, whether wilfully or through habit, dissociation or shock, seems to be part of it. Not to feel one's concerns implicated is not to undergo the situationally relevant emotion; or, as Shweder (2004) puts it, not to *emotionalize* the situation.

What makes the Chewong case unusual, far-out even by low-key Javanese standards, is its (for them) normality. If Chewong are somewhere on the emotional spectrum, it must be at the dimly visible ultraviolet end. Hence, the *non*-Chewong feels bound to look for inarticulate or repressed emotion, hypocognition – whether justifiably or not, who can say?

Without greater narrative depth, which could add plausibility, we lack the detail required for firmer conclusions, conclusions that would contradict almost all emotion theories. (Once again, it needs stressing that lab methods, which remodel the circumstances – clearing the forest to pick out the tree – would exclude the possibility of radical difference.) Nonetheless, the interpretation sketched above might be felt to resonate beyond specific locations. In their *unemotionality*, what the bereaved Tahitian, the stoic Javanese ploughman, the humiliated headman, and the

Perspectives

Chewong forest people all seem to show is that nameless putative emotions need not be emotions at all; nor do such puzzling absences have to imply either repression or cover-up, the love or hate that dare not speak its name. What these cases propose is a different form of adapation of person to context, or – to attribute agency where habit is the likely driver – a difference in personal strategy, a capacity to disengage.

Could it be that the conventions of ethnographic reporting, which downplay the personal perspective in favour of group, habitus or cultural frame – the same format that discounts the personal dimension as a projection of Western ideology – simply miss the factors that comprise emotion? Maybe that Tahitian husband *was* sad in some discoverable sense and the ethnographer, bent on folk psychology, lost for words, failed to pick it up. Maybe the ploughman, bereft of his buffalo, was just putting on a brave face. If I didn't know him, I would say so. (But I didn't know him well enough – as a brother would know him – to *understand*.) Our theoretical training, as much as our unexamined assumptions, directs our interests and determines our blind spots. The ethnographer with a preconceived idea of what emotions are may be unreceptive to different ways of feeling and being, blunting the instrument of the self. Yet, on a practical level, the man or woman in the field still has to deal with fellow humans, work them out, learn their histories and foibles. If the seasoned fieldworker is puzzled, not merely fooled, we can be confident she has good reason.

What we make of ethnographic conundrums will therefore depend not so much on our grasp of ethnopsychology (a theoretical construction, fixed and generic), or semantic meaning (impersonal, cut-and-dried), but on a richer sense of the living context. Which is not – emphatically – another another plea for Geertzian thick description: Geertz too quickly reverts to cultural frames and human types (the stage-struck Balinese, the scheming Moroccan peddler) to illuminate emotion. No, this is a plea for deeper narrative, a dramatic engagement that is sensitive to inconsistencies of language use and that better captures human creativity and

Concepts, Words, Feelings

diversity in an unpredictable world: the unexpected being a factor in many emotion episodes.

Performing shame: A little charade

Space forbids extended illustration, so instead of going deep I shall stay shallow, ending this chapter – rather bathetically after the sensationally nonchalant Chewong – with one of those odd, unclassifiable, lab-proof moments that fieldwork throws up. The point of the example (which also exceeds its point) is to highlight several aspects to the theme of this chapter, language and emotion:

- the difficulty of assigning a precise meaning to an emotion word
- the ambiguity of usage and inference
- the pragmatics of naming
- the emotional framing of a scene
- the efficacy of narrative.

The scene is a dusty backyard in Bayu, a village in East Java; the time, a listless, warm afternoon in June. Ali, a village notable, plump and successful, had dropped by on his moped and was sitting on a bench with Bu Lurah, the headman's wife, watching with amusement their four-year-old grandson Erwin messing about in the yard. (He is the paternal grandfather, she the maternal grandmother.) After a while we heard the rumble of a soup vendor pushing his cart past the house and the chime that announced his wares. Ali drew a banknote from his pocket and dangled it temptingly, shouting, 'Here, lad. Go and buy some meatballs!' But the boy carried on playing, his back turned. To Ali's persistent offers Erwin just wriggled his shoulders and mouthed a rejectful *Emoh!* (Don't want to!). Still wearing his motorbike goggles and not a little ridiculous, Ali got up and followed the little boy round the yard holding out the money. It was a scene in which no one wanted a part. Leaning over the neighbouring fence, an aunt – there is always an

Perspectives

aunt – called out mockingly, 'It's because it's only five hundred rupiah; if it were a thousand, he'd take it!' Bu Lurah, who mostly looked after her grandson and was 'responsible for him', seemed embarrassed and irritated. 'Erwin *isin*', she called out to no one in particular: 'he's embarrassed', which was manifestly untrue. Ali laughed loudly, snatched up the boy and took him off on his moped.

Aside from its potential as a comedy of manners, this little drama illustrates in miniature the difficulties of reading an emotion into a situation, of connecting word and feeling in a straightforward manner. It is framed by the friendly, but slightly tense, relations between maternal and paternal grandparents. Kin through their grandson, they share pride in his achievements, but they are also in-laws and rivals for his affection. (In a curious back and forth kidnapping, the grannies had struggled for possession of the infant grandson.) As his main carer, Bu Lurah could not watch Erwin's display of rudeness without comment. But rather than embarrass his grandfather by correcting the boy and highlighting the snub, she excused him by attributing to him the socially acceptable, indeed praiseworthy, emotion of *isin*, shame/embarrassment. Reference to a socially oriented emotion, however unmerited, serves as a contrivance to enable relations to continue smoothly.

But perhaps even to put it in terms of feelings is to misconstrue the situation. For what is really happening in this scene is that Erwin's rudeness is being passed off, however feebly, as *delicacy*. Small, uncivilized children 'lack shame' and are 'not yet Javanese' (*durung jawa*). Having a sense of shame means, in most cases, simply knowing how to act with decorum, how to 'be Javanese'. Erwin, aged four, stands on that developmental threshold and, to his elders' embarrassment but not his own, he occasionally slips up.

Whether Javanese children learn these emotion words – if that is what they are – in the same way that they learn to discriminate other features of their environment, such as objects or aunts or actions, is a

Concepts, Words, Feelings

moot question. Surely much more is involved. But the fact that emotion words, in adult usage at least, refer to subjective experience as well as objective context, and to a complicated relation between the two, allows for considerable ambiguity and variety of conception. We cannot assume that children understand emotional practices – the display and naming of social emotions – as adults do; and the challenge to *our* understanding is less a matter of embodied differences in emotional development than of something about the constitution of emotions as complex, culturally mediated events. For a paradox frames the way Javanese adults refer to children's social emotions. On the one hand, small children are described as *isin* when they hide behind their mothers, or are tongue-tied before a stranger. On the other, children under five or six are said to lack a *sense* of *isin*.

I believe this folk theory registers the developmental threshold to which Paul Harris (1989) refers when he distinguishes between a child's capacity to experience a complex emotion like shame and his or her having an understanding of shame: of how it interlocks with others' expectations and emotions. As Javanese put it, small children can be or *feel isin*, but they do not yet possess (*nduwe*) *isin*. *Isin*, in the sense of proper social attitude and comportment, is acquired long after the relevant feeling, denoted by the same word. *Isin*, the feeling, develops naturally, spontaneously, through the routines of everyday life; *isin*, the behavioural pattern, must be coached, and therefore typically refers to situations when the child is not feeling *isin* at all. It takes a lot of practice to become Javanese.

Language is our first resource in getting a quick, if unreliable, understanding of what is going on in the field, emotionally-speaking. The second – equally indispensible, equally unreliable – is empathy, focus of the last substantive chapter of this book. Narrative helped with one; will it help with the other?

259

TEN

The Uses of Empathy

The excesses of 'behaviorism' can only be corrected by empathy.
(Bateson 1975: 146)

Outside science fiction, no one these days subscribes to hardcore behaviourism of the rats-in-mazes variety, though it still does occasional duty as a straw man in discussions of softer, humanistic approaches. Gregory Bateson, anthropological sage and grand theoretician, puts the B-word in scare quotes to distinguish a hypothetical type of materialist description, stuck on externals, that cuts out cultural context, intention, and subjectivity. Old-fashioned behaviourism may be dead, but there are lots of newer candidates for the role.

For the human scientist, Bateson writes, 'without identification of context, nothing can be understood. The observed action is utterly meaningless until it is classified as "play," "manipulation," or what not' (ibid.). In humanly constructed worlds – emotional worlds, let's say – everything that happens happens in quotes. Categorization, irony, implication, all depend on processes invisible to the white-coated observer. It follows that a grasp of what the other is about, what they intend, and what they understand demands that we go beyond appearances. 'Only by use of introspection, empathy, and shared cultural premises – the products of socialization – can anybody identify how context appears to another' (ibid. 146).

The Uses of Empathy

Empathy, on this view, is at the heart of sociality and therefore at the heart of ethnography. But Bateson the tough-minded scientist is careful to add a rider to the oracular epigraph that heads this chapter: 'but the hypotheses that empathy proposes must always be tested in the external world'. The risk, otherwise, is of projection, a facile attribution of our own thoughts and emotions to others based on an assumed similarity of context or an unthinking universalism. Like Geertz in his culturalist perspective on the person, and like Wittgenstein in his refutation of 'private language', Bateson wants to insist on the inter-subjective nature of meaning and its validation in the public sphere. Empathy depends on getting the contextual meaning right, the test of which is ethnographic.

Empathy denied: The relativist position

In contemporary anthropological discussions of emotion, the adversary of empathy is no longer behaviourism, or even 'behaviourism'. Other paradigms – evolutionary psychology, affect theory, social construction-ism – vie, in different ways, to diminish or pre-empt human agency and the capacity for reflexive experience in favour of inclusive fitness, non-human 'intensities', groupthink, or distributed personhood. One way or another, empathy loses out.

The antagonism can be sharp. One emotion-themed volume on South Asia, written in constructionism's heyday, hurls at empathy some of anthropology's worst insults. In his introduction, the editor writes: 'attempts to understand them [emotions] through empathy are no more than projections of one's own ideological assumptions about emotional reactions onto the Other ... These essays, then, reject empathy as a naïve and ethnocentric practice, a form of Western imperialism over the emotions of the Other' (Lynch 1990: 11, 17). As usually happens when ideology is assumed to exhaust experience, Lynch hollows out the human subject to a generalized, abstract Other. But abstractions do

Perspectives

not have emotions. The object of empathy slips away. An ethnographer concerned not only with understanding other worlds but with capturing their personal dimensions and internal diversity must preserve the tension between subjectivity and constraint that Bateson identifies. Which does not mean postulating an indivisible, transcendent actor who deals with the world on his or her (or its) own terms: there is no hiding place for the private self, no escape from the cultural embrace or the society of others. No, to maintain the subjective side of the equation requires little more than recognizing biographical difference and the particularity of experience, however culturally framed. An engagement with others, not Others.

Narrative empathy

To concede this point is to recommend a closer approach in ethnography, more involved than ethnopsychology or constructionism, more intimate than Geertz's (1983) 'experience-near' interpretivism that dealt, for the most part, in categories and symbols rather than actual lives. Constructionists and interpretivists alike were, in several senses, out of touch. In an early critique, John Leavitt faults them for '[losing] the feeling side of the phenomenon and reduc[ing] emotion to a kind of meaning' (1996: 522). Leavitt advocates an attunement to other modes of experience, recognizing that 'emotions are no more purely private than are acts of cognition' (529). Empathy, on this view, is not a mystical act of communion, much less a naive projection. To the experienced ethnographer, it becomes a research tool that engages the whole person and demands a different kind of reporting:

The translation of [exotic] emotions can seek to convey something of the feeling-tones as well as the meanings of emotions, using the shared affective system of ethnographer and readers as raw material. This means that ethnographers of affect must work on their feelings, modifying them to

The Uses of Empathy

model the emotional experiences of people of another society, and must recast this experience in language that can have a parallel effect on others in their home societies. (Leavitt 1996: 530)

Deep immersion entails a resocializing of the body – an embodied grasp of cultural codes – as well as a recognition of diverse intersubjectivities (shared emotions, porous personhood) and the distinctive scenarios defining locally construed emotions. The seasoned fieldworker comes to approximate, even share, the emotional experiences of her companions. (Wikan [1990], whose ethnography is based on this principle, calls it resonance.) Leavitt points out that field researchers – even those who deny it in theory – depend on such practical understanding. They connect. Whether they recognize it explicitly or seek to transmit it in their writings is of course another matter. Naturally, the sceptic can always retort, '*Understand*, fine, but at what level?' or 'How can you really know?' How indeed? Leavitt points to the readjustments that ethnographers habitually make to refine their understandings of more obviously cognitive realms like kinship classification. Why should the same not apply to emotion? Emotions, like word-meanings, are calibrated against social reality. Through trial and error you eventually get it right. Hence, 'the problem with empathy is not that it involves feeling but that it assumes that first impressions are true' (530).

I agree. The hazards of empathy are legion, but without it we have a very thin sort of understanding and no possibility of sharing lives. Yet the proof of connection – and the route to genuine understanding – is not to be found in the dubious fieldwork epiphany (a literary conceit) or in reflection on analogous experience, important though that is, but in correctly following the threads of an emotion episode, situating oneself, in fact or imagination, inside the hurly burly, the thick of it. I shall call this form of engaged understanding *narrative empathy* to distinguish it from intuitive or automatic empathy, whether that is based in biological universals or cultivated responses (which may, in turn, have a biological

Perspectives

basis in facial recognition modules and mirror neurons: what Stueber [2017] calls 'mechanisms of basic empathy'). In entering the stream we learn what it is to feel as others feel, if only imperfectly. At a minimum, we apprehend their emotions within the soft, moving structures of emotion episodes even if we do not share them.

Narrative empathy need not actually be *narrated*; but the following of a thread or joining of a current (choose your metaphor), the tracing of plots in emotion episodes, and the ability to respond appropriately in context all depend on a certain narrative capacity, a temporal, recursive linking of character, event, cause and consequence in narrative-like sequences (Carrithers 1992). Psychologists and philosophers have long recognized this (Bruner 1986, 1990; Goldie 2000; Oatley 2012), but not many anthropologists are prepared to sweat over the details; fewer still ponder how the confluence of person, history, and circumstance help constitute specific emotions.[1] And for various reasons – a fear of seeming unscientific or unprofessional; a simplistic view of emotions; the sheer difficulty of the task – few anthropologists trouble to work such things into their ethnographies. Easier to cut to the chase with a capsule event or linguistic analysis. Easier, indeed, to fudge the travails of discovery, the second life of fieldwork. For as Leavitt hints, to carry conviction, an account of others' emotional lives must touch on the sentimental education of the ethnographer. Ethnography in this mode merges with *Bildungsroman*.

The great fear, of course, is that ethnography will descend into confession or autobiography, a fear partially justified in the last thirty years. As readers, we are all embarrassed victims of too much information. (Cue conference joke: What did the postmodernist say to the informant? *Enough about you; let's talk about me!*) But the greater risk, more frequently exemplified, is that ethnographers have assumed what they cannot know; that others' emotions can be grasped, without

---

[1] On narratives of hope in an American hospital, see Mattingly 2010.

The Uses of Empathy

narrative empathy, on the basis of personal conviction, Human Nature, parallel lives, or empathy *tout court.*

The argument from experience

The point can be illustrated with Renato Rosaldo's essay, 'Grief and a headhunter's rage', 'the most celebrated work on affect of the last generation' (Johnson & Michaelsen 2008: 60). First published in 1984 and adapted as manifesto-like introduction to his book *Culture and Truth* (1989), Rosaldo's essay achieved many things. It called time on symbolic anthropology, junking the concept of culture as spectacle, web of meanings, or encrypted text. It renounced ritual as a lens through which to view social processes (standard since Durkheim), arguing that the unscripted emotions surrounding a death, the offstage comings and goings, tell us more than the organized show of a funeral. And it made a brave case for greater honesty about the researcher's personal limitations, developing the concept of positionality: the vantage afforded by age, education, and life experience that enables but also limits the fieldworker's understanding.

All these points were well taken. Around the same time, the *Writing Culture* collection (Clifford & Marcus 1986) lit a bonfire under ethnography, deconstructing its scientific claims, exposing its partiality. As one of the contributors and a fierce critic of his predecessors, Rosaldo fanned the flames. Especially among graduate students (of whom I was one), ultra-relativism tinged with world-weary scepticism became the new orthodoxy. Science was art, the 'field' an epistemological minefield, almost a no-go area. Which made Rosaldo's *post*-postmodernist recantation all the more arresting. For in his headhunting manifesto Rosaldo appealed to the common denominators of raw experience, the school of hard knocks. Against the disembodied, ghostly interpreter, the voice from the field issued a challenge that recalled Dr Johnson's

Perspectives

stone-kicking reply to the idealist: 'I refute it *thus*!' Here, in the theoretical whirlpool, was something like bedrock. Relativism had found its limits.

The crux of the argument, as every student knows, is that the tragic death of his wife in a fieldwork accident granted Rosaldo revelatory insight into the motivation of Ilongot headhunters. Having long struggled to interpret headhunting in symbolic terms, against his own raging grief homicidal violence suddenly made sense. The key was not to be found in arcane symbolism or the bloody calculus of the feud but in something much more basic. Experience amply and horribly confirmed Ilongot assertions that they go headhunting to work off the rage associated with bereavement. Anger was not merely a cultural pretext for violence, as he had assumed; it was the aftershock of loss (1989: 8–10).

Plainly, at a certain level, Rosaldo's thesis must be true. Experience shapes perception, the young cannot know what it is to be old, nor the tall the perspective of the short. To understand another's emotion we must have felt something like it ourselves, stood in their shoes. But the argument is self-limiting. For if common experience is necessary for ethnographic understanding, only the reader who has had a life like Rosaldo's will be capable of accepting his point. As the philosopher Peter Goldie (2000: 33) puts it, there are two senses of 'knowing what someone is feeling': recognizing the 'paradigmatic narrative structure' of an emotion, its typical action context and expression; and knowing what it is like to have that feeling. Rosaldo conflates the two.

The argument from experience is encapsulated in Rosaldo's notion of the 'positioned subject'. Crucially, part of the researcher's take on the world, her 'subject position', will be her affective make-up, the emotional resources and experiences she brings to the encounter. Positioning is synchronic – a matter of structure, status, and analogy – but liable to periodic updates. In Rosaldo's case, 'only after being repositioned through a devastating loss of my own could I better grasp that Ilongot

The Uses of Empathy

men mean precisely what they say when they describe the anger in bereavement as the source of their desire to cut off human heads' (3). What matters is not how one got to a certain point – the incidents of the story, all the things that make it personally significant for the individual involved – but one's having got there, the position and life stage attained. Narrative serves to reveal parallels between author and informants rather than to induce empathy or add temporal depth. Rosaldo is disarmingly explicit on this point. 'My use of personal experience serves as a vehicle for making the quality and intensity of the rage in Ilongot grief more readily accessible to readers than certain more detached modes of composition' (11). But if personal experience is useful in understanding others, its usefulness surely depends on relevance, closeness of fit; and relevance, in turn, depends on the historical particularities – in a word, the story.

Far from home, Rosaldo puts his faith in what he knows, or rather what he feels. It is shock that compels him to accept Ilongot statements. And rather than persuade us (a story persuades by revealing causes and connections), he batters us into submission. You thought emotions were cultural constructions? They are all about force: 'the emotional force of death', 'the force of anger in grief', 'the cultural force of rage', 'the cultural force of emotions'. Behind the battery of assertions different kinds of experience, different sorts of feeling are being equated, particularities erased. Some examples seem more like sorrow than rage. A man's conversion to Christianity following the death of his child is cited, improbably, as 'the force of the grieving man's desire to vent his rage' (5). Listeners to a taped lament – the old ways – seem to express sorrow, regret, and frustration, not rage; but 'rage' is Rosaldo's preferred term. Words are used to obscure rather than illuminate or discriminate experiences.

So why do they do it? The ideal of head-taking, the quest for vengeance, the thirst for fame, the taunts of peers, the fireside retellings of gory deeds, and the years of mourning prohibitions that Rosaldo recounts are among the pressures building the anger that slaughter releases. The

Perspectives

fact that these motives are culturally inspired, not rooted in personal trauma, makes them no less psychologically real; nor does it make them a culturalist's projection.[2] In contrast, the fixing of headhunters' rage in past grief (sometimes generations old) may be a cultural fiction, an alibi. The time-lag makes the explanation implausible. Rosaldo's tragic story does not readily translate to the Ilongot because their experiences are too different, the mechanisms linking grief with rage less direct. What his account reveals, by implication, is the need for an alternative approach: a building of character, circumstance, motivation, and action, all of which are conducive to narrative empathy. Getting the emotions right by getting the story right.

Narrative empathy, again

Around the same time, against the same theoretical foes, Unni Wikan published *Managing Turbulent Hearts: A Balinese Formula for Living* (1990), its zeitgeistlich title slipstreaming *The Managed Heart*, Hochschild's (1983) famous study of smiling air stewardesses. Like Rosaldo, Wikan explores the researcher's ambivalent positioning in the field and the possibility of knowing through feeling – the faculty of empathic understanding she calls resonance. Through her portrait of Suriati, a young Balinese woman, Wikan offers a person-centred perspective on Balinese life, grounded in biographical particulars and strikingly at odds with Geertz's (1973d) static, impersonal, theatrical model. Where Geertz had elegant spectacle, Wikan has backstage melodrama; where Geertz saw polished display, Wikan senses paranoia. Feelings must be 'managed' to present an unemotional, pleasing exterior that will allay resentment, for the Balinese heart harbours evil intentions that must be deflected. Fearful of witches, 'Balinese are perpetually preoccupied to

---

[2] For an Amazonian parallel and similar criticisms, see Robarchek & Robarchek (2005).

268

The Uses of Empathy

decipher each others' hidden hearts' (1990: 43). This is not just a darker view of Bali, but a shift from ideology to everyday encounters, from ritual-as-spectacle to Goffmanesque interaction rituals; a move that opens up unsuspected – though to Balinese, very much suspected – fears and horrors.

If Wikan achieves a rare empathy with her subject, she does so chiefly through narrative means, charting the ups and downs of their relationship as she worries about her friend's debts, offers motherly consolation over lost loves, and accompanies Suriati on tense formal visits to sip tea with dangerous aunts. With her emphasis on people's 'compelling concerns', and on situations rather than symbols, Wikan is well equipped to go after emotions, though her claims to rewrite the Balinese ethos are weakened by the atypicality of her heroine: Muslim, disconnected, urban, English-speaking, in a tightly-knit, agrarian, Hindu-majority society. Suryati's uniqueness gets in the way of what remains, at bottom, a generalizing project, an inversion of standard Bali, a dark side of the Geertzian moon: all sorcery and spite where Geertz is sweetness and light.

Evidently, in reporting emotional episodes, and in attributions of the culture-and-personality variety (which Wikan does not avoid), a balance has to be struck between specificity and typicality. Like Suriati, we are all incorrigibly ourselves in how we feel and act, but our differences are patterned and linked to broader social processes: therein lies the interest. To get the balance right, narrative empathy – which invests in individuals, and in the converging points of view of ethnographer and subject – needs to be sustained by a broader vision, perhaps closer to that of the Malinowskian/Firthian tradition, the contours of each portrait blending into the populous background.

Ethnography's limits and beyond

Where does that leave us? Rosaldo and Wikan brought into focus the interrelations among emotions, engagement in the field, and writing,

Perspectives

showing that what we feel, what we observe, and how we write are intimately connected. Both authors make an appeal to something like authenticity or emotional integrity that puts empathy at the heart of ethnographic understanding. Such an approach appears to place a tremendous burden on the ethnographer to follow through on the routine promise of contextual hi-fidelity. With markets, kinship, or rituals that's already tough; but emotional veracity demands much more.

Can it really be done? Yes, provided the ethnographer resists the urge to turn inward in confessional mode, or outward – away from the field reality – in quest of types and cases. Merging or mystical participation is a failure of empathy, which depends on a degree of separation, a recognition of difference. In fact, empathy is not strictly an emotion but a 'metacognitive ability' (Sherman & Haidt 2011: 250), a disposition to feel an emotion congruent with that of another person that depends on taking their perspective (Cuff et al. 2016). This arms' length apprehension is what permits empathy but blunts its stimulus and follow-through. Empathy is less than a *sharing* of emotion – a feeling of the same kind, force, and reason – because *I* am not quite in *your* position; nor do I have your history or the susceptibilities that got you there in the first place. I am not as irascible as you, but I can empathize with your fury at the parking ticket – even as I am tempted to laugh. This conception of empathy does not demand of the ethnographer a 'pretension to more-than-normal capacities for ego effacement and fellow feeling', as Geertz wrote dismissively (1983: 70). Nor does it require mind-reading of the kind that Evans-Pritchard dubbed 'if I were a horse' theorizing. All it needs is the ability to follow – and enter – a story, the better later to tell it. For which reason the burden is somewhat lighter than that imposed by Wikan and Rosaldo.

Given, also, the mark of separation needed in achieving 'empathic accuracy' (Cuff et al. 2016), we must look a little sceptically on fieldwork accounts that hinge on ethnographic communion, the epiphany

The Uses of Empathy

that illuminates and connects. The trials of fieldwork, epitomized by arrival and departure stories, seldom illuminate the emotional lives of our hosts (Briggs is, once again, the outstanding counter-example).[3] The ethnographer's feelings towards her companions have a shallow past, or their past is rooted in relations with other – quite different – people back home. To the extent that her emotions *do* enter the swim and make sense within others' lifeworlds they cannot readily be captured in conventional ethnographic description, which cuts and pastes between cases, abbreviating backstory and fencing off emotional hinterland. If she wants to write about emotion in the standard mode, she is faced with a dilemma: stick to her own case and admit the limitations of ethnographic reporting, or venture dangerously outside them.

But why respect the limits? The thrust of this book has been to take on board the lessons of other narrative genres. And if by reading between Rosaldo's lines one sees the alternative case – not for positionality, human nature, or analogous experience but for narrative empathy – why not pursue that course? Likewise, if the singular Suriati doesn't quite hit the spot, why not follow the intertwined lives of more typical, less micromanaged figures in the Balinese passion play?

I have argued that a convincing account of emotions – an emotionally alive anthropology – depends on an attention not just to cultural themes and social positions but to the fluctuating narrative context that is their temporal medium. Conventional ethnography has its rules and its disciplinary watchdogs; but if the comparative urge is resisted and the craving for generality checked – the rules of *disengagement* suspended – something can still be done, maybe something important. In this book I have drawn upon some older ethnographies that are rich in

---

[3] Other works that carry off this feat, mostly by adopting a strong narrative line, include Jackson (1989); Read (1965); Scheper-Hughes (1992); and Stoller & Olkes (1989).

Perspectives

narrative empathy and – recall Bateson's empirical test – proof of empathic accuracy. More recent examples, just as emotionally resonant but alert to the epistemological wobbles that, a generation ago, threw ethnography off its stride, are beginning to accumulate. James Staples (2014) has given us the life of a Tamil leprosy sufferer, the author retracing his friend's picaresque life-course, dogging his footsteps as they revisit old haunts: dusty railway stations, race tracks (the scene of gambling triumphs), and city streets where Das made a living as a porter; the leper colony where they first met. In roadside tea stalls and rackety train carriages Staples gets his pal to talk, letting him choose what he finds important, locating the milestones on his erratic journey. This is the ethnographer as *doppelgänger*: empathy enacted.

In *Witchcraft and a Life in the New South Africa* (2012) Isak Niehaus recounts the life and death of his longterm field assistant, Jimmy Mohale, a school teacher and AIDS victim who dies convinced he is the target of his father's sorcery. Jimmy himself sets the bounds to empathy. Visiting his friend for the last time, Niehaus asks if he can do anything for him and receives the reply, 'Sakkie, you cannot be both a player and a referee' (177). A painful predicament for the anthropologist: 'As his biographer, I was a referee who merely had to observe the contest between them [the brothers] and his father.' In the powerful scene of leave-taking that follows, the author conveys with affecting economy his own feelings as he struggles with the conjunction of lives, the tangle of violent, sometimes obscure emotions that fieldwork intrudes upon and opens up.

Both books exemplify the advantages of vernacular mastery and longterm biographical engagement, gains at once scientific and humanistic. As portraits they are affecting; but they have the authority of deep local knowledge and social know-how. Neither has a whiff of the confessional. Indeed, a fully achieved narrative attains a certain objectivity that allows the reader room for interpretation, the characters having a three-dimensionality denied to case studies and confessional

The Uses of Empathy

monologue alike. My own *After the Ancestors: An Anthropologist's Story* (2015) interweaves the story of a tribal feud with the story of fieldwork. Instead of a single biographical thread, it presents a set of evolving dramas and counterpointed voices within an ethnographic *Bildungsroman* whose narrator offers a point of view on the swirl of events: two years of a life, a life in two years. It bears emphasizing that the narrator/ protagonist in such examples is a constructed figure, a creature of fieldwork and text not to be confused with Little Me.

What these recent works attempt – and two, at least, achieve – is a view into other emotional worlds very different from our own but nonetheless comprehensible. The connection is made not through mind-reading, intuition, good vibrations, imported experiences, or even imagination, but through narrative engagement. It follows that the ethnographer's testimony, that of her subjects, *and* their conjoint experience can be shared by the reader. Empathy put to the ethnographic test and recreated on the page.

Self-evidence: Memoir and intimate ethnography

Empathy is difficult abroad, however necessary. But what of anthropologists working 'at home', as so many now do; surely *they* are on safer ground? Doesn't empathy, like charity, begin at home? Though the possibilities of mistaken empathy are diminished in that their pasts are closer to those of their hosts, their situation is not altogether different from that of the desert island ethnographer. They mostly operate outside their habitual circle, among farmers, factory hands, or stockbrokers: they are not really at home. And they are stuck with the same methodological strait-jacket: the descriptive summaries, analytical 'cases', and arguments that traduce emotion. Either that, or as their writing turns inwards and approaches autobiography or family biography, it ceases to do the things expected of ethnography, collapsing context into subject, becoming memoir.

Perspectives

Yet emotional insights can still be had, the self made relevant. In a moving discussion of the life history of her mother, a Polish Catholic caught up in the Holocaust, Barbara Rylko-Bauer introduces the notion of 'intimate ethnography, where the personal and the emotional suffuse the work at all levels' (2005: 12). The anthropologist's own relatives become informants and the mixed feelings called up by efforts to excavate life histories serve as clues to 'how social forces become embodied as individual experience' (Waterston & Rylko-Bauer 2006: 409). Linked essays by Philippe Bourgois (2005) and Alisse Waterston (2005) on similar themes probe the difficulties attending intimate ethnography: the complex negotiation of roles, the painful construction of a 'truthful' account. (Waterston [2013] has developed this approach at book length.) What legitimizes the projects is the authors' insider status as children of their informants, their *necessary* involvement in the reconstitution of personal history.

These diverse uses of the ethnographer's experience can be analyzed without resorting to prescriptive definitions or recipes for empathy. For the anthropologist, it hardly matters whether they count as textbook instances; what matters is whether the chosen frame is helpful or misleading in understanding others.

The pull of the universal

Empathy has no consistent meaning or application among anthropologists. Perhaps because it has largely gone untheorized, there is a consistent strain towards universalism. For some it is a matter of intuition, for others, a product of fellow feeling, 'resonance', countertransference, or a transcultural human condition (Davies & Spencer 2010). The universalist stance has been maintained despite overwhelming evidence of cultural diversity in the shaping of emotion and despite agreement that English psychological terms are inadequate to map such diversity.

The Uses of Empathy

A default relativist position in the analysis of *emotion* is thus contradicted by a default, if by no means unanimous, assumption of the fact and faculty of cross-cultural *empathy*. Which is surely odd, given that empathy and emotional recognition are so intimately related.

To be sure, universalists have gained support from recent work in neuropsychology, especially on mirror neurons, and from older work on mimicry and simulation (Heberlein & Atkinson 2009). We harmonize with others because we automatically simulate their emotions when we grasp their predicaments or perceive their expressions. Yet anthropologists are right to insist that emotional episodes are heavily coloured by cultural context, which makes cross-cultural empathy – the fieldworker's fix – doubly problematic. As the Mayan epic the *Popol Vuh* has it, in our fallen world the mirror of consciousness is clouded and there is no direct view into others' souls (Groark 2008).

It makes sense, therefore, to heed the scientists' distinction between automatic, pre-cultural empathic responses and slower cogitated responses that have to reckon with culturally-inflected intentional states: the clouded mirror. In analysing empathy in the field a moderate relativism is both scientifically justified and practically necessary. Yet, as noted, anthropologists exercising or ruminating on empathy tend to drop the relativist guard. Which rather implies a tacit reversion to the acceptance of emotions as natural kinds. If only we could get past the cultural overlay, we could all connect as citizens of the world! The utopian assumption is that we can identify common instances of an emotion, even across cultures, by reference to some set of essential characteristics, and that our emotions vibrate at the same frequency. Our anger tells us what the other is undergoing; our emotions become a source of information. Or else the headhunter's rage remains an inexplicable tantrum.

Sometimes a combination of reflexivity and universality can, indeed, be informative; in which case it is usually the *disparity* that

Perspectives

is telling. Jean Briggs writes: 'My own reactions to the situations in which I found myself – my empathy and my experience of contrasts between my feelings and those of my hosts – were all invaluable sources of data' (1970: 6). In other cases, the failure of empathy, or a discovery of its limits, points to a different patterning of emotion, a different 'emotion regime' (Reddy 1997). Christine Dureau, who worked in the Solomons, was unsettled by kindly meant words from a Simbo woman when her (Dureau's) daughter fell sick. It prompts her to observe that the 'fact of having children we loved did not grant me privileged understanding of Simbo mothers ... Against ... claims of experiential knowing, I became increasingly aware that with better understanding of women's lives I felt *deeper sympathy but less emotional congruence*, grasping *taru* ("love") as I recognised the relative superficiality of our similarities' (2012: 146; my italics). Against starkly different life chances, mother-love in the Solomons and the industrial West diverged enough to frustrate empathy. Likewise, Scheper-Hughes (1992) struggled with the fact that maternal love in a Brazilian slum did not extend to every dying infant. The refusal to weep for the child who 'wants to die' – a way of coping with poverty and deprivation – stirred her to construct a powerful critique of Brazilian society, in effect a political economy of emotion.

Studies that problematize the ethnographer's empathy are still rare, though a growing number of scholars have become interested in the phenomenon of empathy or its denial in other cultures – a quite different matter (Hollan & Throop 2011). More often the ethnographer's emotional insight is simply taken for granted as reward and proof of being there. Yet, as Leavitt wisely puts it, 'empathy, while perfectly real, is not an end to understanding but the beginning of the search' (1996: 530).

How to clear the clouded mirror and see into others' souls? Short of mystical illumination or paranoid delusion it cannot be done. But to grasp the other's predicament, read their intentions, follow their plots,

The Uses of Empathy

know – in that useful cliché – where they're coming from, we do not need special powers or X-ray specs. Deep immersion, shared experience, and a narrative grasp of intertwined lives will take us most of the way. After all, as Throop (2011) entertainingly informs us, even the sceptical folk of Yap, firm adherents of the opacity doctrine, feel the need to hold conversations back-to-back. Though they cannot know one another's minds, they know one another's stories.

Conclusion
Emotions and Narrative

A book about emotion by an anthropologist might take many forms: *Around the World in Eighty Cultures*; a survey of folk psychology; a close-up of 'anger' and its analogues; a dirge on the trials of fieldwork. Steering between the encyclopedic and the egocentric, macro and micro, I have explored the middle ground of social engagement – what the field reveals that the lab and the library cannot. I have tried to show how emotions shape and are shaped by social relations, how they do so with incredible diversity, and why they matter for anthropology. The major contention is that we can only recover the complexity and immediacy of emotional worlds by a change in ethnographic practice. A move to a more narratively-engaged ethnographic writing is at once a gain in realism and a gain in understanding; a move away, a double loss. Working through examples from classic ethnographies and my own fieldwork, adding in critical readings of innovative studies, I have tried at every stage to show how narrative can enhance and qualify the insights furnished by other approaches.

This is not a conventional textbook: panoramic, impartial, the view from nowhere. Like its theme, emotion, it springs from a particular vantage, offering a personal perspective, an appraisal, motivated and heartfelt, with a definite action tendency, namely, closer engagement. It presents an argument about the narrative structure of emotion and the need for a corresponding method in ethnography.

Conclusion

With this preamble, let me sum up how emotions implicate narrative, and vice versa; how they are made for each other. It will be clear by now that I am not just talking about narrative as *text*, the written ethnography, but about the structuring of emotions as construals of events.

In the cognitivist view, emotions are 'intentional'. One is not just angry, but angry *at* someone or *about* some state of affairs. Dissolve the object, alter the cognition, and the emotion vanishes. To be sure, a mere cognition does not imply much of a narrative. Simple emotions have simple objects. One is angry at having one's rattle removed. One fears the wolf. But most emotions – and especially those with moral content like pride and regret – have a more complex structure; threads in a weave of persons with histories in situations. This is the first sense in which emotions implicate narrative. Goldie and Nussbaum aside, few cognitivists (and fewer still theorists of other persuasions) allow much time-depth to the situational interpretation – of loss, danger, or opportunity. The cognitive package is small. For my purposes, however, it is enough to recognize that in the cognition one grasps a meaningful temporal sequence; and that, in the interesting cases, the sequence links persons in moral frames and reverberates with prior encounters and stories; that the swift narrative of contextual interpretation draws from deeper currents, stories within stories.

A second sense in which emotion implicates narrative is that people refer to hope, guilt, and shame to explain past and predict future behaviour. 'She felt gratitude for the gift.' 'He hung his head in shame.' 'Clear up the mess, your father will be angry!' An attributed emotion is like a chapter heading: we know, roughly, what follows. This is not only because emotion words encode scripts but also because, as Frijda has taught us, emotions comprise action tendencies.

A third connection points to the discursive role of emotion. Anthropologists have done most to show how emotions are manipulated in speech, performed for audiences, and used to persuade, evade, and dominate. Research in Pacific societies has revealed how emotion talk

Conclusion

provides an idiom for political activity, both as a tool of negotiation and as a reflection on political processes (Lutz & Abu-Lughod 1990; White & Kirkpatrick 1985). In Niha oratory we saw how heart idioms function as tactical levers in debate, winning concessions, and fending off demands. They make up a rhetoric of moral suasion rather than a folk psychology. Whether that disqualifies them as emotion words is another question. They are certainly enacted with passion; they provoke an emotional response; and they imply action tendencies, which is why they have rhetorical force. All of these tactical and performative uses of passion imply story-like structures and call, in turn, for narrative treatment.

A fourth connection derives from the patterning of social life. Michael Carrithers (1992) has eloquently shown how our capacity to operate across cultural boundaries, or indeed within them, depends on our skill at reading situations, grasping the plot, and recognizing – or constructing in turn – the narratives that give form to events. Emotions would qualify as a special, highly developed, instance of the capacity to construe form, motive, backstory, personal relevance, and consequence: whether in the snap judgment of a jealous glance or in the more deeply pondered apprehensions of love, hatred, and regret. Owing to their constitutive particularity, however, emotions are especially liable to misconstrual by outsiders; and, for this, detailed narrative is the only remedy. For the same reasons, by filling the gaps that synchronic analysis leaves as enigmas, narrative supplies a defence against the more extravagant claims of cultural relativism – the outlandish emotions that *could* exist in some parallel universe but in practice probably do not. (As the unemotional Chewong show, however, there are exceptions to the exceptions.)

Fifth, as thinkers going back to Aristotle have pointed out, narratives are mostly about emotion-eliciting situations, reversals of fortune (Bruner 1990; Oatley 2012).

Finally, and most importantly, emotions have a time-depth and a biographical resonance that elude synchronic analysis. A grasp of the narrative structure of emotion illuminates not only the tangle of pressures and constraints (those specific to individual characters, those that go with role) but also the possibilities inherent in the situation that the passionate person registers and weighs. A narrative account allows for the subjective experience of free will – however we want to qualify it – and the possibility of reflexive moral action.

None of these points depends on a theory of emotion, as such – the belief, for example, that there is a discrete domain of emotion in nature, or that certain emotions (anger, fear etc.) are natural kinds. The coherence of the concept of emotion, whether in science or folk psychology, is not really an issue for a narrativist, because the relevant units are broadly encompassing episodes, segments of life, not sharp-edged specimens under a microscope. It may be the case that, as Wierzbicka puts it, English does not carve nature at its joints. Yet, as she shows, descriptive definition, if not word-for-word translation, is always possible. And this possibility depends on deeper affinities that undercut linguistic relativism: for the elements of appraisal, feeling, and response do, in practice, tend to hang together, suggesting that emotion words are fuzzy categories with real-world correlates – as always, exceptions aside. The French concept of *sentiment* or the Javanese *rasa* – different in shape but overlapping in substance – could equally serve as starting-points for cross-cultural comparison. We can come at the problem from different angles. Nature's joints, as it turns out, are quite flexible. Even for the emotion-sceptic, culturally varying combinations of wants, feelings, cognitions and actions are no less susceptible to a narrative analysis (Shweder 2004).

But I would add that – whatever their status as cultural inventions, biological states, or constructed social roles – emotions are, by and large, unified *experiences*; and this subjective unity is due to their conceptual or narrative structure as construals of personal situations. We can leave the neuroscientists to quarrel over the milliseconds separating appraisal, visceral feedback, and action-readiness, and the order in which they

Conclusion

occur, rather as we marvel at physicists disputing the moments that follow the Big Bang. The anthropologist's job is to get the experience right and to work out its significance in the stream of life – to recover what Malinowski called the imponderabilia.

That effort will take account of local interpretations, representations, and genres, and of other modes of experience which may be non-verbal, non-narrative, embodied, tacit, or inarticulate (Csordas 1994, 2002; Desjarlais 1992). A sensitive and imaginative account will make something of these cultural differences without denying that people everywhere need to be able to read behaviour, fathom motives, assign significance, and apportion blame; that their emotions take shape within structured, unfolding situations linking persons and events. This is true whether the elements in play are you and me, we and they, ego and id, partible persons, the forces of production, the stars, the humours, or vengeful gods. And it remains true whether narrative looms large as epic, small as anecdote, or hides in accusations and one-word excuses (*'isin'*, 'he's embarrassed!'). For narrative is integral to human sociality. So too, of course, is emotion; and so, for that matter, is each to the other, since anger, hope, and regret are forms of explaining, predicting, judging, and relating. Whether we think in pictures or stories, resist or relish mind-reading, love or loathe anecdotes, we are all narrators because we all have emotions – and emotions tell their own story.

References

Abu-Lughod, Lila. 1986. *Veiled Sentiments: Honor and Poetry in a Bedouin Society*. Berkeley: University of California Press.

1993. *Writing Women's Worlds: Bedouin Stories*. Berkeley: University of California Press.

Anon. 1917. 'Die Erweckungsbewegung auf Nias'. *Berichte der Rheinischen Missions-Gesellschaft*, 7–10, 40–4, 173–174.

Averill, J. R. 1980. 'Emotion and anxiety: Sociocultural, biological, and psychological determinants', in A. Rorty (ed.) *Explaining Emotion*. Berkeley: University of California Press.

1994. 'In the eyes of the beholder', in P. Ekman & R. J. Davidson (eds.) *The Nature of Emotion: Fundamental Questions*. New York: Oxford University Press.

Barrett, Lisa Feldman. 2006. 'Emotions as natural kinds?' *Perspectives on Psychological Science*, 1: 28–58.

2012. 'Emotions are real'. *Emotion*, 12: 413–429.

2017. *How Emotions Are Made: The Secret Life of the Brain*. London: Macmillan.

Barrett, Lisa Feldman & James A. Russell (eds.). 2015. *The Psychological Construction of Emotion*. New York: The Guilford Press.

Barrett, L.F., B. Mesquita, K. Ochsner & J. Gross. 2007. 'The experience of emotion'. *Annual Review of Psychology,* 58: 373–403.

Bateson, Gregory. 1958 (1936). *Naven*. Stanford, CA: Stanford University Press.

1975. 'Some components of socialization for trance'. *Ethos*, 3: 143–155.

Bateson, Gregory & Margaret Mead. 1942. *Balinese Character: A Photographic Analysis*. New York: New York Academy of Sciences.

Bayley, John. 1966. *Tolstoy and the Novel*. London: Chatto & Windus.

Beatty, Andrew. 1992. *Society and Exchange in Nias*. Oxford: Oxford University Press.

References

1999. *Varieties of Javanese Religion: An Anthropological Account.* Cambridge: Cambridge University Press.

2002. 'Changing places: Relatives and relativism in Java'. *Journal of the Royal Anthropological Institute*, 8: 469–691.

2005a. 'Emotions in the field: What are we talking about?' *Journal of the Royal Anthropological Institute*, 11: 17–37.

2005b. 'Feeling your way in Java: An essay on society and emotion'. *Ethnos*, 70: 53–78.

2009. *A Shadow Falls: In the Heart of Java.* London: Faber & Faber.

2010. 'How did it feel for you? Emotion, narrative, and the limits of ethnography'. *American Anthropologist*, 112: 430–443.

2012. 'The tell-tale heart: Conversion and emotion in Nias'. *Ethnos*, 77: 1–26.

2013. 'Current work in anthropology: Reporting the field'. *Emotion Review*, 5 (4): 414–422.

2014. 'Anthropology and emotion'. (Malinowski Memorial Lecture) *Journal of the Royal Anthropological Institute*, 20: 545–563.

2015. *After the Ancestors: An Anthropologist's Story.* Cambridge: Cambridge University Press.

Bedford, Errol. 1984 (1957). 'Emotion', in Cheshire Calhoun and Robert C. Solomon (eds.) *What Is an Emotion: Classic Readings in Philosophical Psychology.* Oxford: Oxford University Press.

Ben-Ze'ev, Aaron. 2010. 'The thing called emotion', in Peter Goldie (ed.), *The Oxford Handbook of Philosophy of Emotion.* Oxford: Oxford University Press.

Benedict, Ruth. 1934. *Patterns of Culture.* Boston: Houghton Mifflin.

Bennett, Maxwell R., Daniel Dennett, Peter Hacker, & John Searle. 2009. *Neuroscience and Philosophy: Mind, Brain and Language.* New York: Columbia University Press.

Bennett, Maxwell R. & P. M. S. Hacker. 2003. *Philosophical Foundations of Neuroscience.* Oxford: Blackwell.

Besnier, Nico. 1990. 'Language and affect'. *Annual Review of Anthropology*, 19: 419–451.

Biehl, João, Byron Good, & Arthur Kleinman (eds.). 2007. *Subjectivity: Ethnographic Investigations.* Berkeley: University of California Press.

Blackman, Lisa & Couze Venn. 2010. 'Affect'. *Body & Society*, 16: 7–28.

Bloch, Maurice. 2012. *Anthropology and the Cognitive Challenge.* Cambridge: Cambridge University Press.

Boon, James A. 1977. *The Anthropological Romance of Bali 1597–1972.* Cambridge: Cambridge University Press.

Boster, James S., James Yost, & Catherine Peeke. 2003. 'Rage, revenge, and religion: Honest signaling of aggression and nonaggression in Waorani coalitional violence'. *Ethos*, 31: 471–494.

References

Bourgois, Philippe. 2005. 'Bringing the past into the present: Family narratives of Holocaust, exile, and diaspora'. *Anthropological Quarterly*, 78: 89–123.

Brennan, Teresa. 2004. *The Transmission of Affect*. Ithaca, NY: Cornell University Press.

Bromwich, David. 2017. 'In praise of ambiguity.' Review of *On Empson*, by Michael Wood. *New York Review of Books*, Oct. 26 issue.

Briggs, Jean. 1970. *Never in Anger: Portrait of an Eskimo Family*. Cambridge, MA: Harvard University Press.

1998. *Inuit Morality Play: The Emotional Education of a Three-Year-Old*. New Haven, CT: Yale University Press.

Brown, Lea. 2001. 'A grammar of Nias Selatan.' Unpublished PhD dissertation. Sydney University.

Bruner, Jerome. 1986. *Actual Minds, Possible Worlds*. Cambridge, MA: Harvard University Press.

1990. *Acts of Meaning*. Cambridge, MA: Harvard University Press.

Burkitt, Ian. 2014. *Emotions and Social Relations*. London & New York: Sage.

Calhoun, Cheshire. 2004. 'Subjectivity and emotion', in Robert C. Solomon (ed.) *Thinking about Feeling: Contemporary Philosophers on Emotions*. Oxford: Oxford University Press.

Calhoun, Cheshire & Robert C. Solomon (eds.). 1984. *What Is an Emotion? Classic Readings in Philosophical Psychology*. New York & Oxford: Oxford University Press.

Carr, David. 2001. 'Getting the story straight: Narrative and historical Knowledge', in Geoffrey Roberts (ed.) *The History and Narrative Reader*. London: Routledge.

Carrithers, Michael. 1992. *Why Humans Have Cultures: Explaining Anthropology and Social Diversity*. Oxford: Oxford University Press.

Charland, Louis C. 2009. 'Affect (philosophical perspectives)', in David Sander and Klaus R. Scherer (eds.) *The Oxford Companion to Emotion and the Affective Sciences*. Oxford: Oxford University Press.

Cohen, Anthony P. 1994. *Self Consciousness: An Alternative Anthropology of Identity*. London: Routledge.

Clifford, James & George Marcus (eds.). 1986. *Writing Culture: The Poetics and Politics of Ethnography*. Berkeley: University of California Press.

Clore, Gerald & Andrew Ortony. 2008. 'Appraisal theories: How cognition shapes affect into emotion', in M. Lewis, J. Haviland-Jones, & L. F. Barrett (eds.) *Handbook of Emotions*. New York & London: The Guilford Press.

Clough, Patricia T. 2007. 'Introduction', in Patricia T. Clough & Jean Halley (eds.) *The Affective Turn: Theorizing the Social*. Durham, NC: Duke University Press.

References

Conrad, Joseph. 2002 (1900). *Lord Jim*. Oxford: Oxford University Press.

Cornelius, Randolph R. 1996. *The Science of Emotion*. Upper Saddle River, NJ: Prentice-Hall.

Crapanzano, Vincent. 1980. *Tuhami: Portrait of a Moroccan*, Chicago: University of Chicago Press.

Crivelli, C., J. A. Russell, S. Jarillo, & J.-M. Fernández-Dols. 2017. 'Recognizing spontaneous facial expressions of emotion in a small-scale society of Papua New Guinea'. *Emotion*, 17 (2): 337–347.

Csordas, Thomas J. (ed.) 1994. *Embodiment and Experience*. Cambridge: Cambridge University Press.

   2002. *Body/Meaning/Healing*. London: Palgrave Macmillan.

Cuff, B. M. P., S. J. Brown, L. Taylor, & D. J. Howat. 2016. 'Empathy: A review of the concept'. *Emotion Review*, 8: 144–153.

Damasio, Antonio. 1999. *The Feeling of What Happens: Body, Emotion and the Making of Consciousness*. London: Heinemann.

   2003. *Looking for Spinoza: Joy, Sorrow, and the Feeling Brain*. New York: Harcourt, Brace & Co.

Darwin, Charles. 1965 (1872). *The Expression of the Emotions in Man and Animals*. Chicago: University of Chicago Press.

Davies, James & Dimitrina Spencer (eds.). 2010. *Emotions in the Field: The Psychology and Anthropology of Fieldwork Experience*. Stanford, CA.: Stanford University Press.

Desjarlais, Robert. 1992. *Body and Emotion: The Aesthetics of Illness and Healing in the Nepal Himalayas*. Philadelphia: University of Pennsylvania Press.

de Sousa, Ronald. 2014. 'Emotion', *The Stanford Encyclopedia of Philosophy,* Spring 2014 Edition (ed.) Edward N. Zalta, https://plato.stanford.edu/archives/spr2014/entries/emotion/.

Dixon, Thomas. 2003. *From Passions to Emotions: The Creation of a Secular Psychological Category*. Cambridge: Cambridge University Press.

   2012. '"Emotion": The history of a keyword in crisis'. *Emotion Review*, 4: 338–344.

   2015. *Weeping Britannia: Portrait of a Nation in Tears*. Oxford: Oxford University Press.

Duffy, Eamon. 2002. *The Voices of Morebath: Reformation and Rebellion in an English Village*. New Haven, CT: Yale University Press.

Dureau, Christine. 2012. 'Translating love'. *Ethos*, 40: 142–163.

Echols, John M. & Hassan Shadily. 1989. *Kamus Indonesia-Inggris*. 3rd edition. Jakarta: Gramedia.

Ekman, Paul. 1999. 'Basic emotions', in T. Dalgleish & M. Power (eds.). *Handbook of Cognition and Emotion*. New York: Wiley.

References

2003. *Emotions Revealed: Understanding Faces and Feelings*. London: Weidenfeld & Nicolson.

Ekman, Paul & Richard J. Davidson (eds.). 1994. *The Nature of Emotion: Fundamental Questions*. New York: Oxford University Press.

Epstein, A. L. 1992. *In the Midst of Life: Affect and Ideation in the World of the Tolai*. Berkeley: University of California Press.

Errington, J. Joseph. 1988. *Structure and Style in Javanese*. Philadelphia: University of Pennsylvania Press.

Fernández-Dols, J.-M. & C. Crivelli. 2013. 'Emotion and expression: Naturalistic studies'. *Emotion Review*, 5: 24–29.

Firth, Raymond. 1936. *We, the Tikopia*. London: Allen & Unwin.

1971. *Elements of Social Organization*. London: Routledge.

1985. 'Degrees of intelligibility', in Joanna Overing (ed.) *Reason and Morality*. ASA Monographs 24. London: Tavistock.

Fontaine, Johnny R., Klaus R. Scherer, & Cristina Soriano (eds.). 2013. *Components of Emotional Meaning: A Sourcebook*. Oxford: Oxford University Press.

Fontaine, Johnny R., Y. H. Poortinga, B. Setiadi, & S. Markam. 2002. 'Cognitive structure of emotion terms in Indonesia and the Netherlands'. *Cognition and Emotion* 16: 61–86.

Fridlund, A. J. 1994. *Human Facial Expression: An Evolutionary View*. San Diego, CA: Academic Press.

Frijda, Nico H. 1986. *The Emotions*. Cambridge: Cambridge University Press.

1994. 'Varieties of affect', in P. Ekman & R. Davidson (eds.) *The Nature of Emotion: Fundamental Questions*. New York: Oxford University Press.

2001 (1988). 'The laws of emotion', in W. Gerrod Parrott (ed.) *Emotions in Social Psychology*. Hove: Taylor & Francis.

2004. 'Emotions and action', in A. S. R. Manstead, N. H. Frijda, & A. Fischer (eds.) *Feelings and Emotions*. New York: Guilford Press.

2008. 'The psychologists' point of view', in M. Lewis, J. Haviland-Jones, & L. F. Barrett (eds.) *Handbook of Emotions*. New York & London: The Guilford Press.

Geertz, Clifford. 1960. *The Religion of Java*. Glencoe: The Free Press.

1973a. 'Ritual and social change: A Javanese example', in C. Geertz, *The Interpretation of Cultures*. New York: Basic Books.

1973b. 'The growth of culture and the evolution of mind', in C. Geertz, *The Interpretation of Cultures*. New York: Basic Books.

1973c. 'Notes on the Balinese cockfight', in C. Geertz, *The Interpretation of Cultures*. New York: Basic Books.

1973d. 'Person, time, and conduct in Bali', in C. Geertz, *The Interpretation of Cultures*. New York: Basic Books.

References

1983. 'From the native's point of view: On the nature of anthropological understanding', in C. Geertz, *Local Knowledge*. New York: Basic Books.

Geertz, Clifford & Hildred Geertz. 1975. *Kinship in Bali*. Chicago: Chicago University Press.

Geertz, Hildred. 1974 (1959). 'The vocabulary of emotion: A study of Javanese socialization processes', in R. A. LeVine (ed.), *Culture and Personality*, Chicago: Aldine.

1961. *The Javanese Family*. Glencoe: The Free Press.

Gellner, Ernest. 1985. *Relativism and the Social Sciences*. Cambridge: Cambridge University Press

Goddard, Cliff. 2001. '*Hati*: A key word in the Malay vocabulary of emotion', in J. Harkins & A. Wierzbicka (eds.) *Emotions in Crosslinguistic Perspective*. Berlin: Mouton de Gruyter.

Goldie, Peter. 2000. *The Emotions: A Philosophical Exploration*. Oxford: Clarendon Press.

2010. *The Oxford Handbook of Philosophy of Emotion*. Oxford: Oxford University Press.

Gombrich, E. H. 1982. 'The mask and the face: The perception of physiognomic likeness in life and in art', in E. H. Gombrich, *The Image and the Eye*. Oxford: Phaidon.

Gonda, J. 1952. *Sanskrit in Indonesia*. Nagpur: International Academy of Indian Culture.

Grandjean, Didier & Klaus R. Scherer. 2009. 'Syncronization (and emotion)', in David Sander & Klaus R. Scherer (eds.) *The Oxford Companion to Emotion and the Affective Sciences*. Oxford: Oxford University Press.

Greenblatt, Stephen. 2007. 'Hamlet in purgatory', in J. Biehl, B. Good, & A. Kleinman (eds.) *Subjectivity: Ethnographic Investigations*. University of California Press.

Gregg, Melissa & Gregory J. Seigworth. 2010. *The Affect Theory Reader*. Durham, NC: Duke University Press.

Grima, Benedicte. 2004. *The Performance of Emotion among Paxtun Women*. Karachi: Oxford University Press, Pakistan.

Griffiths, Paul E. 2004. 'Is emotion a natural kind?' in Robert C. Solomon (ed.), *Thinking about Feeling: Contemporary Philosophers on Emotions*. Oxford: Oxford University Press.

Groark, Kevin P. 2008. 'Social opacity and the dynamic of empathic in-sight among the Tzotzil Maya of Chiapas, Mexico'. *Ethos*, 36: 427–448.

Harré, Rom. 1986. 'Introduction', in Rom Harré (ed.), *The Social Construction of Emotions*. Oxford: Blackwell.

References

Harkness, S. & P. I. Kilbride. '1983. The socialization of affect'. *Ethos*, 11: 215–220.

Harris, Paul L. 1989. *Children and Emotion*. Oxford: Blackwell.

Hasan Ali. 2002. *Kamus bahasa daerah Using-Indonesia*. Banyuwangi: Pemerintah Kabupaten Banyuwangi.

Heberlein, Andrew A. & Anthony P. Atkinson. 2009. 'Neuroscientific evidence for simulation and shared subtrates in emotion recognition: Beyond faces'. *Emotion Review*, 1: 162–177.

Heider, Karl G. 1991. *Landscapes of Emotion: Mapping Three Cultures of Emotion in Indonesia*. Cambridge: Cambridge University Press.

2011. *The Cultural Context of Emotion: Folk Psychology in West Sumatra*. New York: Palgrave Macmillan.

Hemmings, Clare. 2005. 'Invoking affect: Cultural theory and the ontological turn'. *Cultural studies* 19: 548–567.

Herman, David. 2007. 'Introduction', in David Herman (ed.), *The Cambridge Companion to Narrative*. Cambridge: Cambridge University Press.

Hochschild, Arlie R. 1983. *The Managed Heart*. Berkeley: University of California Press.

Hollan, Douglas. 2001. 'Developments in person-centered ethnography', in C. Moore & H. Mathews (eds.) *The Psychology of Cultural Experience*. Cambridge: Cambridge University Press.

Hollan, Douglas W. & C. Jason Throop (eds.). 2011. *The Anthropology of Empathy: Experiencing the Lives of Others in Pacific Societies*. New York & Oxford: Berghahn.

Hollan, Douglas W. & Jane C. Wellenkamp. 1994. *Contentment and Suffering*. New York: Columbia University Press.

Horne, Elinor Clark. 1974. *Javanese–English Dictionary*. New Haven, CT: Yale University Press.

Howell, Signe. 1981. 'Rules not words', in Paul Heelas & Andrew Lock (eds.) *Indigenous Psychologies*. London: Academic Press.

1984. *Society and Cosmos: Chewong of Peninsula Malaysia*. Chicago: University of Chicago Press.

1988. 'From child to human: Chewong concepts of self', in G. Jahoda & I. M. Lewis (eds.) *Acquiring Culture: Cross Cultural Studies in Child Development*. London: Croom Helm.

1989. '"To be angry is not to be human, but to be fearful is": Chewong concepts of human nature', in Signe Howell & Roy Willis (eds.) *Societies at Peace: Anthropological Perspectives*.

Izard, Carroll E. 2010. 'More meanings and more questions for the term "emotion"'. *Emotion Review*, 2: 383–385.

References

Jackson, Michael. 1989. *Paths towards a Clearing: Radical Empiricism and Ethnographic Enquiry*. Bloomington: Indiana University Press.

James, Henry. 1972 (1884). 'The art of fiction', in J. E. Miller (ed.), *Theory of Fiction: Henry James*. Lincoln: University of Nebraska Press.

   1984 (1876). *Preface to Roderick Hudson*. In *Literary Criticism*. New York: The Library of America.

James, William. 1884. 'What is an emotion?' *Mind* 9: 188–205.

Jay, Robert T. 1969. *Javanese Villagers: Social Relations in Rural Modjokuto*. Cambridge, MA: MIT Press.

Johnson, David E. & Scott Michaelsen. 2008. *Anthropology's Wake: Attending to the End of Culture*. New York: Fordham University Press.

Kearney, Richard. 2002. *On Stories*. London: Routledge.

Keeler, Ward. 1983. 'Shame and stage fright in Java'. *Ethos*, 11: 152–165.

Keesing, Roger M. 1994. 'Radical cultural difference. Anthropology's myth?' In Martin Pütz (ed.), *Language Contact and Language Conflict*. Amsterdam: John Benjamins Publishing.

Kirmayer, L. 2000. 'Broken narratives: Clinical encounters and the poetics of illness experience', in Cheryl Mattingly & Linda Garro (eds), *Narrative and the Cultural Construction of Illness and Healing*. Berkeley: University of California Press.

Krause, Elizabeth L. 2010. Review of K. Stewart, *Ordinary Affects. Anthropology & Humanism*, 35: 128–129.

Kriele, Ed. 1927. 'The Nias revival'. *International Review of Missions*, 26 (61): 91–102.

Kuper, Adam. 1999. *Culture: The Anthropologists' Account*. Cambridge, MA: Harvard University Press.

Kuppens, Peter. 2015. 'It's about time: A special section on affect dynamics'. *Emotion Review*, 7: 397–400.

Lakoff, George. 2016. 'Language and emotion'. *Emotion Review*, 8: 269–273.

Lase, Apolonius. 2011. *Kamus li Niha. Nias-Indonesia*. Jakarta: Buku Kompas.

Laszczkowski, Mateusz & Madeleine Reeves (eds.). 2017. *Affective States: Entanglements, Suspensions, Suspicions*. Oxford: Berghahn.

Latour, Bruno. 2005. *Reassembling the Social*. Oxford: Oxford University Press.

Lazarus, Richard S. 1991. *Emotion and Adaptation*. New York: Oxford University Press.

   1994. 'The past and the present in emotion', in P. Ekman & R. Davidson (eds.) *The Nature of Emotion: Fundamental Questions*. New York: Oxford University Press.

Leach, E. R. 1966. 'Virgin birth'. *Proceedings of the Royal Anthropological Institute*, 1966: 39–49

References

Leavitt, John. 1996. 'Meaning and feeling in the anthropology of emotions'. *American Ethnologist*, 23: 514–539.

Lebra, Takie. 1983. 'Shame and guilt: A psychocultural view of the Japanese self'. *Ethos*, 11: 192–209.

Lévi-Strauss, Claude. 1962. *Totemism*. Trans. R. Needham. London: Merlin Press.

  1981. *The Naked Man. Introduction to a Science of Mythology*, 4. Trans. J. & D. Weightman. London: Jonathan Cape.

Leys, Ruth. 2011. 'The turn to affect: A critique'. *Critical inquiry*, 37: 434–472.

Levy, Robert I. 1973. *Tahitians: Mind and Experience in the Society Islands*. Chicago: University of Chicago Press.

  1984. 'Emotion, knowing, and culture', in R. A. Shweder & R. A. Levine (eds.) *Culture Theory: Essays on Mind, Self, and Emotion*. Cambridge: Cambridge University Press.

  1994. 'Person-centered anthropology', in Robert Borofsky (ed.), *Assessing Cultural Anthropology*. New York: McGraw-Hill.

Lutz, Catherine A. 1982. 'The domain of emotion words on Ifaluk'. *American Ethnologist*, 9: 113–128.

  1988. *Unnatural Emotions: Everyday Sentiments on a Micronesian Atoll and their Challenge to Western Theory*. Chicago: University of Chicago Press.

Lutz, Catherine & Lila Abu-Lughod (eds.). 1990. *Language and the Politics of Emotion*. Cambridge: Cambridge University Press.

Lynch, Owen M. 1990. 'The social construction of emotion in India', in O. M. Lynch (ed.), *Divine Passions: The Social Construction of Emotion in India*. Berkeley: University of California Press.

Lyons, John. 1977. *Semantics*, vol. 1. Cambridge: Cambridge University Press.

Malcolm, Janet. 2015. 'Dreams and Anna Karenina'. *New York Review of Books*, June 25 issue.

Malinowski, Bronislaw. 1922. *Argonauts of the Western Pacific*. London: Routledge.

  1926. *Crime and Custom in Savage Society*. New York: Harcourt, Brace.

  1929. *The Sexual Life of Savages in North-Western Melanesia*. London: Routledge.

Mandelstam, Nadezhda. 1970. *Hope against Hope: A Memoir*. Trans. Max Hayward. London: Collins & Harvill Press.

Manstead, A. S. R., Frijda, N. H., & Fischer, A. (eds.). 2004. *Feelings and Emotions*. New York: Guilford Press.

Markus H. R. & S. Kitayama. 1991. 'Culture and the self: Implications for cognition, emotion and motivation'. *Psychological Review*, 98: 224–253.

Martin, Emily. 2013. 'The potentiality of ethnography and the limits of Affect Theory'. *Current Anthropology*, 54, Supplement 7: 149–158.

References

Massumi, Brian. 2002. *Parables for the Virtual: Movement, Affect, Sensation.* Durham, NC: Duke University Press.

Matt, Susan J. 2011. 'Current emotion research in history'. *Emotion Review*, 3: 117–124.

Matt, Susan J. & Peter N. Stearns (eds.). 2014. *Doing Emotions History.* Urbana: University of Illinois Press.

Mattingly, Cheryl. 2010. *The Paradox of Hope: Journeys through a Clinical Borderland.* London, Berkeley: University of California Press.

Mead, Margaret. 1972 (1928). *Coming of Age in Samoa.* Harmondsworth: Penguin.
  1963 (1935). *Sex and Temperament in Three Primitive Societies.* London: William Morrow.

Mimica, Jadran (ed.). 2007. *Explorations in Psychoanalytic Ethnography.* Oxford: Berghahn.

Mink, Louis O. 2001. 'Narrative form as cognitive instrument', in Geoffrey Roberts (ed.) *The History and Narrative Reader.* London: Routledge.

Mulligan, K., & Scherer, K. R. 2012. 'Toward a working definition of emotion'. *Emotion Review*, 4: 345–357.

Musil, Robert. 1995. *The Man without Qualities.* Trans. Sophie Wilkins & Burton Pike. New York: Alfred A. Knopf.

Myers, Fred R. 1986. *Pintupi Country, Pintupi Self.* Berkeley: University of California Press.

Nabokov, Vladimir. 1981. *Lectures on Russian Literature.* Ed. F. Bowers. San Diego/New York: Harcourt Brace & Company.

Navaro-Yashin, Yael. 2009. 'Affective spaces, melancholic objects: Ruination and the production of anthropological knowledge'. *Journal of the Royal Anthropological Institute*, 15: 1–18.
  2012. *The Make-Believe Space: Affective Geography in a Postwar Polity.* London, Durham, NC: Duke University Press.

Needham, Rodney. 1975. 'Polythetic classification'. *Man* 10, 349–367.

Niedenthal, Paula M. 2008. 'Emotion concepts', in M. Lewis, J. Haviland-Jones & L. F. Barrett (eds.) *Handbook of Emotions.* New York and London: The Guilford Press.

Niehaus, Isak. 2012. *Witchcraft and a Life in the New South Africa.* Cambridge: Cambridge University Press.

Nussbaum, Martha C. 2001. *Upheavals of Thought: The Intelligence of Emotions.* Cambridge: Cambridge University Press.

Oatley, Keith. 1992. *Best Laid Schemes: The Psychology of Emotions.* Cambridge: Cambridge University Press.
  2012. *The Passionate Muse: Exploring Emotion in Stories.* Oxford: Oxford University Press.

References

Oatley, Keith & P. N. Johnson-Laird. 2014. 'Cognitive approaches to emotions'. *Trends in Cognitive Sciences*, 18 (3): 134–140.

Oatley, Keith, Dacher Keltner, & Jennifer M. Jenkins. 2006. *Understanding Emotions*. 2nd edition. Oxford: Blackwell.

Obeyesekere, Gananath. 1981. *Medusa's Hair: An Essay on Personal Symbols and Religious Experience*. Chicago: University of Chicago Press.

Ochs, Elinor. 1988. *Culture and Language Development: Language Acquisition and Language Socialization in a Samoan Village*. Cambridge: Cambridge University Press.

Ogarkova, Anna. 2013. 'Folk emotion concepts: Lexicalization of emotional experiences across languages and cultures', in Johnny R. J. Fontaine, Klaus R. Scherer, Cristina Soriano (eds.) *Components of Emotional Meaning: A Sourcebook*. Oxford: Oxford University Press.

Okely, Judith. 2012. *Anthropological Practice: Fieldwork and the Ethnographic Method*. Oxford: Berg.

Ots, T. 1994. 'The silenced body – the expressive *Leib*: On the dialectic of mind and life in Chinese cathartic healing', in T. Csordas (ed.), *Embodiment and Experience*. Cambridge: Cambridge University Press.

Papoulis, Constantina & Felicity Callard. 2010. 'Biology's gift: Interrogating the turn to affect'. *Body & Society*, 16: 29–56.

Parish, Steven M. 1994. *Moral Knowing in a Hindu Sacred City: An Exploration of Mind, Emotion, and Self*. New York: Columbia University Press.

Parkinson, Brian, Agneta H. Fischer, & Antony S. R. Manstead. 2005. *Emotions in Social Relations*. New York/Hove: Psychology Press.

Parr, Adrian (ed.). 2005. *The Deleuze Dictionary*. Edinburgh: Edinburgh University Press.

Parrott, W. Gerrod. 2001. 'The emotional experiences of envy and jealousy', in W. Gerrod Parrott (ed.), *Emotions in Social Psychology*. Hove: Taylor & Francis.

Pile, Steve. 2010. 'Emotions and affect in recent human geography'. *Transactions of the Institute of British Geographers*, 35: 5–20.

Pinker, Steven. 1997. *How the Mind Works*. New York & London: Norton.

Plamper, Jan. 2015. *The History of Emotions*. Oxford: Oxford University Press.

Pollock, Linda A. 1983. *Forgotten Children: Parent–Child Relations from 1500 to 1900*. Cambridge: Cambridge University Press.

Postert, Christian. 2012. 'Emotion in exchange: Situating Hmong depressed mood in social context'. *Ethos*, 40: 453–475.

Pugmire, David. 1998. *Rediscovering Emotion*. Edinburgh: Edinburgh University Press.

References

Quinn, Naomi. 2015 'A critique of Wierzbicka's theory of cultural scripts: The case of Ifaluk fago'. *Ethos*, 43: 165–186.

Radcliffe-Brown. A. R. 1922. *The Andaman Islanders*. Cambridge: Cambridge University Press.

Ratcliffe, Matthew. 2010. 'The phenomenology of mood and the meaning of life', in Peter Goldie (ed.) *The Oxford Handbook of Philosophy of Emotion*. Oxford: Oxford University Press.

Read, Kenneth E. 1965. *The High Valley*. New York: Charles Scribner's Sons.

Reddy, William. 1997. 'Against constructionism: The historical ethnography of Emotions'. *Current Anthropology*, 38: 327–351.

　　2001. *The Navigation of Feeling: A Framework for the History of Emotions*. Cambridge: Cambridge University Press.

Riemer, N., 2006. 'Reductive paraphrase and meaning: A critique of Wierzbickian Semantics'. *Linguistics and Philosophy*, 29: 347–379.

Robarchek, C. & C. Robarchek. 2005. 'Waorani grief and the witch-killer's rage: Worldview, emotion, and anthropological explanation'. *Ethos*, 33: 206–230.

Robbe-Grillet, Alain. 1965. *Jealousy*, tr. Richard Howard. New York: Grove Press.

Roberts, Robert C. 1988. 'What an emotion is: A sketch'. *The Philosophical Review*, 97: 183–209.

Robinson, Jenefer. 2004. 'Emotion: Biological fact or social construction?' In R. Solomon (ed.), *Thinking about Feeling: Contemporary Philosophers on Emotions*. Oxford: Oxford University Press.

　　2007. *Deeper than Reason: Emotion and Its Role in Literature, Music, and Art*. Oxford: Oxford University Press.

Robson, Stuart & Singgih Wibisono. 2002. *Javanese–English Dictionary*. Singapore: Periplus Editions.

Rosaldo, Michelle Z. 1980. *Knowledge and Passion: Ilongot Notions of Self and Social Life*. Cambridge: Cambridge University Press.

　　1984. 'Toward an anthropology of self and feeling', in R. A. Shweder & R. A. Levine (eds.) *Culture Theory: Essays on Mind, Self, and Emotion*. Cambridge: Cambridge University Press.

Rosaldo, Renato. 1989. 'Grief and a headhunter's rage: On the cultural force of emotions', in R. Rosaldo, *Culture and Truth*. Boston: Beacon Press.

Rosenberg, Daniel V. 1990. 'Language in the discourse of the emotions', in C. A. Lutz & L. Abu-Lughod (eds.) *Language and the Politics of Emotion*. Cambridge: Cambridge University Press.

Rosenwein, Barbara H. 2006. *Emotional Communities in the Early Middle Ages*. Ithaca, NY: Cornell University Press.

References

Rosi, Francesco. 2014 (1962). *Salvatore Giuliano*. DVD, including interviews with the director. Arrow Academy.

Russell, James A. 1991. 'Culture and the categorization of emotions'. *Psychological Bulletin*, 110: 426–450.

  1994. 'Is there universal recognition of emotion from facial expressions? A review of the cross-cultural studies'. *Psychological Bulletin*, 115: 102–141.

  2003. 'Core affect and the psychological construction of emotion'. *Psychological Review*, 110: 145–172.

  2009. 'Emotion, core affect, and psychological construction'. *Cognition and Emotion*, 23: 1259–1283.

Rylko-Bauer, Barbara. 2005. 'Lessons about humanity and survival from my mother and from the Holocaust'. *Anthropological Quarterly*, 78: 11–41.

Salovey, Peter, Christopher K. Hsee, & John D. Mayer. 2001. 'Emotional intelligence and the self-regulation of affect', in W. Gerrod Parrott (ed.), *Emotions in Social Psychology*. Hove: Taylor and Francis.

Sanjek, Roger. 1990. 'The secret life of fieldnotes', in Roger Sanjek (ed.), *Fieldnotes: The Makings of Anthropology*. Ithaca and London: Cornell University Press.

Sapir, Edward. 1994. *The Psychology of Culture*. Lectures reconstructed and edited by Judith T. Irvine. New York & Berlin: Mouton de Gruyter.

Scarantino, Andrea. 2012. 'How to define emotions scientifically'. *Emotion Review*, 4: 358–368.

Scheper-Hughes, Nancy. 1992. *Death without Weeping: The Violence of Everyday Life in Brazil*. Berkeley: University of California Press.

Scherer, Klaus R. 2004. 'Feelings integrate the central representation of appraisal-driven response organization in emotion', in A. S. R. Manstead, N. H. Frijda, & A. Fischer (eds.) *Feelings and Emotions*. New York: Guilford Press.

  2005. 'What are emotions? And how can they be measured?' *Social Science Information*, 44: 695–729.

  2009. 'Emotion definitions (psychological perspectives)', in David Sander & Klaus R. Scherer (eds.) *The Oxford Companion to Emotion and the Affective Sciences*. Oxford: Oxford University Press.

Scruton, Roger. 2014. *The Soul of the World*. Princeton, NJ: Princeton University Press.

Sherman, Gary D. & Jonathan Haidt. 2011. 'Cuteness and disgust: The humanizing and dehumanizing effects of emotion'. *Emotion Review*, 3: 245–251.

Schmidgall-Tellings, A. & Alan M. Stevens. 1981. *Contemporary Indonesian-English Dictionary*. Ohio University Press: Athens, Ohio.

Shaver, P., J. Schwartz, D. Kirson, & C. O'Connor. 1987. 'Emotion knowledge: Further exploration of a prototype approach'. *Journal of personality and social psychology*, 52: 1061–1086.

References

Shore, Bradd. 1996. *Culture in Mind: Cognition, Culture, and the Problem of Meaning*. Oxford: University Press.

Shweder, Richard A. 1994. '"You're not sick, you're just in love": Emotion as an interpretive system', in P. Ekman & R. Davidson (eds.) *The Nature of Emotion: Fundamental Questions*. New York: Oxford University Press.

2004. 'Deconstructing the emotions for the sake of comparative research', in A. S. R. Manstead, N. H. Frijda, & A. Fischer (eds.) *Feelings and Emotions*. New York: Guilford Press.

Sobo, E. J. 1996. 'The Jamaican body's role in emotional experience and sense perception: Feelings, hearts, minds, and nerves'. *Culture, Medicine and Psychiatry*, 20: 313–342.

Solomon, Robert C. 1980. 'Emotions and choice', in A. Rorty (ed.), *Explaining Emotions*. Berkeley: University of California Press..

1993 (1976). *The Passions: Emotions and the Meaning of Life*. 2nd edition. Indianapolis: Hackett.

1995. 'Some notes on emotion, "East and West"'. *Philosophy East and West*, 45: 171–202.

2004. 'Emotions, thoughts, and feelings: Emotions as engagements with the world', in R. Solomon (ed.) *Thinking about Feeling: Contemporary Philosophers on Emotions*. Oxford: Oxford University Press.

2008. 'The philosophy of emotions', in M. Lewis, J. Haviland-Jones, & L. F. Barrett (eds.) *Handbook of Emotions*. New York and London: The Guilford Press.

Stange, Paul. 1984. 'The logic of rasa in Java'. *Indonesia*, 38: 113–134.

Staples, David. 2008. Review of K. Stewart, *Ordinary Affects*. *American Ethnologist*, 35: 3047–3050.

Staples, James. 2014. *Leprosy and a Life in South India: Journeys with a Tamil Brahmin*. Lanham, MD: Lexington Books.

Stearns, Peter N. 2008. 'History of emotions: Issues of change and impact', in M. Lewis, J. M. Haviland-Jones, & L. F. Barrett (eds.) *Handbook of Emotions*. New York & London: Guildford Press.

Stewart, Kathleen. 2007. *Ordinary Affects*. London, Durham, NC: Duke University Press.

Stoller, Paul & Cheryl Olkes. 1989. *In Sorcery's Shadow: A Memoir of Apprenticeship among the Songhay of Niger*. Chicago: University of Chicago Press.

Stueber, Karsten. 2017/2008. 'Empathy', in Edward N. Zalta (ed.), The Stanford Encyclopedia of Philosophy https://plato.stanford.edu/archives/spr2017/entries/empathy/.

Sundermann, Heinrich. 1887. 'Die Psychologie des Niassers'. *Allgemeine Missions-Zeitschrift*, 14: 289–302.

1905. *Niassisch-Deutsches Wörterbuch*. Moers: J. W. Spaarmann.

References

Tallis, Raymond. 2011. *Aping Mankind: Neuromania, Darwinitis and the Misrepresentation of Humanity*. Durham: Acumen.

Thrift, Nigel. 2004. 'Intensities of feeling: Towards a spatial politics of affect'. *Geografiska Annaler*, 86B (1): 57–78.

Tolstoy, Leo. 1973 (1865–1868). *War and Peace*. Trans. Rosemary Edmonds. Harmondsworth: Penguin.

  1901 (1873–1877). *Anna Karenina*. Trans. Constance Garnett. London: William Heinemann.

Tomkins, Silvan S. 1984. 'Affect theory', in Klaus R. Scherer & Paul Ekman (eds.) *Approaches to Emotion*. Psychology Press: New York.

Turner, Victor W. 1957. *Schism and Continuity in an African Society*. Manchester: Manchester University Press.

  1981. 'Social dramas and stories about them', in W. J. T. Mitchell (ed.), *On Narrative*. Chicago: University of Chicago Press.

Van Bunge, W., H. Krop, P. Steenbakkers, & J. van de Ven (eds.). 2011. *The Bloomsbury Companion to Spinoza*. London: Bloomsbury.

Vogel, Shane. 2009. 'By the light of what comes after: Eventologies of the ordinary'. *Women & performance*, 19: 247–260.

Warner, Sara L. 2009. Review of K. Stewart, *Ordinary Affects*. *Feminist Theory* 10: 258–259

Waterston, Alisse. 2005. 'The story of my story: An anthropology of violence, dispossession, and diaspora'. *Anthropological Quarterly*, 78: 43–61

  2013. *My Father's Wars: Migration, Memory and the Violence of a Century*. London: Routledge.

Waterston, Alisse & Barbara Rylko-Bauer. 2006. 'Out of the shadows of history and memory: Personal family narratives in ethnographies of rediscovery'. *American Ethnologist*, 33: 397–412.

Wawrzyniak, J. K. 2010. 'Native speakers, mother tongues and natural semantic Metalanguages'. *Language Sciences*, 32: 648–670.

Weber, Max. 1968 (1922). *Economy and Society*. G. Roth & K. Wittich (eds.). New York: Bedminster.

Wetherell, Margaret. 2012. *Affect and Emotion: A New Social Science Understanding*. London: Sage.

White, Daniel. 2017. 'Affect: An introduction'. *Cultural Anthropology* 32: 175–180.

White, Geoffrey M. 1990. 'Moral discourse and the rhetoric of emotion', in C. Lutz & L. Abu-Lughod. *Language and the Politics of Emotion*. Cambridge: Cambridge University Press.

  1992. 'Ethnopsychology', in T. Schwartz, G. M. White, & C. A. Lutz (eds.) *New Directions in Psychological Anthropology*. Cambridge: Cambridge University Press.

References

2005. 'Emotive institutions', in Conerly Casey & Robert B. Edgerton (eds.) *A Companion to Psychological Anthropology*. Oxford: Blackwell.

White, Geoffrey M. & John Kirkpatrick (eds.). 1985. *Person, Self, and Experience: Exploring Pacific Ethnopsychologies*. Berkeley: University of California Press.

White, Hayden. 1981. 'The value of narrativity in the representation of reality', in W. J. T. Mitchell (ed.), *On Narrative*. Chicago: University of Chicago Press.

2001. 'The historical text as literary artifact', in Geoffrey Roberts (ed.), *The History and Narrative Reader*. London: Routledge.

Widen, Sherri C & James A. Russell. 2010. 'Descriptive and prescriptive definitions of emotion'. *Emotion Review*, 2: 377–378.

Wierzbicka, Anna. 1994. 'Emotion, language, and "cultural scripts"', in S. Kitayama & H. Markus (eds.) *Emotion and Culture: Empirical Studies of Mutual Influence*. Washington: American Psychological Association.

1999. *Emotions across Languages and Cultures: Diversity and Universals*. Cambridge: Cambridge University Press.

2009. 'Language and metalanguage: Key issues in emotion research'. *Emotion review*, 1: 3–14.

2010. 'On emotions and on definitions: A response to Izard'. *Emotion review*, 2: 379–380.

Wikan, Unni. 1990. *Managing Turbulent Hearts: A Balinese Formula for Living*. Chicago: Chicago University Press.

1992. 'Beyond the words: The power of resonance'. *American Ethnologist*, 19: 460–482.

Wilce, James M. 2009. *Language and Emotion*. Cambridge: Cambridge University Press.

Wittgenstein, L. 1953. *Philosophical Investigations*. Trans. G. E. M. Anscombe. Oxford: Basil Blackwell.

1967. *Zettel*. Trans. G .E .M. Anscombe. Oxford: Basil Blackwell.

Young, Michael W. 2004. *Malinowski: Odyssey of an Anthropologist, 1884–1920*. New Haven, CT: Yale University Press.

Zajonc, Robert. 1980. 'Feeling and thinking: Preferences need no inferences'. *American psychologist*, 35: 151–175.

Zoetmulder 1995. *Pantheism and Monism in Javanese Suluk literature: Islamic and Indian Mysticism in an Indonesian Setting*. Trans. M. C. Ricklefs. Leiden: KITLV Press.

Zweig, Stefan. 2011 (1939). *Beware of Pity*. Trans. Anthea Bell. London: Pushkin Press.

Index

A'ara (New Hebrides), 55
Abu-Lughod, Lila, 143–146
action tendencies, 36, 59, 83, 279
Actor Network Theory, 220, 225
affect, 72, *See also* core affect
  in anthropology, 198
  and cognition, 39
  definitions of, 198–199, 206–207, 223
  and emotion, 200, 225–226
  etymology of, 197
  in psychology, 197–203
Affect Theory, 197, 205–209, 226–227
  emancipatory agenda of, 207
  and fieldwork, 225
  as new paradigm, 197
  and science, 205
Afghanistan, 127
afökho dödö. See resentment, Nias
amok, 99
Andaman Islands, 154
anger, 26, 54, 111, 128, 137, 140, 151, 242–243, 253, 266
appraisal theory, 19, 38, 40, 127, 229
Arapesh (New Guinea), 121
Aristotle, 111, 151, 161, 253, 280
Arnold, Magda, 20
Averill, James, 32, 283
avoidance relationships, 98, 127, 129

Bali, 85, 90, 178, 181, 268
Banyuwangi (Java), 85, 241
Barrett, Lisa Feldman, 18, 21, 126
basic emotions, 17, 19, 108, 156, 163, 201, 203, 205–206, 246
Bateson, Gregory, 119, 178–180, 260
Bedford, Erroll, 54, 60–62, 132
Bedouin, 143–146
behaviourism, 260
Benedict, Ruth, 74
Bennett, M. and P. Hacker, 162
Ben-Ze'ev, Aaron, 20, 155, 229
Besnier, Niko, 199
Bible, 3, 251
biographical perspectives, 126–131, 178, 181–182, 192–193, 201, 268, 272–273, 280
blush, 164–166
Boas, Franz, 10, 178
Boster, James, 252
Bourgois, P., 274
Brazil, 276
bridewealth, 48
Briggs, Jean, 128, 136–142, 153, 186, 271, 276
Bruner, Jerome, 113–114

Calhoun, Cheshire, 126
Carr, David, 113

Index

Carrithers, Michael, 174, 176, 264, 280
Carver, Raymond, 213
Charland, Louis, 199
Chewong, 6, 252–256, 280, 289
Clore, G. and A. Ortony, 201
cockfight, 181
Cohen, Anthony, 135
Conceptual Act Theory, 231
Conrad, Joseph, 165–167
constructionism
  cultural and social, 61, 237, 261
  psychological, 202, 220, 231
conversion, 57, 69, 72–73, 251
core affect, 201, 208, 220
core relational themes, 36, 42, 111, 139,
  174, 192, 230, 238
Crivelli, C., 158
cross-cultural comparison, 244
Culture and Personality, 119, 128, 178,
  180
Cyprus, 216, 219

Damasio, Antonio, 39, 205
dance, 154
De Niro, Robert, 157
Deleuze, Gilles, 197, 214, 221
Desjarlais, Robert, 148
dimensional models, 201, 247
discourse, 132, 227
disentangling, 55, 233
display rules, 19, 37, 131, 141, 201
dispositions, 26
documentary, 108, 169
Duffy, Eamon, 10
Dureau, Christine, 276
Durkheim, Emile, 84, 176–177, 265

egocentric perspectives, 115, 126, 130, 155
Ekman, Paul, 156
embarrassment, 60, 83, 90, 92
emotion language
  body phrases, 57, 252
  discursive practices, 231

diversity of usage, 235, 239
domain of emotion words, 242–243
and granularity, 60, 231, 252
as labels, 59, 231
and meaning, 60, 232–240
metaphors, 247
as moral discourse, 54, 132, 232–233
performativity of, 55
as political rhetoric, 55, 62, 133
pragmatic usage, 60, 233, 279
reference of. *See* reference
semantic clusterings, 236–237, 239
emotional contagion, 154
emotional episode, 4, 17, 20, 30, 38, 45,
  109, 159, 163, 174–175, 178, 201, 230,
  263, 281
emotional intelligence, 154
emotional meaning, 93, 130, 229–239
emotionalization, 34–35, 41, 255
emotionology, 234
emotions
  boundaries, 18, 33, 200
  categorization, 19, 203, 231, 250–251
  cognitive theories, 20, 192
  communicative theory, 161
  complexity of, 26, 29
  components of, 17, 110, 201
  and consciousness, 18, 27, 34, 39, 72
  control of, 37, 97, 139, 254
  cross-cultural comparison, 19, 31, 43
  definition, 5–6, 13, 19, 31–32, 58, 84, 115,
    132, 163, 247–248, 281, 292
  domain, 32, 219, 281
  dramatic nature of, 30, 167
  as emergent, 18, 200
  as English folk category, 17, 248
  and etiquette, 1–2, 31, 87, 94–95, 241,
    258, *See* Java
  expression, 153
  first- and third-person perspectives
    on, 25, 29–30, 126
  generic category, 235, 241
  heterogeneity of, 5, 31, 240

300

Index

history of, 6, 8–10
in history of anthropology, 8, 170–183
and ideology, 132–133, 239, 243, 261
and illness, 34–35, 42, 242
as inner states, 29–30, 39–40, 60–61,
77, 130, 224, 226, 238, 242
as judgments, 28, 83, 93, 230
and kinship, 127
locus of, 62, 100, 239
and morality, 89, 91, 94, 166
natural kinds, 6, 13, 32, 178, 203, 231,
242, 275, 281
performativity of, 54
personal frame of reference, 20, 126,
155, 262, 281
phenomenology of, 19, 101, 110, 124,
229, 239–240, 247
privacy of, 28–30, 61, 131, 188, 247
psychological reality of, 2, 229, 242,
249, 256
putative coherence of, 18, 32, 34, 112,
281
scepticism about, 13, 18, 33, 41, 45, 124,
163, 193, 200, 281
scripts, 38, 111, 120, 133, 203, 230, 241,
246
theories of, 13, 17–21, 44
and time, 111, 130, 136, 155, 159, 183, 188,
190, 192, 279
emotives, 55, 67, 254
empathic accuracy, 270, 272
empathy, 81, 147, 151–153
defined, 270
failure of, 270
narrative empathy, 263
as research tool, 262–263
and sociality, 261
as universal, 275
Empson, William, 25
envy, 110
Epstein, A.L., 118–124, 188
ethnography. *See* empathy, fieldwork,
methodology, narrative, realism

ethnopsychology, 231, 256
ethos, 46, 98, 179, 234, 269
Evans-Pritchard, E., 270
extended case method, 118, 122, 172

facial expressions, 154, 156–157, 164
fear, 89
feeling, 30, 39, 59–60, 77, 233, 247, 252
feeling theory, 5, 19, 38, 40, *See also*
James, William
Fernandez-Dols, J.-M., 158
fiction and ethnography, 151–152,
184–185
fiction, psychology of, 151
fieldwork, 3–4, 15, 46, 65–66, 116, 122,
130, 135, 137, 172, 225, 273
fieldwork emotions, 152, 263–264, 269,
271
Firth, Raymond, 173–176
folk psychology, 133, 135, 231
Forster, E. M., 188
Freud, Sigmund, 72, 180, 191
Frijda, Nico, 32, 36, 96, 117, 127, 160, 198,
230, 279
functionalism, 173
funeral, 43, 64, 82, 175, 179, 188, 193

Geertz, Clifford, 37, 113, 180–182, 226,
250, 261, 268, 270
Geertz, Hildred, 94, 96, 240
gender, 127, 129
general and particular, 14, 42, 126, 145
generalization, deficiency of, 20, 117, 135,
269
German, 254
Gluckman, Max, 117
Goddard, Cliff, 235, 245
Goldie, Peter, 29, 111, 159–160, 266, 279
Gombrich, E., 157
gossip, 65, 147
Great Repentance, 57, 69–74, 214–215
grief, 43, 122, 134, 242, 268
guilt, 95, 247

Index

Hamlet, 134, 183
happy, 245
Harré, Rom, 59
Harris, Paul, 259
headhunters, 70, 134, 191, 266–268
heart idioms, 54, 62
Heider, Karl, 81, 234, 251
Herman, David, 115
historiography, 112–113
Hmong (Laos), 68
Hollan, D. & J. Wellenkamp, 182
Hollan, D. and J. Throop, 147
honour, 127
Howell, Signe, 253–254
hypocognition, 41, 97, 253

Iatmul (New Guinea), 178–179
Ifaluk (Micronesia), 131, 147, *See also* Lutz
Ilongot (Philippines), 134, 266–268
Indonesian language, 234, 251
intentionality, 27, 229, 279
interpretative genres, 148
interpretivism, 181, 262
intuition, 153
isin, 2, 87, 89, 94, 240, 258

James, Henry, 123, 185
James, William, 5, 38, 40, 202, 204
Japan, 240
Java
    domestic space, 85–86
    emotional navigation, 83, 87, 89, 92
    etiquette, 2, 86
    family dynamics, 95
    focal emotions, 4, 83
    interiority, 75, 77, 134
    kinship and emotion, 95
    Muslim tradition, 77, 97
    mysticism, 82, 94, 100
    reflexivity, 79, 97, 99
    social emotions, 94–97, 240, 259
    social structure, 83, 86, 90
    syncretism, 77

Java, examples
    child with guests, 2
    father-in-law avoidance, 129
    headman's defeat, 35–36
    poisoned buffalo, 36
    runaway youth, 101
    shameless toddler, 257–259
Javanese, 78, 80–81, 235
    speech levels, 81
Javanism, 77–78, 97
Jay, Robert, 84
jealousy, 26, 29, 66, 110

Kant, 7
Keeler, Ward, 95

Lakoff, George, 247
Latour, Bruno, 223
Lazarus, Richard, 36, 111, 160
Leavitt, John, 262–264, 276
Lévi-Strauss, Claude, 177
Levy, Robert, 34, 41–43, 82, 147, 183, 186, 252–253
lexicalization, 110, 252
Leys, Ruth, 205–206, 221
Lingis, Alphonso, 213
linguistic primes, 245
linguistic relativity, 244
literature as evidence, 160, 163–164
Lord Jim. See Conrad
love, 204
Lutz, Catherine, 34, 131–133, 237–240
Lynch, Owen, 261

Malay, 235
Malinowski, Bronislaw, 171–173, 177
Mandelstam, Nadezhda, 186
Massumi, Brian, 205, 221
Maya, 275
Mead, Margaret, 119, 121, 134, 178
meta-emotions, 203
methodology
    discourse, 132, 134

302

Index

interviews, 183
naturalistic observation, 131
naturalistic v. experimental, 137, 158,
  239, 242–243, 249
object-oriented, 225
participant-observation, 171, 237
self-report, 239
semantic analysis, 234, 238, 241
Minangkabau (Sumatra), 234
Mink, Louis, 112
mirror neurons, 153, 264, 275
misattribution, 186
misrecognition, 27, 186
missionaries, 70–71, 251
modular mind, 161–163
mood, 26
mourning, 134, 175
Musil, Robert, 159–160
Myers, Fred, 87, 230

narrative, 4, 184, 205, 249, 279–282
  construction of emotion, 109–110, 114,
    116, 120, 144
  features of, 114
  understanding of emotions, 110,
    151–152
narrative empathy, 263, 265, 269, 273
narrative ethnography, 130, 143, 146, 176,
  192
narrativity, 112–113, 116, 135
Natural Semantic Metalanguage, 245,
  247, 249
Navaro-Yashin, Yael, 216–225
Naven, 178–179, *See* Bateson
Needham, Rodney, 32
neo-realism, 170
Nepal, 82
Nias, 47
  afökho dödö, 63–68
  bridewealth debate, 48–50
  death of chief, 188–193
  emotive speeches, 50–53
  heart speech, 3, 56–59, 62, 254

oratorical style, 1, 53–54, 62, 74
  staging emotion, 53–56
Niehaus, Isak, 272
Nietzsche, 69–70, 73
Nussbaum, Martha, 112, 160, 192,
  279

Oatley, Keith, 19, 116, 151, 160–163
Ordinary affects. See Stewart, Kathleen
Osing, 81, 88
other minds, 147, 181, 277

Pacific societies, 147, 233
Pakistan, 127, 230
Pakthun, 129
Parish, Steven, 183
Parrott, Gerrod, 64, 73
Parsons, Talcott, 180
particularity, 280
  egocentric and biographical, 130
particulars, 14, 42, 44, 116, 123, 125, 128,
  146, 159, 184, 244, 268
passions, 9
perasaan, 80, 235
pernah, 87–88, 91, 93, 102
person-centred ethnography, 43,
  182
phenomenology, 148, 182, 191
Pile, Steve, 197
Pintupi (Australia), 87, 230
plot, 161, 164, 184, 264
Poe, Edgar Allan, 57
polythetic classification, 32, 45, 244
positioned subject, 266
Postert, Christian, 68
psychoanalysis, 124, 129

qualia, 60, 247

Radcliffe-Brown, A.R., 154, 176
rage, 267
Ramayana, 79
rasa, 77–78, 100, 235, 281

303

Index

realism
  in emotion theories, 32
  in reporting and depiction, 17, 125,
    170, 183–185, 187
Reddy, William, 55
reference, 61, 232–234, 241–242
reflexivity, 120, 261, 281
relativism, cultural, 4, 10, 17, 19, 59, 113,
    159, 199, 253, 266
reluctance, 4, 83, 87, 89, 92–93, 95
resentment, 53, 56, 63–68, 74, 99, 188, 268
resonance, 263, 268
respect, 2, 87, 95, 240
ressentiment, 69–70, 73
revenge, 251
Roberts, Robert, 20
Robinson, Jenefer, 231
Rosaldo, Michelle, 20, 134, 199
Rosaldo, Renato, 182, 184, 265–269, 271
Rosenberg, D., 132
Rosenwein, Barbara, 29
Rosi, Francesco, 168–169, 184
Russell, James, 6, 19, 31, 90, 200–203,
    207–208, 220, 225, 230, 241, 243, 249
Russians, 187
Rylko-Bauer, B., 274

sadness, 41, 111, 186
Salvatore Giuliano (film), 168
Samoa, 147, 178
Sapir, Edward, 128
Schachter and Singer, 199
Scheper-Hughes, N., 276
schismogenesis, 178
Scruton, Roger, 162
Sedgwick, Eve Kosofsky, 207
shame, 2, 4, 95, 127, 166, 258–259
Shweder, Richard, 33–35, 39, 41–42, 111,
    255
sincerity, 54
social dramas, 117, 120
socialization, 94–95, 98, 258
Solomon Islands, 233, 276

Solomon, Robert, 27, 54, 60, 93, 96, 160,
    191, 198, 204, 230
Soviet Union, 186
spatial feelings, 90, 101
Spinoza, 161, 197, 221–222
Staples, James, 272
Stearns, Peter, 234
Stewart, Kathleen, 210–216
structural functionalism, 176
structuralism, 177
subjectivity, 15, 126, 262
Sundermann, 3, 56–59
sungkan, 87, 89, 94, 96, 240

Tahiti, 185, 252
Tahitian widower, case of, 41–43
Tallis, Raymond, 162
tepa slira, 81, 96
terror, 187
The make-believe space. See Navaro-
    Yashin
Thrift, Nigel, 207, 223, 226
Throop, Jason, 276
Tikopia. *See* Firth
Todorov, Tzvetan, 115
Tolai (New Hebrides). *See* Epstein
Tolstoy, Leo, 160, 165, 185
    Anna Karenina, 161–163, 165, 204
    War and Peace, 27–29, 42, 185
Tomkins, Silvan, 118, 203, 207, 221
trance, 71
translation, 6, 56–58, 102, 242, 245–251,
    262, 281
Trobriand Islands, 172–173
Tulpan (film), 107–110
Turner, Victor, 73, 117, 120
two-factor theories, 40, 199

uncanny, 73, 224
universals, 31, 113, 174, 244
unnamed emotions, 6, 243,
    250–255
Utku (Canada). *See* Briggs

Index

valence, 199
verisimilitude, 185

Waorani (Ecuador), 251
Weber, Max, 13
Wetherell, Margaret, 209
White, Geoffrey, 233
White, Hayden, 112
Wierzbicka, Anna, 33, 57, 243–250, 252, 255

Wikan, Unni, 182, 263, 268–269
Wilce, James, 232
Wittgenstein, Ludwig, 41, 60, 171, 180, 261
Writing Culture, 265

Yap (Micronesia), 147, 277

Zajonc, Robert, 39
Zweig, Stefan, 112